Encouragement Takes Courage: Building Each Other Up in Him

Christine C Sponsler

Cover design by Cristian Mihai

Encouragement Takes Courage: Building Each Other Up in Him

Copyright © 2021 by Christine C Sponsler
Published by Sponsler Ink
https://sponsler.ink

ISBN 978-1-7371852-1-5 (print)

About the Author:
Christine C Sponsler
Master of Divinity (M.Div.), Liberty Baptist Theological Seminary
Master of Arts (MA), Liberty University

Christine is about halfway through her Ph.D. in Forensic Psychology.
Her M.Div. is in Professional Ministry and her M.A. is in Human Service
Counseling/Life Coaching which gives her the edge in sharing the Lord's
purpose in other people's lives. She enjoys helping people to move
forward toward their life goals.

Christine C Sponsler M-Div., MA, CLC
Encouraging Circle of Life-Coaching
Email: cc@sponsler.ink
Website: https://sponsler.ink

Dedications

First, I would like to dedicate this book to our Father God in heaven, to our Lord and Savior Jesus Christ, and to our guide the Holy Spirit.

Next, I dedicate this book to my husband...boy did he put up with a lot. I love you Cutie!

Next, to my children, all of them! They watched as I would disappear into my office, coming out exhausted and went along for this ride.

Next, to two of the most prayerful people that I know, my brother-in-law and his beautiful wife...thank you for all your prayers.

Next, to one of the sweetest people that I know...my mother-in-law. Her questions helped me to focus more which I needed often.

Finally, to my four family members who have watched me struggle the longest...my mom, stepdad, sister, and brother-in-law, thank you.

Table of Contents

Encouragement is the empowerment to build each other up into the person God has created us to be.

Preface

A generous person will prosper;
> whoever refreshes others will be refreshed.
> **Proverbs 11:25, NIV**

Now faith is confidence in what we hope for and assurance about what we do not see.
> **Hebrews 11:1, NIV**

I urge you, first of all, to pray for all people. Ask God to help them; intercede on their behalf, and give thanks for them.
> **1 Timothy 2:1, NLT**

Be strong and courageous. Do not be afraid or terrified because of them, for the LORD your God goes with you; he will never leave you nor forsake you.
> **Deuteronomy 31:6, NIV**

Encouraging, building up and refreshing others includes being their spiritual cheerleader. How many times have any of us felt down, sad or upset and along came a good friend or family member who cheered us up? This is encouragement, at its finest. Then, there are the numerous prayer chains which encourage us to pray for others and have them pray for us. This is another example of encouragement, at its finest. Finally, have any of us ever felt fear was going to choke us to death? Then, your friend, family member or even your devotionals send you an encouraging message? More encouragement, at its finest.

Christine C. Sponsler

*****

May we all strive to be another person's encouragement today, and every day!

Encouragement

We can find our encouragement through promises from God. His promises include "there is now no condemnation" (Romans 8:1, NIV). We no longer live in guilt and shame but under His grace and mercy instead. Encouraging others will begin to come naturally when we live and stand on the promises of God and under His grace and mercy.

> 1 Brothers and sisters, if someone is caught in a sin, you who live by the Spirit should restore that person gently. But watch yourselves, or you also may be tempted. 2 Carry each other's burdens, and in this way you will fulfill the law of Christ. 3 If anyone thinks they are something when they are not, they deceive themselves. 4 Each one should test their own actions. Then they can take pride in themselves alone, without comparing themselves to someone else, 5 for each one should carry their own load. 6 Nevertheless, the one who receives instruction in the word should share all good things with their instructor.
>
> 7 Do not be deceived: God cannot be mocked. A man reaps what he sows. 8 Whoever sows to please their flesh, from the flesh will reap destruction; whoever sows to please the Spirit, from the Spirit will reap eternal life. 9 Let us not become weary in doing good, for at the proper time we will reap a harvest if we do not give up. 10 Therefore, as we have opportunity, let us do good to all people, especially to those who belong to the family of believers.
> **Galatians 6:1–10, NIV**

While encouraging each other, we find encouragement for ourselves. I am not suggesting that we encourage each other simply to receive our own encouragement. I am, however, saying that is how strong and necessary encouragement is. We all suffer from various pains. However, God is always there to heal that pain and when we encourage others, we feel loved almost instantaneously.

> 9 Love must be sincere. Hate what is evil; cling to what is good. 10 Be devoted to one another in love. Honor one

3

another above yourselves. 11 Never be lacking in zeal, but keep your spiritual fervor, serving the Lord. 12 Be joyful in hope, patient in affliction, faithful in prayer. 13 Share with the Lord's people who are in need. Practice hospitality.
Romans 12:9–13, NIV

It is difficult to love each other while we are hurting. However, God has called each of us to "Love your neighbor as yourself" (Matthew 22:39; Mark 12:31, NIV) and to even love your enemies (see Matthew 5:43-48 and Luke 6:27-36). Love is not discouraging. Therefore, our call includes love, because through love we can encourage and lift each other up during the most important and impactful times.

Encouraging words contain the necessary godly love to move through the struggles and trials of this lifetime. Remember Jesus' words of encouragement,

"I have told you these things, so that in me you may have peace. In this world you will have trouble. But take heart! I have overcome the world."
John 16:33, NIV

Jesus did not say, oh well, that's just the way things happen. He said to take heart because we can find encouragement in His promises and in His love.

Encouragement does not mean that all worry and struggle will immediately disappear (although they might); it does mean that while we struggle, He is with us and we can encourage each other to persevere. Encouraging other people is as Christlike as it gets. Christ did not discourage people because of who they are, or what they had done. He encourages each of us to "Go and sin no more" (John 8:11, NLT). This is one of the most encouraging verses in Scripture. After reading this book, the importance of encouraging words should become more apparent and the encouragement toward others will be supported by Scripture.

4 As you come to him, the living Stone—rejected by humans but chosen by God and precious to him—5 you also, like living stones, are being built into a spiritual house to be a holy priesthood, offering spiritual sacrifices

acceptable to God through Jesus Christ. 6 For in Scripture it says:

> "See, I lay a stone in Zion,
>   a chosen and precious cornerstone,
> and the one who trusts in him
>   will never be put to shame."

7 Now to you who believe, this stone is precious. But to those who do not believe,

> "The stone the builders rejected
>   has become the cornerstone,"

8 and,

> "A stone that causes people to stumble
>   and a rock that makes them fall."

They stumble because they disobey the message—which is also what they were destined for.

9 But you are a chosen people, a royal priesthood, a holy nation, God's special possession, that you may declare the praises of him who called you out of darkness into his wonderful light. 10 Once you were not a people, but now you are the people of God; once you had not received mercy, but now you have received mercy.

1 Peter 2:4–10, NIV

21 To this you were called, because Christ suffered for you, leaving you an example, that you should follow in his steps.

> 22 "He committed no sin,
>   and no deceit was found in his mouth."

23 When they hurled their insults at him, he did not retaliate; when he suffered, he made no threats. Instead, he entrusted himself to him who judges justly. 24 "He himself bore our sins" in his body on the cross, so that we might

die to sins and live for righteousness; "by his wounds you have been healed." 25 For "you were like sheep going astray," but now you have returned to the Shepherd and Overseer of your souls.

1 Peter 2:21–25, NIV

Jesus died for our sins. How can we keep this to ourselves? We need to encourage as many people as we can with this Good News. He is the cornerstone of our salvation. Our salvation is built around what He did for us on Calvary. Destructive people (us included) attempted to harm the Lord, yet He died for us while we were still sinners (see Romans 5:8) because He loves us.

We have become His royal family, adopted into the Lord's family of encouragers. He did not sin, but all of us have. Even though we are sinners, Christ still gave His life to save us. All of us have gone astray in some way or another and Christ still died for these sins. We must encourage others to find this truth and allow them to live inside of His salvation for their lives.

I hope and pray that each of these words finds you and your family and friends encouraged and beloved! I know that without the love of Christ, we are all discouraged and doomed. However, I hope and pray that you find the hope, love, and encouragement of Christ throughout this book. God is good all the time; we are not and that is fine. He and His love make us good!

Christ's sacrifice has become our ultimate encouragement. Share it every single day of our lives and watch the Lord work in other people's lives too!

PART 1: Overview of Encouragement vs. Discouragement

Whoever pursues righteousness and unfailing love
will find life, righteousness, and honor.
Proverbs 21:21, NLT

Do nothing out of selfish ambition or vain conceit.
Rather, in humility value others above yourselves,
Philippians 2:3, NIV

Do to others as you would like them to do to you.
Luke 6:31, NLT

Christine C. Sponsler

Jesus did not spend His days discouraging His disciples because there was a lot of work to be done. He did challenge them so that they felt His strength and encouragement. If the disciples felt discouraged, then why would they desire to follow Jesus and hold tight to His ministry for all the years that they followed Him? They wouldn't. Even Jesus had to encourage His disciples. How much more should each of us desire to encourage each other? Jesus' encouragement is unequaled because it is the hope of eternity with Him. Life is difficult even without the discouraging words of family, friends, society and even our colleagues. Therefore, let's begin this encouraging journey together and bring some joy to a hurting world.

*****

Blessings and honor to each person reading this book, today and always!

Chapter 1: What is Encouragement?

Your word is a lamp to my feet
    and a light to my path.
    Psalm 119:105, ESV

Submit yourselves therefore to God. Resist the devil,
and he will flee from you.
    James 4:7, ESV

We have all found ourselves unable to smile at times. Sometimes this leads to words we regret. God's Word can change our attitudes toward ourselves, our circumstances and even toward others. His truths and promises are encouraging and filled with joy.

Therefore, getting daily alone time with God is an important part of each of His believers' lives. I encourage each person reading these words to get alone with God and be encouraged by His Word so that you may encourage others.

*****

May you be an encourager and also be encouraged today and always!

Christine C. Sponsler

Encouragement Defined

> 2 Be completely humble and gentle; be patient, bearing with one another in love. 3 Make every effort to keep the unity of the Spirit through the bond of peace. 4 There is one body and one Spirit, just as you were called to one hope when you were called; 5 one Lord, one faith, one baptism; 6 one God and Father of all, who is over all and through all and in all.
> **Ephesians 4:2–6, NIV**

When searching through various texts, there are numerous definitions associated with the word encourage. There are terms from the Bible and the dictionary.

Merriam-Webster's dictionary states that encourage means, "to inspire with courage, spirit, or hope" (Merriam-Webster). While the Holy Bible is filled with encouraging scripture such as,

> 16 May our Lord Jesus Christ himself and God our Father, who loved us and by his grace gave us eternal encouragement and good hope, 17 encourage your hearts and strengthen you in every good deed and word.
> **2 Thessalonians 2:16–17, NIV**

I almost got misty-eyed after reading this a few times. How about you? It's all right to admit it; we are here to encourage each other to find hope in His Word.

Can you imagine if everyone in the world would inspire others in this way? It would be the "world peace" that every pageant contestant strives for, and that nations claim to desire. It would be wonderful. However, it is not in human nature (the flesh anyhow) to be so encouraging. It is simpler to cut each other down, to lift ourselves up and to feel better about ourselves. While this might sound gross and unrealistic, it has some truth to it. However, we can be the beginning of the changes seen throughout our own communities, at the very least. Society simply needs a little push in the godly direction.

In today's society, it is difficult to find encouragement from almost anyone. Each person has their own agenda, their own issues, and their own pain. They cannot be troubled by attempting to help others unless it benefits their agenda, issues, or pain. However, becoming a person who enjoys encouraging others is possible when we seek out and find the encouraging words of our Lord, and then share them with as many people as possible.

Encouragement takes Courage is not simply something to read, say aloud and repeat. It takes a special kind of strength to be an encourager. For sure, being an encourager will accelerate our lives into the realm of the Spirit's strength. God's very strength becomes something that we can use to strengthen others. Think of it this way, you can either spread "good cheer," (see John 16:33) and find true joy, or you can spread negativity and find yourself lost in a web of unfulfillment and pain.

Now it is time to learn what encouragement can do for us so that we can share it with others. Encouragement has been defined as support which builds confidence and "to inspire with courage, spirit, or hope" (Merriam-Webster). Finding strength in Him includes listening to what He has said about loving others and honoring our Father. Courage and strength usually go hand-in-hand and encouraging others strengthens those people.

Courage and Strength Defined

> I tell you the truth, those who listen to my message and believe in God who sent me have eternal life. They will never be condemned for their sins, but they have already passed from death into life.
> **John 5:24, NLT**

> Be devoted to one another in love. Honor one another above yourselves.
> **Romans 12:10, NIV**

> The fear of the LORD is a fountain of life,
> turning a person from the snares of death.
> **Proverbs 14:27, NIV**

Courage is the power found from grasping His strength in our lives so that we can share this strength with others. Have you ever tried to accomplish something in your own strength? How did that work out? Yes,

11

we are capable people. However, when we believe in Christ, we understand where this capability comes from. It is not simply our own power and strength that we work with, it is His power and strength which works in and through us. This is pure courage, to give glory to God for something He did through you to encourage His children. What an honor!

Finding His Strength

Next, we share the definition and application of finding His strength. Look out because these next few pages are intense but inviting. They are new, old and usable. His Word is the ultimate encouragement, and this section demonstrates this through His Word and what it means for us as encouragers.

> Search for the LORD and for his strength;
> continually seek him.
> **1 Chronicles 16:11, NLT**

> Look to the LORD and his strength;
> seek his face always.
> **1 Chronicles 16:11, NIV**

First, let's discuss what strength truly is. We have either read or heard of the David and Goliath story from the Bible (see 1 Samuel 17). Therefore, we know that the strength which David has comes straight from the Lord. However, do we know how to harness this strength? Re-read the verse above (1 Chronicles 16:11) and ask yourself, what does it mean to search (or look) for the Lord and his strength? Read His Word and find His strength! When we seek after the Lord, we will find Him and His strength throughout His Word...the Holy Bible!

> 13 Be on your guard; stand firm in the faith; be courageous; be strong. 14 Do everything in love.
> **1 Corinthians 16:13–14, NIV**

When we seek after the Lord and read His Word, we will find His strength and stand firm in the faith that our Lord and Savior Jesus Christ will strengthen our hearts and our minds. The strength of the Lord has caused many small-minded and narrow-minded people to turn from their selfish ways (myself included) and rejoice in knowing that we share in the encouragement of His strength and power.

> fear not, for I am with you;
> be not dismayed, for I am your God;
> I will strengthen you, I will help you,
> I will uphold you with my righteous right hand.
> **Isaiah 41:10, ESV**

Fear is not a spiritual feeling. It tries to extinguish any hope, love and faith that we possess. However, when fear does peek into our lives, we turn back to the Lord and stand upon His strength, again. His strength will help each of us to move forward and stand tall upon our faith. Courage is the theme throughout this text. Therefore, finding courage and using it to encourage each other is the key component to our standing firm in our faith.

> Be strong and courageous. Do not fear or be in dread
> of them, for it is the LORD your God who goes with you.
> He will not leave you or forsake you."
> **Deuteronomy 31:6, ESV**

We no longer have to dread the future. Our future is in Him. We no longer need to dread our past for He has forgotten all our sins (see Psalm 103:3-13). We will spend eternity praising Him and rejoicing in His presence. He is with us and will never forsake us…Hallelujah!

> They want to be teachers of the law, but they do not know what they are talking about or what they so confidently affirm.
> **1 Timothy 1:7, NIV**

> They want to be known as teachers of the law of Moses, but they don't know what they are talking about, even though they speak so confidently.
> **1 Timothy 1:7, NLT**

He has taken our heart of fear and replaced it with one of faith, hope and love (see 1 Corinthians 13). His spirit lives within our hearts. How encouraging! Now turn to the person next to you (or anyone you desire to) and encourage them with this same hope that we have found in His Word. Our spirit is now filled with power, not timidity. He is our strength and our power.

> If anyone speaks, they should do so as one who speaks the very words of God. If anyone serves, they should do so with the strength God provides, so that in all things God may be praised through Jesus Christ. To him be the glory and the power for ever and ever. Amen.
> **1 Peter 4:11, NIV**

How encouraged do you feel right now?

I hope and pray that encouragement comes easy to most of us. However, the people who struggle (including myself) with the natural feeling of encouragement found throughout the Bible can also encourage others through their dedication to the Lord and His Word.

When we speak to each other, we need to remember to do so as if God were speaking through us. God can reach others through our kind words because the Holy Spirit is present when we do. God does use us to get His message out to others and this should encourage both us and the people we share this with.

When we serve people, whether it is at home, in the community, or during missionary trips, we need to be so fed by His Word that it is as though the people that we are serving are reading the Bible, through our Christlike actions.

When we serve people and/or speak to people, we must do so in a way that God, through Christ Jesus, can be praised and honored. We must be people who are so thoroughly drenched in His Word that it overflows into other people's lives. We found salvation, the ultimate encouragement. Therefore, we must share this encouragement with as many other people as we possibly can.

> The LORD is my strength and my defense;
>> he has become my salvation.
> **Psalm 118:14, NIV**

> The LORD is my strength and my song;
> > he has given me victory.
> **Psalm 118:14, NLT**

The Lord is our strength, our hope, our guidance and our encouragement. This goes to prove that with this strength, we are not able to keep it all to ourselves. Sharing His encouraging Word with the world is our goal and our honor. Let's get out there and share it!

How to Be Courageous

God desires to have a relationship with all His creation (children). He also desires that His children inspire relationships with each other. If we are ready, willing and able to share the Gospel, then we must share the love of Christ by encouraging each other. Do any of us remember when your mommy would drop you off at preschool and you felt all alone? How about when she finally returned to pick you up? Did you feel encouraged and filled with hope? Probably!

How about, if you are like me and heard of a mommy and her son in the above-mentioned story, would it encourage you vicariously? Vicarious encouragement is just as effective as first-hand encouragement. That is the simplicity of encouragement. Do not forget testimonies. Share the love you have felt and/or feel with others. It takes courage to share this type of mommy story and the encouraging words can help another person see what love looks like. We must be careful not to hold back these encouraging words. It could be the only glimpse of Christ's love a person might encounter.

Another way to be courageous is to realize where our strength comes from.

> 1 I lift up my eyes to the hills.
> > From where does my help come?
> 2 My help comes from the LORD,
> > who made heaven and earth.
> **Psalm 121:1–2, ESV**

Christine C. Sponsler

Our help, our strength and the desire to encourage others come from the Lord. He is our strength (see Psalm 28:7). He is our refuge (see Psalm 46:1-2) and He is our Abba-Father (see Mark 14:36; Romans 8:15; Galatians 4:6). I hope these truths give you as much encouragement as they do for me. He is our everything! He loves us unconditionally! It is exceedingly difficult not to be encouraged by these hope-filled words of truth. Thank you, Lord!

We have many challenges every single day. However, those challenges are met with His strength when we truly trust in Him and His Word. We must find time to meditate on His Word so that we can meet the challenges of life with hope and find encouragement from His truth and promises. He will meet us amidst our struggles. He will give us His strength to endure and we must share this encouragement with others. Otherwise, we become those discouraging people that knock people down with their words and/or actions. Yikes!

Knocking people down does not always take negative words. We are also capable of knocking people down when we do not listen to their needs. Therefore, it is up to us to read His Word and find out how He would like us to care for each person we listen to. We need to be able to get past our own hurt and pain so that we can encourage others to do the same. If we find His strength, we can lead others to His strength also.

I hope and pray that these words are read as they are meant to be…revelations of what God's Word, promises and love mean to the world. They mean eternity with our Lord and Savior Jesus Christ and our Abba Father. OMGoodness, I am encouraged so much right now that I could shout from the rooftop (and probably get arrested, since it is after 10p.m.). Oh well, Paul was arrested for his dedication to Christ. It's worth getting arrested if even one person hears and believes what Christ will do for them!

People make assumptions about what a normal Christian life is supposed to look like. The best example of what any life is supposed to look like is in Christ's life. He died for our sins. He laid down His life for us (see 1 John 3:16). Christ gives us the strength to live a Christian life which means that we lay our lives down for one another.

Let us be encouraging, as You are Lord. Let us not be the discouraging people who knock people down with our words or our actions. We love You so much Lord, that we want to shout Your glorious name from the rooftops. Give us Your strength and power to accomplish this so that we can encourage many people today! Amen!

Pitfalls Which Lead to Discouragement

Discouragement includes holding back encouraging words because someone may take offense. Let's look at a scenario that all of us may have encountered before. You want to talk to someone in your family, community or workplace and you get scared because you overheard them talking about, "where was God when _____ happened?" Now, do you need to walk up to them and tell them that He was there during this struggle? Of course not; they probably would not hear you and this could be viewed as offensive (eavesdropping and all). However, you can talk to them another time and share what God has done in your life during a similar struggle. This may not change their minds right then and there, but it is a seed planted in their hearts for the Holy Spirit to nurture. Encouraging, huh? Another issue related to discouragement can stem from not taking better care of ourselves.

Please do not get this mixed up with "self-help." As Christians, we all know what kind of "help" we can give to ourselves; believing in Christ our Savior! Without Christ, we are useless, hopeless, and doomed. Lack of self-care will eventually lead a person to become discouraging toward others, rather than the encouraging person that God desires us to be.

Encouraging others takes courage and the Bible reminds us to care and love ourselves as well as to care for and love others, "…as ourselves" (see Mark 12:30-31). Our bodies are the temple of God. Therefore, caring for ourselves is not selfish, it is biblically encouraging.

If we do not take care of ourselves, how can we expect to care for others? It is not possible. I am always reminded about what self-care looks like when I go flying. The flight attendant instructs us to place our own air mask on and then place one on our child or another loved one. We cannot help anyone else, without helping ourselves first.

God has shown us, through the ministry of Jesus Christ, that caring for others comes naturally when we become more Christlike. When we start to drift away from the ministry of Christ, we tend to lose sight of caring for others. Jesus had to rest, pray, fast and meditate to hear from the Father. How much more sense does it make that we must do this daily also? Delve into the Word of God, and be encouraged by His truth, love, promises and hope.

Be encouraged, so that you can encourage others!

Chapter 2: What is Discouragement?

It would be better for him if a millstone were hung around his neck and he were cast into the sea than that he should cause one of these little ones to sin.
Luke 17:2, ESV

Encouragement has a strong counterpart. However, discouragement is only as strong as we allow it to be. We give it strength when we do not encourage a brother or sister. We give it strength when we forget our hope and promises and discourage another person, for any reason. Discouragement is more than a lack of encouragement. It is also part of unforgiveness in our own hearts. We must forgive and encourage others to do the same.

*****

Let's learn what it means to be discouraging and remember that we can draw on our encouragement to find His strength to encourage others!

Christine C. Sponsler

Disheartening Words about Discouragement

This is definitely my least favorite part of the book. However, it is necessary to enlighten people about discouragement, so they are more capable of recognizing encouragement. The words that we use can become either a blessing or a curse (see James 3:9-10). Therefore, we must use our words carefully. To encourage others with our words, it would be best for us to gather the proper words from the Bible. The Bible is filled with God's truth and hope. Knowing how to speak to others is the beginning of encouraging others.

Be careful of the effect that your words can have on someone. If your words do not encourage, build up or help others, they are not of God (see 1 Thessalonians 5:9-11). Discouraging words are dangerous and not godly. There are many reasons for the Bible to mention using our words wisely. Encouraging each other is one of those reasons. Encouragement comes from the heart of God. Therefore, find as much time to spend with Him daily, and notice how encouraged you become and how encouraging you become to others.

Discouraging words, no more. Be encouraging instead!

Discouragement Defined

We are not the judge. Christ is the Judge. His actions prove that only He can judge people and that we are not to judge each other. When we judge others, we are discouraging them and acting as if we are God.

> 37 "Do not judge, and you will not be judged. Do not condemn, and you will not be condemned. Forgive, and you will be forgiven. 38 Give, and it will be given to you. A good measure, pressed down, shaken together and running over, will be poured into your lap. For with the measure you use, it will be measured to you."
> 39 He also told them this parable: "Can the blind lead the blind? Will they not both fall into a pit? 40 The student is not above the teacher, but everyone who is fully trained will be like their teacher.
> 41 "Why do you look at the speck of sawdust in your brother's eye and pay no attention to the plank in your own

eye? 42 How can you say to your brother, 'Brother, let me take the speck out of your eye,' when you yourself fail to see the plank in your own eye? You hypocrite, first take the plank out of your eye, and then you will see clearly to remove the speck from your brother's eye."
Luke 6:37–42, NIV

The Bible states that we are not to judge each other. Judgment is one way to discourage people. The verses from above in Luke chapter 6 should help us all to realize the dangers of judging each other, for ourselves and others.

How many of us have ever felt unwelcomed in a church? Did it feel as though every single eye in the sanctuary was staring at you and judging who you are? And how many of us were on the judging end of this scenario? It is probably safe to say that both scenarios have happened to all of us.

It feels discouraging when someone judges us. Therefore, as it reads in the Bible, "Do unto others as you would have them do unto you" (Matthew 7:12; Luke 6:31). The golden rule is the best way to empathize with every person the Lord blesses you with. If we all put ourselves in other people's shoes, the world would be a much shinier place to live. We can be the representation of His shining light and help others come to know and love Him.

It might seem as though words are just that...words. And this adage might sound all right, "sticks and stones may break my bones but, names (words) will never hurt me." However, this adage was created so that people could act as though someone's opinion of them did not matter.

In this day and age, we find people not loving each other enough to be encouraging. How dreadful. How biblical also. Let me explain. God sent His Son to this earth to challenge His children and to spread the Good News.

However, prior to Christ visiting us on earth there was Babel. The Tower of Babel made changes which were explained in Genesis 11:1-9. Please read this passage and then return to this book.

It appeared that God caused chaos just to be mean. However, the whole world was about to create something which would cause them to believe that they did not need God anymore.

Building the tower was going to make a name for themselves, rather than relying on God anymore. Therefore, instead of losing even one (see 2 Peter 3:9), He presented the need for His guidance through creating separate languages. Encouraging His children to rely upon Him to understand each other and to know Him more. Words were no longer the thing that kept people together...it became God Himself, again.

Discouraging words are the most harmful things that a person can use against another person. Other than actual weapons, words are harmful and cause pain. Courageous steps toward becoming the Christlike encourager is to build up strength through His Word.

Scripture does not mince words. There is no reason to mince words when these words are the truth. Therefore, with each disciplined word comes the promise of His hope for our future.

Who doesn't want to share this hope with the world? It starts with you, with me, and each hope-filled word we can share with our own communities. Begin by taking time to be immersed in His Word.

Part 2 of this text discusses, in detail, how to strengthen the 'self' so that there is enough strength to share with others. For now, we continue with discouragement and how to avoid it as much as possible!

Discouragement Without Hope

Using our words to discourage people is not biblical. When we do not use encouraging words with those who are hurting, the pain will become greater and the Lord will hear their cries (see Exodus 22:23; Psalm 34:6-17; Psalm 91:15; Psalm 107:6-19). The reason for encouraging others is not simply because we do not want God to hear their cries against us. Encouraging others must come from our hearts because our hearts are filled with His never-ending love.

When people who struggle to find hope in this world are met with discouraging words from those of us who claim to be Christians, how do we think this makes Christianity look? It makes us look as though we are nothing but hypocrites. Jesus warned the Pharisees and Sadducees about hypocrisy.

> 1 Then Jesus said to the crowds and to his disciples: 2 "The teachers of the law and the Pharisees sit in Moses' seat. 3 So you must be careful to do everything they tell

you. But do not do what they do, for they do not practice what they preach. 4 They tie up heavy, cumbersome loads and put them on other people's shoulders, but they themselves are not willing to lift a finger to move them.

5 "Everything they do is done for people to see: They make their phylacteries wide and the tassels on their garments long; 6 they love the place of honor at banquets and the most important seats in the synagogues; 7 they love to be greeted with respect in the marketplaces and to be called 'Rabbi' by others.

8 "But you are not to be called 'Rabbi,' for you have one Teacher, and you are all brothers. 9 And do not call anyone on earth 'father,' for you have one Father, and he is in heaven. 10 Nor are you to be called instructors, for you have one Instructor, the Messiah. 11 The greatest among you will be your servant. 12 For those who exalt themselves will be humbled, and those who humble themselves will be exalted.

Matthew 23:1–12, NIV

We are to heed this same advice from our Lord and Savior, today. The Bible's lessons do not change and when we strive to hear from God, we are capable of encouraging more people. Discouraging words are useless, dangerous, and completely deadly.

Will we find times when we suffer from discouragement? Yes. However, we find our hope in God. Let's share this with the world around us!

Discouragement with Hope

It is sad to see discouraging news. When we read or watch the news, how often do we claim that we will never watch again, only to watch again tomorrow? People have been discouraged since the fall of man.

> Why am I discouraged?
>   Why is my heart so sad?
> I will put my hope in God!
>   I will praise him again—

Christine C. Sponsler

my Savior and my God!
Psalm 42:11, NLT

King David found himself discouraged numerous times. His words of discouraging events are read throughout the Book of Psalms. His laments are some of the words we can relate to still today. He never left the words in the discouraging stage though. He would find ways to see, hear and feel God's true love.

1 In you, LORD my God,
    I put my trust.

2 I trust in you;
    do not let me be put to shame,
    nor let my enemies triumph over me.
3 No one who hopes in you
    will ever be put to shame,
but shame will come on those
    who are treacherous without cause.

4 Show me your ways, LORD,
    teach me your paths.
5 Guide me in your truth and teach me,
    for you are God my Savior,
    and my hope is in you all day long.
6 Remember, LORD, your great mercy and love,
    for they are from of old.
7 Do not remember the sins of my youth
    and my rebellious ways;
according to your love remember me,
    for you, LORD, are good.

8 Good and upright is the LORD;
    therefore he instructs sinners in his ways.
9 He guides the humble in what is right
    and teaches them his way.
10 All the ways of the LORD are loving and faithful
    toward those who keep the demands of his covenant.
11 For the sake of your name, LORD,

forgive my iniquity, though it is great.

12 Who, then, are those who fear the LORD?
　　He will instruct them in the ways they should choose.
13 They will spend their days in prosperity,
　　and their descendants will inherit the land.
14 The LORD confides in those who fear him;
　　he makes his covenant known to them.
15 My eyes are ever on the LORD,
　　for only he will release my feet from the snare.

16 Turn to me and be gracious to me,
　　for I am lonely and afflicted.
17 Relieve the troubles of my heart
　　and free me from my anguish.
18 Look on my affliction and my distress
　　and take away all my sins.
19 See how numerous are my enemies
　　and how fiercely they hate me!

20 Guard my life and rescue me;
　　do not let me be put to shame,
　　for I take refuge in you.
21 May integrity and uprightness protect me,
　　because my hope, LORD, is in you.

22 Deliver Israel, O God,
　　from all their troubles!
　　Psalm 25:1–22, NIV

People are lonely, afflicted with their sins and we have their saving grace right here in our hearts. Sharing this grace and His promises will allow the afflicted to live inside of their salvation. King David found hope through his dedication to God and so can we. This is an example of what is meant by discouragement with hope. We will all be afflicted and have trials (see John 16:33). However, we do not have to wallow in these trials because we have the only hope, Jesus Christ, our Lord and Savior.

We are all given the opportunity to find this same hope in God because the Bible is still the Word of God. Therefore, no matter our circumstances, we have hope in the one true God. We all have days when we feel distant from God and discouraged with how things have turned out in our lives. However, since we are believers, we can (and do) rely on God and His promises to "never leave nor forsake us" (Deuteronomy 31:6; Hebrews 13:5). Hallelujah! Praise His holy name!

Hope is probably the most rewarding and strengthening word. God's promises are supported in our hope through His gift of faith to us. How many of us have broken a promise? How many of us have had a promise to us broken? Well, God's promises are never broken. Now that's hope!

He has blessed us with a Lord and Savior named Jesus and we are reconciled to Him through Jesus. More hope! It seems as though we don't deserve this gift. Trust me, we don't. This is why God calls it a gift! We will still find discouragement in this world. Discouragement is temporary for us because we already know our Savior. We must share this hope with others. We must strive to not discourage others because they may not yet know Him!

Let's all go and be the only Christ that someone sees. Share the hope with all the people we know and never discourage, on purpose again. Commitments are stronger when there are three or more like a braid or a rope (see Ecclesiastes 4:12). His strength is in us. Now is the time to share it with others!

Chapter 3: Tearing Each Other Down

They cause the poor to cry out, catching God's attention.
He hears the cries of the needy.
Job 34:28, NLT

11 Brothers and sisters, do not slander one another. Anyone who speaks against a brother or sister or judges them speaks against the law and judges it. When you judge the law, you are not keeping it, but sitting in judgment on it. 12 There is only one Lawgiver and Judge, the one who is able to save and destroy. But you—who are you to judge your neighbor?
James 4:11–12, NIV

How often has each of us felt torn down, brushed aside or outcast from groups and families? How many of us are guilty of being the one who tears down, brushes aside and outcasts people? The answer to the second question is probably most painful for me to admit.

I wish that I could say, "I have never done this to anyone." However, I am guilty. It is hard to be Christlike when someone hurts you. We are called to work through this pain by calling on the Lord. Do we call upon Him before or after being guilty of shunning people? Hopefully, we get better at calling upon Him before this occurs, but until then, we must repent and ask for forgiveness when we shun anyone.

Throughout the Book of James, we read about how to tame the tongue, how to not be harsh toward each other and how to not judge each other. How does it feel when someone misjudges us? It's as though they are trying to recreate who we are, right? Well, I believe that we can safely say that no matter what, when we judge someone, we are always misjudging them. Let me explain.

Judgment toward another human being is left for only One Person, Jesus Christ. Therefore, if we judge someone, we are always getting it wrong, no matter how close to the truth it may seem. We are not judges, we are encouragers and to encourage each other we ask questions instead of guessing, judging or assuming.

James states that when we judge we are judging the law of God and this means that we are not obeying the law. What happens when we disobey the law? We get into trouble. Who wants to be in trouble with God? Not me! Encouraging others helps us to steer clear of judging them.

*****

Here's to building each other up and not tearing each other down; Encouragers unite!

Changing Attitudes Toward Our Brother and Sister

Forgiveness is the best way to be an encourager rather than striving to be such a discourager (see Matthew 6:14; Luke 6:37). Forgiveness is how we can get closer to the Lord. Through forgiveness, He can forgive us and have conversations with us. We are (technically) able to talk to Him, just as much as Peter did. Therefore, encouraging another person can help them to find this same forgiveness.

When Jesus asked His disciple Simon Peter who people said He was, Peter answered to the best of his ability by stating that some said He was John the Baptist, some said Elijah and others claimed He was Jeremiah or another prophet (see Matthew 16:13-14). Then, Jesus asked Peter who he thought He was, and Peter stated, "You are the Messiah, the Son of the living God" (Matthew 16:15-16). As followers of the Son of the living God, we are not to be so discouraging to each other.

We are simple human beings and need His strength to accomplish this task. Therefore, we need to read His Word daily and apply it to our lives. His strength and love are enough to be the encourager that He has asked us to be, and we can do this for Him and for ourselves.

Loving the Lord your God with all your strength does not mean that we are so strong. No, it means that we are blessed to have His strength to fall back upon (see Mark 12:30). All of this means that we are to love. We are to love our neighbors (see Mark 12:31) and even our enemies (see Matthew 5:43-48; Luke 6:27-36). If we love our enemies, we are less likely to judge others.

The Danger of Judging Others

We are not here to judge each other. We are here to allow God to use us for His Kingdom's sake. Therefore, understanding the dangers of judging each other is necessary and could save our lives (see Matthew 7:1-2) When we are using the Lord's strength to encourage each other, we are truly becoming more Christlike. However, if we judge and condemn each other, we will be judged harsher and condemned by the Lord (see Luke 6:37). It feels better when we encourage each other anyway.

How often have we felt torn down, persecuted and judged for something we wish we hadn't done? It has happened to me, often. It seemed as though I could never do anything right, even when I changed routes and did it the way I was told to do it. Do I really want to instill this pain on other people? No, I enjoy watching people smile and enjoy their encouraging words, especially His Word. Therefore, even when someone tries to hurt me, I (try to) change my attitude and become encouraging to them. I hope this is simple enough to understand. We were meant to encourage each other. Let's do this!

God Hears the Cries of the Needy

I know that we are not to do things simply because we think that it might harm our relationship with the Lord. We are to do things with a joyful heart. However, there are certain things that the Lord made clear and one of them is that we are to love!

When we cause people harm and discourage them, the Lord hears their cries, especially widows and orphans. We are never to cause another person harm, discouragement or discomfort because then the Lord's anger will be aroused (see Exodus 22:23, 27; Job 34:28). I don't know about you, but I am not trying to upset the Lord!

When we decide to be discouraging, the Lord knows. He knows everything! Job said it well, "Can anyone teach knowledge to God, since he judges even the highest?" (Job 21:22, NIV). Nobody can teach the Lord. However, we are taught to be more like Him. One of the main ways to be more like Him is through helping the needy and the poor.

How often do we simply pass by someone in need out of fear of saying the wrong thing to them and making matters worse? I am guilty of this. However, if all we do is encourage and lift their spirits, the Holy Spirit will do the rest. The people that we ignore, look away from and even shun will be heard by the Lord. It is so rewarding to be the person He uses to encourage others.

Let's get out there and change the discouraging words of the world into the encouraging Words of the Lord! Be blessed!

Chapter 4: Building Each Other Up

Do not be afraid or discouraged, for the LORD will personally go ahead of you. He will be with you; he will neither fail you nor abandon you.
Deuteronomy 31:8, NLT

This is all that I have learnt: God made us plain and simple, but we have made ourselves very complicated.
Ecclesiastes 7:29, GNB

7 None of us lives for himself only, none of us dies for himself only. 8 If we live, it is for the Lord that we live, and if we die, it is for the Lord that we die. So whether we live or die, we belong to the Lord. 9 For Christ died and rose to life in order to be the Lord of the living and of the dead. 10 You then, who eat only vegetables—why do you pass judgement on others? And you who eat anything—why do you despise other believers? All of us will stand before God to be judged by him. 11 For the scripture says:
"As surely as I am the living God, says the Lord,
    everyone will kneel before me,
    and everyone will confess that I am God."
12 Every one of us, then, will have to give an account of ourselves to God.
Romans 14:7–12, GNB

9 For God has not destined us for wrath, but to obtain salvation through our Lord Jesus Christ, 10 who died for us so that whether we are awake or asleep we might live with him. 11 Therefore encourage one another and build one another up, just as you are doing.
1 Thessalonians 5:9–11, ESV

Christine C. Sponsler

God desires for everyone to know Him and to believe in His salvation, so we may receive eternal life. It is with Christ's strength and encouraging words that we can encourage others. Christ died for everyone's sins. He did not pick and choose people that He desired to save. He chose to save us all. He loves us all this much!

*****

Be the encouragement that God has called you to be!

The Lord is Our Strength

The Lord is our strength, our hope and our courage. There, that is all we need to know. He guides us so that we can encourage the people that He places in our lives. The Father desires for His children to share Him with the world. If we keep His love to ourselves, we are guilty of selfish gain. We cannot gain anything by not sharing the love of God. We gain everything when we share His love with the world.

> 17 But you, my dear friends, must remember what the apostles of our Lord Jesus Christ predicted. 18 They told you that in the last times there would be scoffers whose purpose in life is to satisfy their ungodly desires. 19 These people are the ones who are creating divisions among you. They follow their natural instincts because they do not have God's Spirit in them.
>
> 20 But you, dear friends, must build each other up in your most holy faith, pray in the power of the Holy Spirit, 21 and await the mercy of our Lord Jesus Christ, who will bring you eternal life. In this way, you will keep yourselves safe in God's love.
>
> 22 And you must show mercy to those whose faith is wavering. 23 Rescue others by snatching them from the flames of judgment. Show mercy to still others, but do so with great caution, hating the sins that contaminate their lives.
>
> 24 Now all glory to God, who is able to keep you from falling away and will bring you with great joy into his glorious presence without a single fault. 25 All glory to him who alone is God, our Savior through Jesus Christ our Lord. All glory, majesty, power, and authority are his before all time, and in the present, and beyond all time! Amen.
>
> **Jude 17–25, NLT**

This scripture is great news because it means that we are saved from our sins, now go, and bring this very same good news to those who are still lost. And do not fall into their sinful ways. But share the good news of salvation in Christ Jesus our Lord! Amen!

Living for Him…Living for Ourselves

The world has become more and more complicated. More people believe in themselves than in God. However, we will all answer to the Lord one day. Therefore, it is up to us to share His love with the hurting world. We are to live a life which glorifies God. How can we glorify God if we do not share Him with the world? It is impossible. With God, nothing is impossible (see Luke 1:37). He created us from dust. He can help us to spread His Good News.

People are led by their desires every day. When they are left to their own beliefs, without hearing the Good News, it becomes something that we need to begin sharing with them, to bring them the hope of His salvation. God desires that no one shall perish (see 2 Peter 3:9). He has given us His Manual to share His promises with all we meet. Loving our brothers and sisters is a great start but sharing the Word of God with the lost is another way to be the encouragers that He designed us to be.

Using the Bible as our guide and manual is only the beginning. We are called to use the Word of God to help others find encouragement. Reading the Bible, praying and meditating are not meant to be done only when things are difficult. The Word of God is the light of the world! Embrace it! Share it!

How Good We Have It

I am often reminded of just how good we have it as believers. Even when I do not want to complain, I do. I can complain, just as much as anyone else (sometimes even more) and when I complain it is usually not about anything too tragic. Finding His strength to share His promises brings about the desired emotional relief that we tend to need, especially at the end of the day. Or even at the end of an era.

Not too long ago, someone I knew a long time ago lost their home to fire. When I went to see the damage, it was overwhelmingly tragic. It left me shocked and I began to cry because I had just been angry about making a devastating real estate investment for our company. And here I stood, in a place where I used to live, and there was no more house, no more deck, no more yard. The next few houses were even worse. Yet, I complained about trivial problems without turning to God for help. I say all of this because my nephew came over and held me as I cried. He encouraged me by letting me know that I was already forgiven. Wow, thank you Jesus!

The Cost of Encouragement

Encouraging people does not have to cost an arm and a leg either. We probably all remember the parable that Jesus told about it being easier for a camel to pass through the eye of a needle than a rich man to make it into heaven (see Matthew 19:24; Mark 10:25). This is true because we tend to find too much value in the almighty dollar. Value must be found in the joy that we share with the lost and outcasts of the world.

The more that we give to the poor, the more that we gain. We may not see it while we are here (though we may), but we will see it when we get to heaven. It is written,

> 19 Do not store up for yourselves treasures on earth, where moths and vermin destroy, and where thieves break in and steal. 20 But store up for yourselves treasures in heaven, where moths and vermin do not destroy, and where thieves do not break in and steal. 21 For where your treasure is, there your heart will be also.
> **Matthew 6:19–21, NIV**

Encouraging people costs us nothing. Discouraging people can cost us, and them, everything.

> Give, and you will receive. Your gift will return to you in full—pressed down, shaken together to make room for more, running over, and poured into your lap. The amount you give will determine the amount you get back.
> **Luke 6:38, NLT**

Encourage each other today, and every day!

His Strength or Our Pity

If we gave thanks as often as we threw ourselves a pity party, our lives would be the abundant life He desires for us. We would be joyful and would share this joy with others. However, it takes sitting down, getting into His Word and meditating on what the Word has to say to us. His words are living and breathing words.

> 11 Let us therefore be diligent to enter that rest, lest anyone fall according to the same example of disobedience. 12 For the word of God is living and powerful, and sharper than any two-edged sword, piercing even to the division of soul and spirit, and of joints and marrow, and is a discerner of the thoughts and intents of the heart. 13 And there is no creature hidden from His sight, but all things are naked and open to the eyes of Him to whom we must give account.
> **Hebrews 4:11–13, NKJV**

Our hope is in the Lord. Therefore, we share this hope and encourage others to find the hope, peace and joy that He has to offer them also. We will find rest in Him if we seek His Kingdom first.

Resting is not always easy. However, it is necessary. We were made in His image and the Lord rested.

> And on the seventh day God finished his work that he had done, and he rested on the seventh day from all his work that he had done.
> **Genesis 2:2, ESV**

Since God rested, so should we. Since God proclaimed His glory, then so should we.

As we just read in Hebrews 4:11-13, the Word is alive. He is alive. We must also remember to find rest (sitting down and reading His Word) in Him. Sharing the Word also helps other people find this rest. The intentions of our hearts are made known when we either discourage people or encourage them. Let's trek on together and find out how we can be the God-given encourager He desires for us to be.

Even though there are days that we do not feel like encouraging others, we must try to push through and encourage at least one person. When we can push through the discouraging feelings, we are not only able to encourage others, but we also become encouraged again. Giving thanks to the Lord is another way to find encouragement.

The Encouragement of Giving Thanks in All Circumstances

Giving thanks is not always easy. Sometimes our lives are hard to bear. However, we can always rely upon God to help us through whatever is troubling us. Let's read the entirety of Psalm 107 and heal from anything that might be troubling us so that we can encourage others more.

1 Give thanks to the LORD, for he is good;
    his love endures forever.

2 Let the redeemed of the LORD tell their story—
    those he redeemed from the hand of the foe,
3 those he gathered from the lands,
    from east and west, from north and south.

4 Some wandered in desert wastelands,
    finding no way to a city where they could settle.
5 They were hungry and thirsty,
    and their lives ebbed away.
6 Then they cried out to the LORD in their trouble,
    and he delivered them from their distress.
7 He led them by a straight way
    to a city where they could settle.
8 Let them give thanks to the LORD for his unfailing love
    and his wonderful deeds for mankind,
9 for he satisfies the thirsty
    and fills the hungry with good things.

10 Some sat in darkness, in utter darkness,
    prisoners suffering in iron chains,
11 because they rebelled against God's commands
    and despised the plans of the Most High.
12 So he subjected them to bitter labor;
    they stumbled, and there was no one to help.
13 Then they cried to the LORD in their trouble,

and he saved them from their distress.
14 He brought them out of darkness, the utter darkness,
     and broke away their chains.
15 Let them give thanks to the LORD for his unfailing love
     and his wonderful deeds for mankind,
16 for he breaks down gates of bronze
     and cuts through bars of iron.

17 Some became fools through their rebellious ways
     and suffered affliction because of their iniquities.
18 They loathed all food
     and drew near the gates of death.
19 Then they cried to the LORD in their trouble,
     and he saved them from their distress.
20 He sent out his word and healed them;
     he rescued them from the grave.
21 Let them give thanks to the LORD for his unfailing love
     and his wonderful deeds for mankind.
22 Let them sacrifice thank offerings
     and tell of his works with songs of joy.

23 Some went out on the sea in ships;
     they were merchants on the mighty waters.
24 They saw the works of the LORD,
     his wonderful deeds in the deep.
25 For he spoke and stirred up a tempest
     that lifted high the waves.
26 They mounted up to the heavens and went down to the
          depths;
     in their peril their courage melted away.
27 They reeled and staggered like drunkards;
     they were at their wits' end.
28 Then they cried out to the LORD in their trouble,
     and he brought them out of their distress.
29 He stilled the storm to a whisper;
     the waves of the sea were hushed.
30 They were glad when it grew calm,
     and he guided them to their desired haven.
31 Let them give thanks to the LORD for his unfailing love

and his wonderful deeds for mankind.
32 Let them exalt him in the assembly of the people
and praise him in the council of the elders.

33 He turned rivers into a desert,
flowing springs into thirsty ground,
34 and fruitful land into a salt waste,
because of the wickedness of those who lived there.
35 He turned the desert into pools of water
and the parched ground into flowing springs;
36 there he brought the hungry to live,
and they founded a city where they could settle.
37 They sowed fields and planted vineyards
that yielded a fruitful harvest;
38 he blessed them, and their numbers greatly increased,
and he did not let their herds diminish.

39 Then their numbers decreased, and they were humbled
by oppression, calamity and sorrow;
40 he who pours contempt on nobles
made them wander in a trackless waste.
41 But he lifted the needy out of their affliction
and increased their families like flocks.
42 The upright see and rejoice,
but all the wicked shut their mouths.

43 Let the one who is wise heed these things
and ponder the loving deeds of the LORD.
Psalm 107, NIV

Reading this Psalm brings about encouragement. This Psalm is the encouragement toward the reunion (or the first union) with our God! God will always keep us near Himself. He desires that we share His promise with others, and He desires that we share intimate times with Him as well.

How many times in this life have we felt hungry for more? More of what? More of Who? When we are hungry, He gives us His Word to feed off and we drink in His promises. He shares His promises with us. We are encouraged and blessed through His Word. Now, we must share this same miraculous love with others.

He satisfies the thirsty. He satisfies the hungry. He asks us to be the vessels for which He brings this satisfaction to others. The Holy Spirit is awakened and filled with joy as we share the encouraging words and promises of God. Each time a person is encouraged, they have the opportunity to give thanks to the Lord. We are not the reason they can do this. We are the vessel that God uses to share His encouraging words.

There are times when we all suffer from darkness in our lives. When the lost struggle with this darkness, they either have someone like you or me to help them through the struggle, or they struggle alone. God can hear their cries, whether we encourage them or not. Therefore, it makes sense to be a part of what He is doing in their lives. Share His encouraging Word and watch their lives finally have meaning.

After struggling through the darkest parts of their lives, they will be so encouraged that they will sing praises to the Lord. Their chains are broken. Their lives are freed from the slavery of sin and their cries to the Lord have been heard. Hallelujah!

Has anyone reading this not been rebellious to the Lord? Has anyone reading this ever cried out to the Lord during that rebellion? I believe that we all can answer yes to both questions. Therefore, through our encouraging words to others, we can watch the same 'aha' moments arrive in their lives. Witnessing their discovery of the grace for which we all find hope. How exciting!

When we cry out to the Lord, He saves us from the grave. Our hearts and souls deserve death and destruction. However, through the grace of God, we are saved…all of us! So, let's share this salvation, as often as we can. Jesus sacrificed His life so that we could all share in His salvation. How encouraging is that?!

Metaphorically (some of us literally), we have all been to the depths of the sea. In the depths, we could still cry out to God. Do you believe that someone that you know is struggling with these depths right now?

We must encourage them! Share the Good News of their salvation with them. We must bless them, as the Lord has blessed us.

Not only does the Lord quench our thirst. He also dries up our lives when we feel as though we are drowning. Life is difficult. Without the encouragement of His Good News, we are devastated, distraught and drowning. However, when we cry out to the Lord, He answers with His blessings, grace, and mercy. To help others find this hope, we must try to remain encouraging in all that we do and say.

One way or another, we are to become humble. When we exalt ourselves, He will humble us. When we humble ourselves, He will exalt us (see James 4:10; 1 Peter 5:6). It is wasteful to try to be exalted on our own strength. The Lord is our strength, and He is the only One Who has the power and strength to exalt us. God is love and the only One to be praised and exalted by us. Encouraging others helps to share His love, strength and promise of eternal life with Him.

Did anyone encourage us when we were struggling with the darkness of this world? Have we ever felt alone, and then someone shared the encouraging words of the Lord's promises? Were we ever stuck in our own world and pushing forward on our own strength?

Well, trust me; we can encourage others who are struggling with these issues right now. We are a part of a much bigger thing. Eternity is not a journey to take alone. We must encourage someone else to take this journey with us today.

Christine C. Sponsler

Chapter 5: Taming the Tongue

1 Not many of you should become teachers, my brothers, for you know that we who teach will be judged with greater strictness. 2 For we all stumble in many ways. And if anyone does not stumble in what he says, he is a perfect man, able also to bridle his whole body. 3 If we put bits into the mouths of horses so that they obey us, we guide their whole bodies as well. 4 Look at the ships also: though they are so large and are driven by strong winds, they are guided by a very small rudder wherever the will of the pilot directs. 5 So also the tongue is a small member, yet it boasts of great things.

How great a forest is set ablaze by such a small fire! 6 And the tongue is a fire, a world of unrighteousness. The tongue is set among our members, staining the whole body, setting on fire the entire course of life, and set on fire by hell. 7 For every kind of beast and bird, of reptile and sea creature, can be tamed and has been tamed by mankind, 8 but no human being can tame the tongue. It is a restless evil, full of deadly poison. 9 With it we bless our Lord and Father, and with it we curse people who are made in the likeness of God. 10 From the same mouth come blessing and cursing. My brothers, these things ought not to be so. 11 Does a spring pour forth from the same opening both fresh and salt water? 12 Can a fig tree, my brothers, bear olives, or a grapevine produce figs? Neither can a salt pond yield fresh water.
James 3:1–12, ESV

The Lord desires that we tame our tongues. I have a prayer that goes like this, "Lord, please bite my tongue for me, because I am no good at doing it myself. Amen!" He usually helps a little bit, but mostly directs me to His Word for this help.

Christine C. Sponsler

*****

Let's encourage others with our tongues! Let's not use our tongues as the weapon it is capable of being.

Words are Dangerous...or Encouraging

Words, or the lack thereof, are usually the worst part of shunning people. We must learn to ask God to tame our tongues. I have another saying that makes me laugh but is profoundly serious also. It is, "Lord, bite my tongue for me, so that it is with Your strength that I do not say harmful words to others." I simply desire not to harm anyone with my words and the old saying to "bite your tongue" is not quite strong enough in certain situations. If the Lord bites my tongue for me, I have a better chance of using biblical, godly words, instead of harmful words.

Can we tame our own tongues? Do we have enough power and strength to accomplish this? Are we capable of 'always' watching our mouths? Or do we need the Savior, the Father, and the Spirit to guide us in all that we do and say?

The obvious answer is that we need His guidance. However, the not so obvious part of this answer is how do we tap into this strength and power? Through daily devotions, meditation, prayer and allowing the Word of God to flow through everything that we do. Will we mess up? YEP! We are human beings, not God. This is where His guidance comes in...to help us when we mess up.

The tongue is one of the smallest members of the body. Yet, it can do the most damage. James reminds us that our words can do more harm than good unless we decide to use them to encourage people. Unfortunately, we use the same tongue to bless the Lord and then turn around and discourage our neighbor, friend, or family member. This will not do!

As we read James and realize that each of us is not perfect and cannot tame our tongues, we can be encouraged by the Word of God, that He forgives our shortcomings. Therefore, we can encourage each other so that we desire to press on toward the goal of becoming more Christlike. Taming the tongue takes strength beyond ourselves and encouraging each other to seek His strength is the goal for believers.

Biting our tongues might hurt for the moment. However, allowing our words to fall out of our mouths will hurt for much longer! Taming the tongue can be fun. Ask the Lord to bite your tongue so that you do not discourage people with your words and see what happens!

Christine C. Sponsler

Reaping What We Sow

We will reap what we sow. Therefore, it is important to sow encouraging words to others. Helping each other to make it through another day is encouraging. Guidance from people is good, but when the Holy Spirit is guiding us, we can show others how He can guide them too.

> 1 Brothers and sisters, if someone is caught in a sin, you who live by the Spirit should restore that person gently. But watch yourselves, or you also may be tempted. 2 Carry each other's burdens, and in this way you will fulfill the law of Christ. 3 If anyone thinks they are something when they are not, they deceive themselves. 4 Each one should test their own actions. Then they can take pride in themselves alone, without comparing themselves to someone else, 5 for each one should carry their own load. 6 Nevertheless, the one who receives instruction in the word should share all good things with their instructor.
>
> 7 Do not be deceived: God cannot be mocked. A man reaps what he sows. 8 Whoever sows to please their flesh, from the flesh will reap destruction; whoever sows to please the Spirit, from the Spirit will reap eternal life. 9 Let us not become weary in doing good, for at the proper time we will reap a harvest if we do not give up. 10 Therefore, as we have opportunity, let us do good to all people, especially to those who belong to the family of believers.
> **Galatians 6:1–10, NIV**

When the Word reads brothers or sisters, it is directed toward you and me. We are brothers and sisters, in Christ. Therefore, encouraging each other should come easier. However, do we always rely on God to be our strength? I know that I fall short of this often. I also know that He is forgiving, and this encourages me to carry on and not live in guilt and shame. We live by His grace and mercy, not guilt and shame.

Restoring our brother and sister should also be easy. However, I have found that when I am struggling, I have a smaller amount of forgiveness in my heart. I try to remember to call upon God and His strength during these times but still fall short. How about you?

It's okay to fall short because "...all have sinned and fall short of the glory of God" (Romans 3:23, ESV). Asking for His encouraging words is how we recover from this fall. Also, when we fall short, it helps us to remember that we should never judge someone else who has fallen short. Encouraging people to turn to the Word will help them find forgiveness, grace, and mercy.

Whenever we use our tongues to harm others, we reap a heap of trouble upon ourselves. Sometimes, we even heap the same trouble on the person whom we just discouraged with our words. When we heap this mess upon others, it is better for us to have a millstone tied around our necks and jump into the sea (see Matthew 18:6; Mark 9:42; Luke 17:2). We are in big trouble.

Yes, we can and should repent, but we must reconcile with this person as soon as possible.

We reap what we sow. Do we truly want to reap discouragement? Are we ready (in our own strength) to face the discouraging words that we used on someone else? No!

All of this means that we should be sowing encouraging words from the Word of God so that this is what we reap. It is better to trust our guts than to say something and then try to take it back. Words cannot be taken back. Will there be forgiveness when we reap discouragement? Yes, but at what cost? Has anyone ever lost a friend because we used the wrong words? I have and I regret this often.

Does this mean that I am not forgiven? No! Does it mean that I am wrong, and the other person is right? Not necessarily! But it does mean that I said something that I should not have said. So, I reaped the loss of a friend.

As we already know, the flesh is present during our entire lives. However, so is our Spirit! Our strength comes from above. We encourage others to find this out through His Word and reap another friend set for heaven. What an awesome thing to reap. When we sow discord, we will receive discord. When we sow encouragement, we reap encouragement. God is faithful and we can trust Him to present encouraging words to us so that we can share them with the world. Let's try it today!

Christine C. Sponsler

Chapter 6: The Importance of Encouragement

Light shines on the godly,
and joy on those whose hearts are right.
Psalm 97:11, NLT

…but those who hope in the LORD
will renew their strength.
They will soar on wings like eagles;
they will run and not grow weary,
they will walk and not be faint.
Isaiah 40:31, NIV

1 We who are strong have an obligation to bear with the failings of the weak, and not to please ourselves. 2 Let each of us please his neighbor for his good, to build him up. 3 For Christ did not please himself, but as it is written, "The reproaches of those who reproached you fell on me." 4 For whatever was written in former days was written for our instruction, that through endurance and through the encouragement of the Scriptures we might have hope. 5 May the God of endurance and encouragement grant you to live in such harmony with one another, in accord with Christ Jesus, 6 that together you may with one voice glorify the God and Father of our Lord Jesus Christ. 7 Therefore welcome one another as Christ has welcomed you, for the glory of God.
Romans 15:1–7, ESV

Where seldom is heard a discouraging word and the skies are not cloudy all day. Home, home on the range.
Lomax, J.A.

Christine C. Sponsler

Hopefully, this can be said about the church without isolating them from people. It is all right to be alone sometimes, but God created us to be relational beings; relational with Him and His people. Recently, we have been forced to be relational from afar and that's okay. We still encourage each other and demonstrate His love to each other.

*****

May God bless and keep you, always.

Isolation vs. Alone Time

Forced isolation can feel like a prison. However, it can also cause us to rely completely on the Lord. Therefore, gathering together might have to wait a little while but remember, we have eternity together. Isolation must be temporary. Alone time with God is an eternal investment!

Isolation is not biblical. However, taking time to be alone with God is not only biblical but necessary so that He may feed you and supply your needs so that you may supply people's needs. When we have our alone time with God, He can equip us so that we can encourage other people. Encouragement is important because without it, we are hopeless.

Finding people who encourage us is very important also. If we are discouraged, it is more difficult to support others with encouraging words. When we spend time in God's Word, we are equipped, supported and strengthened so that we are an encouragement to other people. If you will notice, there are very few people in the Bible who are alone for any significant amount of time. Gathering together with other people helps us to share His love and to receive His love from others.

His Strength Builds Our Courage

When we rely upon His strength, we become invincible. He is our strength and our courage. When we share this with others, He becomes their strength and courage also. These are words of encouragement. Let's find His strength in one of the most treasured Psalms.

The Encouraging Words of Psalm 91

1 Whoever dwells in the shelter of the Most High
   will rest in the shadow of the Almighty.
2 I will say of the LORD, "He is my refuge and my fortress,
   my God, in whom I trust."

3 Surely he will save you
   from the fowler's snare
   and from the deadly pestilence.
4 He will cover you with his feathers,
   and under his wings you will find refuge;

>his faithfulness will be your shield and rampart.
> 5 You will not fear the terror of night,
>   nor the arrow that flies by day,
> 6 nor the pestilence that stalks in the darkness,
>   nor the plague that destroys at midday.
> 7 A thousand may fall at your side,
>   ten thousand at your right hand,
>   but it will not come near you.
> 8 You will only observe with your eyes
>   and see the punishment of the wicked.
>
> 9 If you say, "The LORD is my refuge,"
>   and you make the Most High your dwelling,
> 10 no harm will overtake you,
>   no disaster will come near your tent.
> 11 For he will command his angels concerning you
>   to guard you in all your ways;
> 12 they will lift you up in their hands,
>   so that you will not strike your foot against a stone.
> 13 You will tread on the lion and the cobra;
>   you will trample the great lion and the serpent.
>
> 14 "Because he loves me," says the LORD, "I will rescue him;
>   I will protect him, for he acknowledges my name.
> 15 He will call on me, and I will answer him;
>   I will be with him in trouble,
>   I will deliver him and honor him.
> 16 With long life I will satisfy him
>   and show him my salvation."

Psalm 91, NIV

When we discover the shelter of the Most High, we have found the most worthwhile treasure of our lives. He covers us with His protective wings and creates a place to dwell which is safe and secure. However, nowhere in this Psalm does it read that we are to keep all of this to ourselves. We encourage others with His shelter of safety.

God is the only Person we can always trust. He will never leave nor forsake us, but He will also never lie to us. He teaches us that a lying tongue is not honorable (see Proverbs 6:16-19). His desire is for us to encourage each other and do this through His Truth.

Nightmares still occur when we trust in the Lord. However, since He is our fortress, we can trust that He will not allow us to be consumed by these dreams. Darkness is all around us, and sometimes we fall prey to the darkness. The Lord reroutes us into the light (see 1 Peter 2:9). Jesus is the way, the truth, and the life (see John 14:6) which means that we live in the light and must share the light with others.

He commands His angels to care for us and to lift us up. We need to encourage others with this hope. He rescues us from ourselves, others and the enemy. Therefore, we are called His sons and daughters (see 2 Corinthians 6:18). Since we are His sons and daughters, we can hold fast to His salvation and then encourage others to do the same.

Love is…Courage

Love stems from courage; God is our courage… God is love!

7 Dear friends, let us love one another, for love comes from God. Everyone who loves has been born of God and knows God. 8 Whoever does not love does not know God, because God is love. 9 This is how God showed his love among us: He sent his one and only Son into the world that we might live through him. 10 This is love: not that we loved God, but that he loved us and sent his Son as an atoning sacrifice for our sins. 11 Dear friends, since God so loved us, we also ought to love one another. 12 No one has ever seen God; but if we love one another, God lives in us and his love is made complete in us.

13 This is how we know that we live in him and he in us: He has given us of his Spirit. 14 And we have seen and testify that the Father has sent his Son to be the Savior of the world. 15 If anyone acknowledges that Jesus is the Son of God, God lives in them and they in God. 16 And so we know and rely on the love God has for us.

God is love. Whoever lives in love lives in God, and God in them. 17 This is how love is made complete among us so that we will have confidence on the day of judgment:

Christine C. Sponsler

In this world we are like Jesus. 18 There is no fear in love. But perfect love drives out fear, because fear has to do with punishment. The one who fears is not made perfect in love.

19 We love because he first loved us. 20 Whoever claims to love God yet hates a brother or sister is a liar. For whoever does not love their brother and sister, whom they have seen, cannot love God, whom they have not seen. 21 And he has given us this command: Anyone who loves God must also love their brother and sister.

1 John 4:7–21, NIV

As the title of this text reads, "Encouragement takes Courage." What this means is that since we have a great inheritance, we are to share it with our brothers and sisters. We are also to share it with the lost to bring them into the adoption of God, and then they become sons and daughters of God.

It takes courage to share things with a world that is not ready to hear the Good News.

> The Spirit of the Sovereign LORD is on me,
>   because the LORD has anointed me
>   to proclaim good news to the poor.
> He has sent me to bind up the brokenhearted,
>   to proclaim freedom for the captives
>   and release from darkness for the prisoners,
> **Isaiah 61:1, NIV**

The Spirit of the Lord is upon us, we need to bring this into a broken and troubled world. Freedom for the captives is necessary so that they will be encouraged enough not to dwell in darkness anymore. The light will appear to the lost. However, it is up to us to be the vessels He uses to present the light. All of this takes…you guessed it, Courage!

Let's find our courage to be a part of what God is doing in the lives of others!

Love is…Strength

Love requires strength; God is our strength…God is love!

7 Dear friends, let us continue to love one another, for love comes from God. Anyone who loves is a child of God and knows God. 8 But anyone who does not love does not know God, for God is love.

9 God showed how much he loved us by sending his one and only Son into the world so that we might have eternal life through him. 10 This is real love—not that we loved God, but that he loved us and sent his Son as a sacrifice to take away our sins.

11 Dear friends, since God loved us that much, we surely ought to love each other. 12 No one has ever seen God. But if we love each other, God lives in us, and his love is brought to full expression in us.

13 And God has given us his Spirit as proof that we live in him and he in us. 14 Furthermore, we have seen with our own eyes and now testify that the Father sent his Son to be the Savior of the world. 15 All who declare that Jesus is the Son of God have God living in them, and they live in God. 16 We know how much God loves us, and we have put our trust in his love.

God is love, and all who live in love live in God, and God lives in them. 17 And as we live in God, our love grows more perfect. So we will not be afraid on the day of judgment, but we can face him with confidence because we live like Jesus here in this world.

18 Such love has no fear, because perfect love expels all fear. If we are afraid, it is for fear of punishment, and this shows that we have not fully experienced his perfect love. 19 We love each other because he loved us first.

20 If someone says, "I love God," but hates a fellow believer, that person is a liar; for if we don't love people we can see, how can we love God, whom we cannot see? 21 And he has given us this command: Those who love God must also love their fellow believers.

1 John 4:7–21, NLT

Finding the strength to get by each day can be rather tough these days and here we are reading about having to have enough strength to encourage others…Yikes!

How are we to find this strength on our own? We aren't! God is our strength! I don't know about you, but I find this refreshing and rewarding. I do not have to find the strength to encourage others by myself. He will show me through his Word. Hallelujah!

Since God is our strength and our comfort, we can easily share this with others…right?

Not always! We must be able to gather His strength in time spent in His Word, through prayer and petition (see Philippians 4:6). Encouraging others to share in the time they spend with the Lord. When we share what we hear, see and read from the Lord, we are able to be more encouraging to others and to feel their encouraging words too. Sharing His strength is encouragement.

Let's spread His love and strength throughout the land today and every day!

The Courage to Love

When we read that God is love, what comes to mind? Is it that He loves you? Is it that He loves me? Or is it that He loves the world?

> For God so loved the world, that he gave his only Son, that whoever believes in him should not perish but have eternal life.
> **John 3:16, ESV**

We must find the courage to share this with all the lost and outcasts of this world.

His courage is coursing through our veins. His strength is a part of our core values and morals. His promises share that we are not alone while accomplishing what He asks of us.

> This is my command—be strong and courageous! Do not be afraid or discouraged. For the LORD your God is with you wherever you go.
> **Joshua 1:9, NLT**

Have I not commanded you? Be strong and courageous. Do not be afraid; do not be discouraged, for the LORD your God will be with you wherever you go.
Joshua 1:9, NIV

The two versions of this verse are powerful. They pretty much say the same thing, but there is something we could miss each time we read this verse. God is with us! Since He is with us, we are carrying on through His strength!

> When you go through deep waters,
>   I will be with you.
> When you go through rivers of difficulty,
>   you will not drown.
> When you walk through the fire of oppression,
>   you will not be burned up;
>   the flames will not consume you.
> **Isaiah 43:2, NLT**

Each of us is going to have trouble and difficulties in this world. We also know that we can still be encouraged because God has overcome this world (see John 16:33). When we share these encouraging words with the world, His promises are seen by others. They do not need to be afraid anymore either.

> Don't be afraid, for I am with you.
>   Don't be discouraged, for I am your God.
> I will strengthen you and help you.
>   I will hold you up with my victorious right hand.
> **Isaiah 41:10, NLT**

Discouragement is no longer an integral part of their lives. God is with them, just as He is with us. His victorious right hand is holding all of us and we are powered through His strength.

There is also strength in numbers. The enemy has helpers supporting his agenda. The enemy is not omnipresent. This means that he needs helpers. Therefore, we must encourage others to be supporters of the

Christine C. Sponsler

Word of God. We could all use the help of others to gain the upper hand with the enemy. God is our upper hand and He will conquer the enemy, always!

The Strength of Three

In the Book of Ecclesiastes, we read that a three-strand cord is much stronger. We also read that when a person falls alone there is no one there to help them back up (see Ecclesiastes 4:9-12). Strength comes in numbers.

The most important number that a believer knows is three. Noah's three sons (see Genesis 6:10), a three-strand cord (see Ecclesiastes 4:12), the three Scripture references of Jesus while Satan was trying to tempt Him (Matthew 4:1-11), and the Trinity of God the Father, God the Son and God the Holy Spirit (see Genesis 1:1-2; John 14:16-17; Romans 14:17-18). There are many other representations of three in the Bible and reading the Bible daily will help us to find all the other references.

The importance of three is that it is not one! "One is the loneliest number that you'll ever do" (One Lyrics). This is a great song. It has much meaning behind the lyrics. It reminds us that without each other and God, we are too lonely to be encouraging to each other.

The only time the number one is glorious is when we are referring to God. "Hear, O Israel: The LORD our God, the LORD is one" (Deuteronomy 6:4, NIV). Be encouraged by the Bible and by a person who loves the Word of God. Encouraging each other with His Love helps multiply residents in heaven.

Godly people encourage with His love!

PART 2: Self-Encouragement

So God created mankind in his own image,
in the image of God he created them;
male and female he created them.
Genesis 1:27, NIV

10 This is what the LORD says: "When seventy years are completed for Babylon, I will come to you and fulfill my good promise to bring you back to this place. 11 For I know the plans I have for you," declares the LORD, "plans to prosper you and not to harm you, plans to give you hope and a future. 12 Then you will call on me and come and pray to me, and I will listen to you. 13 You will seek me and find me when you seek me with all your heart. 14 I will be found by you," declares the LORD, "and will bring you back from captivity. I will gather you from all the nations

and places where I have banished you," declares the LORD, "and will bring you back to the place from which I carried you into exile."
Jeremiah 29:10–14, NIV

I absolutely love these Scripture verses. We were created in His image, asked to 'go' be His ambassador and spread the hope of His future in eternity with Him. We must allow Him to cast out all fear and remember what Jesus did for us. We are not to hoard but share his love with everyone and plant the seeds to watch new brothers and sisters find their 'aha' moments.

*****

Be Encouraged today and every day!

Chapter 7: How Encouragement Toward Others Encourages the Self Also

A generous person will prosper;
    whoever refreshes others will be refreshed.
Proverbs 11:25, NIV

I urge you, first of all, to pray for all people. Ask God to help them; intercede on their behalf, and give thanks for them.
1 Timothy 2:1, NLT

3 Praise be to the God and Father of our Lord Jesus Christ, the Father of compassion and the God of all comfort, 4 who comforts us in all our troubles, so that we can comfort those in any trouble with the comfort we ourselves receive from God. 5 For just as we share abundantly in the sufferings of Christ, so also our comfort abounds through Christ. 6 If we are distressed, it is for your comfort and salvation; if we are comforted, it is for your comfort, which produces in you patient endurance of the same sufferings we suffer. 7 And our hope for you is firm, because we know that just as you share in our sufferings, so also you share in our comfort.

8 We do not want you to be uninformed, brothers and sisters, about the troubles we experienced in the province of Asia. We were under great pressure, far beyond our ability to endure, so that we despaired of life itself. 9 Indeed, we felt we had received the sentence of death. But this happened that we might not rely on ourselves but on God, who raises the dead. 10 He has delivered us from such a deadly peril, and he will deliver us again. On him we have set our hope that he will continue to deliver us, 11 as you help us by your prayers. Then many will give thanks

on our behalf for the gracious favor granted us in answer
to the prayers of many.
2 Corinthians 1:3–11, NIV

As the title of this book states, encouraging others not only takes
courage, it also takes strength and a willingness to share His promises with
others. Sharing encouraging words not only helps the person we share
these words with, but it also creates spiritual growth in us. Our growth
relies heavily on sharing the Word of God with the world. Have you ever
shared His Word with someone, and you could see the light bulb flip on?
Well, this can happen more often, if we share His love with more people.

We are not to do things to receive something from Him. However, we
can expect that His love is present when we obey His command to
support, love, and encourage each other. We are to selflessly encourage as
many people as we can.

*****

Encouraging our 'self' is not a selfish act. It is an important part of
encouraging other people!

In His Image

Hello again my brothers and sisters. I wish you and yours a wonderful journey through the gloriousness of His encouraging love. Go look in the mirror right now and tell yourself, "I am a child of the one true God and I am fearfully and wonderfully made in His image!"

We are made in His image. Can you fathom what that even means? It means that He created us to represent Him to the world. Humbling and honoring to think about, right? We can be in awe of Him and take this admiration of Him into the world, today. I don't know about you, but this excites me. Our 'self' comes from His 'self' and we are to share this with our family, friends, neighbors, the rest of the communities which we live in and with the world.

Anyone else feeling motivated to get out there and shout from the rooftops? Okay, let's go!

Go...

I like to think of 'ready, set, go' here. God is calling us to 'go' and make disciples. How do we do this? We take Him with us and encourage others to come to know Him as their God too. It sounds simple, but it is also difficult. We, as human beings, fear rejection. However, this fear is met with His faithfulness and the fear of rejection is easier to get rid of.

> 5 "Woe to me!" I cried. "I am ruined! For I am a man of unclean lips, and I live among a people of unclean lips, and my eyes have seen the King, the LORD Almighty."
> 6 Then one of the seraphim flew to me with a live coal in his hand, which he had taken with tongs from the altar. 7 With it he touched my mouth and said, "See, this has touched your lips; your guilt is taken away and your sin atoned for."
> 8 Then I heard the voice of the Lord saying, "Whom shall I send? And who will go for us?"
> And I said, "Here am I. Send me!"
> **Isaiah 6:5–8, NIV**

The prophet Isaiah made sure that God's people knew what they had to do to further His Kingdom. When the Lord needed people to take the Word of God to the ends of the earth, Isaiah had the desire in his heart to say, "Here am I. Send me!" (v.8) because he knew that the people needed repentance from their sins. We have been called to 'go' also. Are we prepared to say, "Here I am, send me"? Let's try it today. Share the Good News with someone that has been on your heart. Jesus is with us while we 'go.'

Jesus said, "go and make disciples" (see Matthew 28:18-20) because He made us in His image to share His image with the rest of the world. I can hardly contain myself right now. Do you know what this means? It means that we can encourage people to believe in Christ, through our actions and our words. It takes courage to bring encouraging words to other people, especially hurting people.

The Hope for His Future

Reading the Scripture from above makes it even more profound that He chose us to represent Him and His Kingdom. Think about that for a moment! He chose you, He chose me, He chose us as His ambassadors.

> 11 Because we understand our fearful responsibility to the Lord, we work hard to persuade others. God knows we are sincere, and I hope you know this, too. 12 Are we commending ourselves to you again? No, we are giving you a reason to be proud of us, so you can answer those who brag about having a spectacular ministry rather than having a sincere heart. 13 If it seems we are crazy, it is to bring glory to God. And if we are in our right minds, it is for your benefit. 14 Either way, Christ's love controls us. Since we believe that Christ died for all, we also believe that we have all died to our old life. 15 He died for everyone so that those who receive his new life will no longer live for themselves. Instead, they will live for Christ, who died and was raised for them.
>
> 16 So we have stopped evaluating others from a human point of view. At one time we thought of Christ merely from a human point of view. How differently we know him

now! 17 This means that anyone who belongs to Christ has become a new person. The old life is gone; a new life has begun!

18 And all of this is a gift from God, who brought us back to himself through Christ. And God has given us this task of reconciling people to him. 19 For God was in Christ, reconciling the world to himself, no longer counting people's sins against them. And he gave us this wonderful message of reconciliation. 20 So we are Christ's ambassadors; God is making his appeal through us. We speak for Christ when we plead, "Come back to God!" 21 For God made Christ, who never sinned, to be the offering for our sin, so that we could be made right with God through Christ.

2 Corinthians 5:11–21, NLT

So let us get this straight, God created us in His image and we are His ambassadors so that we can bring the hope of His future to everyone. Wow, I don't know about you all, but I am not only excited, but encouraged!

We share in the hope of the Lord's future for us. We are His ambassadors to 'go' and share this Good News with everyone we meet. We share the Good News as often as we can.

We share it gently and directly. This does not mean that we cram the Lord down their throats. It simply means that we share His hope for the future with everyone and allow the Holy Spirit to move in them.

We no longer need to fear what people will say or do with this information because we have the spirit of power and love, not of fear (see 2 Timothy 1:7). We might even have someone directly reject the Good News, but we also know that the Holy Spirit can use this to move in their hearts.

The Fear of Rejection Cast Out

We are no longer to fear rejection. The 'self' of the one true God lives with the Spirit of power and love now. We are not to fear anymore (see Isaiah 41:10; Philippians 4:6-7). We are to boldly come to the throne, to obtain His strength to share His love with everybody we meet.

Let us then approach God's throne of grace with confidence, so that we may receive mercy and find grace to help us in our time of need.

Hebrews 4:16, NIV

Intimidating? Yes, but necessary, for without deeds, faith is dead.

14 What good is it, my brothers and sisters, if someone claims to have faith but has no deeds? Can such faith save them? 15 Suppose a brother or a sister is without clothes and daily food. 16 If one of you says to them, "Go in peace; keep warm and well fed," but does nothing about their physical needs, what good is it? 17 In the same way, faith by itself, if it is not accompanied by action, is dead.

18 But someone will say, "You have faith; I have deeds."

Show me your faith without deeds, and I will show you my faith by my deeds. 19 You believe that there is one God. Good! Even the demons believe that—and shudder.

20 You foolish person, do you want evidence that faith without deeds is useless? 21 Was not our father Abraham considered righteous for what he did when he offered his son Isaac on the altar? 22 You see that his faith and his actions were working together, and his faith was made complete by what he did. 23 And the scripture was fulfilled that says, "Abraham believed God, and it was credited to him as righteousness," and he was called God's friend. 24 You see that a person is considered righteous by what they do and not by faith alone.

25 In the same way, was not even Rahab the prostitute considered righteous for what she did when she gave lodging to the spies and sent them off in a different direction? 26 As the body without the spirit is dead, so faith without deeds is dead.

James 2:14–26, NIV

Godly deeds include sharing encouraging words with both believers and unbelievers alike. Planting the seed of the Good News is an honor. He has called us to do this. When we share His hope for the eternal future, we are planting seeds of love and encouraging someone to live inside of His love.

> I planted the seed, Apollos watered it, but God has been making it grow. 7 So neither the one who plants nor the one who waters is anything, but only God, who makes things grow. 8 The one who plants and the one who waters have one purpose, and they will each be rewarded according to their own labor. 9 For we are co-workers in God's service; you are God's field, God's building.
> **1 Corinthians 3:6–9, NIV**

We can plant a seed, another person can water it, and then God makes it grow into the healing truth of His Salvation. The Holy Spirit works in other people's lives, even if we do not witness it right away. We can stand on His promise that our prayers will be answered, even when we are in pain.

The Lord Took Our Pain Away

What pain? You might say. I say congratulations if you can ask this question. It is true joy and faith which can honestly ask this question. However, our bodies and our hearts can cause us pain. Christ died for this pain though.

> 4 Surely he took up our pain
> and bore our suffering,
> yet we considered him punished by God,
> stricken by him, and afflicted.
> 5 But he was pierced for our transgressions,
> he was crushed for our iniquities;
> the punishment that brought us peace was on him,
> and by his wounds we are healed.
> **Isaiah 53:4–5, NIV**

Christine C. Sponsler

As mentioned before, some fears are associated with sharing the Gospel with people. He has taken these fears and replaced them with His strength, power, courage, love and hope. His image is carried on through the sharing of His Word. Watch for the 'aha' moments in the eyes of the people that you share His Word with. It will be an encouragement to you too.

Jesus went to the Cross for our punishment. Think about that again, Jesus took our place on the Cross. His pain and suffering have saved us from the death that we all deserve—the death that keeps us from God for eternity. Jesus' sacrifice made a way for us to approach the Father. What this means is that we can find the Father now. Therefore, it is up to us to share Him with everyone.

The 'Aha' Moments in Life

It is fun to watch the 'aha' moments in our lives and other people's lives also. They pop up in the most interesting places and times. One of those 'aha' moments happened to me when I began thanking God for things that I have and not complaining (as much) about the things I do not have. When we focus on the good things God has done for us, we are more encouraging to others also.

Another similar 'aha' moment was when I noticed that encouraging people gave me His joy in my life. I intend to share His love with everyone and in return He creates 'aha' moments for me and the person I am sharing with. The 'aha' moments are usually about figuring out that we are saved through the blood of Christ.

> In him we have redemption through his blood, the forgiveness of sins, in accordance with the riches of God's grace 8 that he lavished on us. With all wisdom and understanding, 9 he made known to us the mystery of his will according to his good pleasure, which he purposed in Christ, 10 to be put into effect when the times reach their fulfillment—to bring unity to all things in heaven and on earth under Christ.
> **Ephesians 1:7–10, NIV**

We are shown 'aha' moments every day; do we actually see them? I hope to see them more often. Then we can share them with others.

Shared Spiritual Blessings in Christ

We are blessed with the spiritual relationship we have with Christ. Praise the Lord that we not only have this blessing, but we share it with others, and they have it to share with even more people. We are chosen and so are the people we sow seeds with. The faith in the Lord creates an encouraging atmosphere, no matter the circumstances in our lives. We have become blameless through the gift of faith.

The Lord desires to lavish His love upon us and we are to not only receive this love but to encourage others with this same love. His grace and mercy fill our hearts. This fulfillment of grace, mercy—and the joy with it—is to be shared with the world.

> 3 Praise be to the God and Father of our Lord Jesus Christ, who has blessed us in the heavenly realms with every spiritual blessing in Christ. 4 For he chose us in him before the creation of the world to be holy and blameless in his sight. In love 5 he predestined us for adoption to sonship through Jesus Christ, in accordance with his pleasure and will—6 to the praise of his glorious grace, which he has freely given us in the One he loves. 7 In him we have redemption through his blood, the forgiveness of sins, in accordance with the riches of God's grace 8 that he lavished on us. With all wisdom and understanding, 9 he made known to us the mystery of his will according to his good pleasure, which he purposed in Christ, 10 to be put into effect when the times reach their fulfillment—to bring unity to all things in heaven and on earth under Christ.
>
> 11 In him we were also chosen, having been predestined according to the plan of him who works out everything in conformity with the purpose of his will, 12 in order that we, who were the first to put our hope in Christ, might be for the praise of his glory. 13 And you also were included in Christ when you heard the message of truth, the gospel of your salvation. When you believed, you were marked in him with a seal, the promised Holy Spirit, 14 who is a deposit guaranteeing our inheritance until the

redemption of those who are God's possession—to the praise of his glory.

Ephesians 1:3–14, NIV

Our inheritance is to be shared with others to encourage them to know the relationship with the Lord.

His salvation is a gift from Jesus to share and to open while encouraging each other. Hearing His message of truth creates a stronger bond for His children. Therefore, as His children, we are to encourage as many people as possible with this Good News.

Hoarding His Love, Or Not

Encouraging other people brings hope, joy and encouragement back into our lives also. What a concept…give and you shall receive (see Luke 6:38). This type of concept reminds me of people who excessively horde stuff in their homes.

People who hoard things usually do not have anything else in their lives because they are too busy hanging onto things they could not possibly need, they are too embarrassed to invite people over and they sometimes get stuck in the mess of the stuff they possess. Their possessions begin to possess them. If they would give some of their stuff away, they could invite people over and not be stuck inside of their homes.

I feel as though I get stuffed when I have not shared Christ with people enough. The buildup of things that could benefit me starts hindering my life because I have not given them to other people. In the same manner as someone who hoards things they do not need, it is also a form of hoarding when we have something that someone else needs and we do not share it with them. That something is the Love of God!

Sharing His love will release some of the stress build-up that we carry every day. We are meant to share the truth with as many people as we can. We are not meant to hoard His love from other people. Does this mean that we empty ourselves of Him? No, it simply means that we share enough to help others find Him too.

Brothers and Sisters

We are sisters and brothers in the name of the Lord. He has adopted us (see Ephesians 1:5) into His family. How many of us lived a life without the love of an earthly parent? It is difficult to find true love if we have never felt it before. However, as brothers and sisters, we can share a love some of us may have never known; His love is the all-time best love and He desires to share it with everyone.

We were created in His image and we are to act as family members because we are 'blood' related—Jesus' blood! How exciting! We are all family, not strangers and not simply friends, but family!

Share His love today and recognize that person in heaven! Inspiring!

Christine C. Sponsler

Chapter 8: The Importance of Daily Devotions

16 Don't you know that you yourselves are God's temple and that God's Spirit dwells in your midst? 17 If anyone destroys God's temple, God will destroy that person; for God's temple is sacred, and you together are that temple.
1 Corinthians 3:16–17, NIV

19 Do you not know that your bodies are temples of the Holy Spirit, who is in you, whom you have received from God? You are not your own; 20 you were bought at a price. Therefore honor God with your bodies.
1 Corinthians 6:19–20, NIV

1 Therefore, I urge you, brothers and sisters, in view of God's mercy, to offer your bodies as a living sacrifice, holy and pleasing to God—this is your true and proper worship. 2 Do not conform to the pattern of this world, but be transformed by the renewing of your mind. Then you will be able to test and approve what God's will is—his good, pleasing and perfect will.
Romans 12:1–2, NIV

10 Create in me a pure heart, O God,
    and renew a steadfast spirit within me.
11 Do not cast me from your presence
    or take your Holy Spirit from me.
12 Restore to me the joy of your salvation
    and grant me a willing spirit, to sustain me.

13 Then I will teach transgressors your ways,
    so that sinners will turn back to you.
Psalm 51:10–13, NIV

The renewing of our bodies, mind, heart and spirit will help us to present His encouraging words to the world. Do any of us feel the same as we did before we came to (or returned to) Christ? Do we still have that hopelessness in our minds or hearts? The answer might seem like yes, at times. However, we can call upon the Lord day and night (see Psalm 50:14-15). We have hope in the hopelessness of this life. We are to share this hope with encouraging words for other people to hear.

> And the peace of God, which transcends all understanding, will guard your hearts and your minds in Christ Jesus.
> **Philippians 4:7, NIV**

*****

Let's encourage ourselves (through devotions) and then other people (through sharing His love), today and every day!

Renew Our Bodies

Use it or lose it! This goes for our bodies too. Our bodies are the temple of the Holy Spirit (see 1 Corinthians 3:16-17). We must take care of our bodies as well as we can, so that He may use us for His glorification and to encourage others.

I recently started a dance routine again to better my body and mind. I have been a dancer all my life (off and on…mostly on) and dancing renews the joy I have found most of my life. When I do this as a way to renew the temple of God, it is even more rewarding. The Lord desires for us to be healthy so that when we bring His Good News to others, it does not drain us of energy.

The body that I use right now is borrowed. I will get another body when I meet my Lord and Savior in heaven. However, that does not mean that I allow my temporary temple (body) to deteriorate, simply because I will get another one. It does mean that as a representative of God, I must try to keep this body ready, willing, and able to share the Good News.

Renew Our Minds

Our minds (brains, really) are a muscle. Therefore, we must exercise them daily to keep them strong, capable, and alert. I have an M.Div. and genuinely enjoy learning as much about our Lord as possible. I am also halfway through my PhD/Forensic Psychology to support treatment of psychopathy and sociopathy and to bring hope to the people who suffer from these personality disorders. This is a form of renewing my mind, but the ultimate renewing of the mind is through His Word.

Reading the Bible is exciting and allows the mind to be renewed through what He has to say to us. When we 'go' and share the Good News, are we expected to do this in our own power? Let's hope not because my power runs out from time to time. His power is never-ending. Renewing our minds will remind us through who's power we work.

Renew Our Hearts

What is in our hearts comes out of our mouths (see Matthew 15:18; Luke 6:45). The more that we are in the Word of God, the more His love will come out of our mouths, and this is very encouraging to anyone who hears about His love.

God creates a pure heart in us when we desire to know Him more. Our hearts are not to be filled with fluff; they are to be filled with His Word. When the Lord asks us to encourage others, He must be able to fill our hearts with the necessary love to accomplish this task. Therefore, we must allow Him to fill our hearts.

This means that we are to listen to what God has to say to us. He speaks to us in different ways—through other people, through His Word and during times of meditation. Yes, we know that we need to pray to communicate with Him. But do we know that we need to listen to what He says after we finish praying? This is a renewal of the heart.

Renew Our Spirit

The Spirit of God dwells inside of us (see Ezekiel 36:27; Romans 8:11; Galatians 4:6). The Spirit moves through us and into the lives of other people, many times, through encouraging words. It's extremely difficult to encourage people when we are feeling discouraged. Therefore, we must allow the Lord to renew our spirits.

Jesus offers to take our yoke so that our spirit can be renewed as we rest in Him (see Matthew 11:29; 2 Corinthians 4:16). To find a true renewal of the spirit, we must also repent of our sins. Repentance is necessary for everyone. We are all sinners and while we were still sinners, Christ died for our sins (see Romans 5:8). The renewal of our spirit will allow us to encourage others even when there are certain discouraging circumstances in our lives.

Renewal of our bodies, our minds, our hearts, and our spirits can be fully supported through the next Psalm…

> Create in me a clean heart, O God,
>   And renew a steadfast spirit within me.
> 11 Do not cast me away from Your presence,
>   And do not take Your Holy Spirit from me.
>
> 12 Restore to me the joy of Your salvation,
>   And uphold me by Your generous Spirit.
>   **Psalm 51:10–12, NKJV**

Daily Devotions

When we rise in the morning, we must remember to thank God for this new day. This is the day that the Lord made, let's rejoice and be glad in it (see Psalm 118:24). Today is here, let's rejoice that He allowed us to wake up and seek Him more.

Daily devotions are not simply reading the Bible, although this is great. It also includes journaling, prayer and meditation. To be renewed, we must dive into His Word, have a communicative relationship with Him and encourage others to do the same.

Encouragement takes self-renewal. Let's get renewed and encourage each other to do the same!

Christine C. Sponsler

Chapter 9: The Importance of Prayer and Meditation

1 "I am the true vine, and my Father is the gardener. 2 He cuts off every branch in me that bears no fruit, while every branch that does bear fruit he prunes so that it will be even more fruitful. 3 You are already clean because of the word I have spoken to you. 4 Remain in me, as I also remain in you. No branch can bear fruit by itself; it must remain in the vine. Neither can you bear fruit unless you remain in me.

5 "I am the vine; you are the branches. If you remain in me and I in you, you will bear much fruit; apart from me you can do nothing. 6 If you do not remain in me, you are like a branch that is thrown away and withers; such branches are picked up, thrown into the fire and burned. 7 If you remain in me and my words remain in you, ask whatever you wish, and it will be done for you. 8 This is to my Father's glory, that you bear much fruit, showing yourselves to be my disciples.

9 "As the Father has loved me, so have I loved you. Now remain in my love. 10 If you keep my commands, you will remain in my love, just as I have kept my Father's commands and remain in his love. 11 I have told you this so that my joy may be in you and that your joy may be complete."

John 15:1–11, NIV

Our Father is the vine for which we find our nourishment. He feeds us with His Word. His promises sustain us, and we are to share His promises with others. When we do, this produces good fruit, and the Father is pleased.

Even though we are already clean, we need to share His love to bring the cleanliness to others and encourage them to share His love also. As a branch from His vine, we only thrive through His guidance. The Holy Spirit is with us and we share Him with others as often as possible.

We must remain in His Word so that we have something hopeful and encouraging to share with others. God will work in a person's life without our help, but don't we desire to be a part of what He will be doing in their lives? Of course, we do. He puts that on our hearts so that we are more eager to share Him with others.

Jesus is the Way to the Father. He has shown us how to approach the Father and now we must share this with others to encourage them to walk with God. His love will shine through our words and our hearts if we remain in Him and He in us.

*****

Share the exciting Good News and encourage others to do the same today and every day!

Knowing God

Who really knows God? We do. We are His believers and already know Him as our Father. We are still to seek Him and discover new things about Him daily. His gift of faith and grace creates a relationship with His creations… us.

> But grow in the grace and knowledge of our Lord and Savior Jesus Christ. To him be glory both now and forever! Amen.
> **2 Peter 3:18, NIV**

How do we come to know the Lord? Through His Word and through time spent in prayer and meditation. Growing in the knowledge of our Lord and Savior is the focal point of true Christian believers. To share this with others brings joy to us, others and God. We are then giving Him the glory and honor that He deserves.

We will then spend eternity with Him. We can look toward heaven and know God more intimately because of Christ's sacrifice. Christ glorified God so that we could witness God-glorifying Christ. This is another way to encourage ourselves and then others.

God granted Christ authority over us all so that we could, through our gift of faith, live in eternity. We know Christ. He knows us and this means that the Father knows us also. God sent His Son and we are saved from our sins because He did. We can approach God without feelings of shame and guilt.

> 1 After Jesus said this, he looked toward heaven and prayed:
> "Father, the hour has come. Glorify your Son, that your Son may glorify you. 2 For you granted him authority over all people that he might give eternal life to all those you have given him. 3 Now this is eternal life: that they know you, the only true God, and Jesus Christ, whom you have sent. 4 I have brought you glory on earth by finishing the work you gave me to do. 5 And now, Father, glorify me in your presence with the glory I had with you before the world began."

Christine C. Sponsler

John 17:1–5, NIV

Christ glorified God, we glorify Christ and find salvation for eternal life in heaven. Christ's obedience to the Father is our ultimate example of how we are to live. We encourage each other when we share this truth. Christ returns to the Father so that He can share in the glory again.

God sent us His only Son to save us and to show us how to live a selfless life. Through prayer and meditation, we can get closer to living the Christlike life that God intended for us. We also gain the strength of the Lord so that we can share His loving kindness with others. All of this takes prayer and meditation.

A Prayerful Life

We are not to pretend to be prayerful by conducting ourselves as the hypocrites did (see Matthew 6:5) but pray alone with the Lord and then pray with others to encourage their prayer lives. Praying for and with others does not have to be robotic or uncomfortable. Simply talk to God as if He were with you because He is. Making time to pray helps an encourager to remain filled enough to share what they are filled with, His hope.

Prayer for Ourselves

It may seem selfish to list prayers for ourselves first among all the people we are called to pray for. However, it goes back to the airplane example of placing your own oxygen mask on first and then helping others.

God feeds us with His Word. He also answers prayers. Therefore, getting the answers to our own needs first can help us when we go to help others. We need to be fed by His food (the Bible) and this way we have His strength to speak to and pray for other people.

It might be difficult to pray for ourselves at first. However, we must pray for His strength and the right encouraging words to use when we talk to people. God does not desire that we do this all on our own. As a matter of fact, He reminds us that His strength is what we need to help others.

"This, then, is how you should pray:

"'Our Father in heaven,

82

hallowed be your name,
10 your kingdom come,
your will be done,
    on earth as it is in heaven.
11 Give us today our daily bread.
12 And forgive us our debts,
    as we also have forgiven our debtors.
13 And lead us not into temptation,
    but deliver us from the evil one.'
Matthew 6:9–13, NIV

This prayer is popular, and it should be listened to rather than simply repeated. Our Father is in heaven. We are going to join Him in His timing. His name is to be adored. His Kingdom is to be sought after. We are to share this encouragement with others as much as we possibly can. Even though we have memorized this prayer, we must stop and really listen to it also.

Prayers for Others

Our prayers are not meant only for us and our loved ones. We need to pray for our communities, our states, our nation, and our world. We are to remember that our faith can move mountains and pray for our leaders.

We must pray that our leaders come to know Him. We must pray that God is put back into schools, the government, and the hearts of our people. We are to hold fast to our faith in Him and demonstrate this with love and conviction. Our conviction to His Word must be heard and seen by others to encourage them to turn back to Him.

22 "Have faith in God," Jesus answered. 23 "Truly I tell you, if anyone says to this mountain, 'Go, throw yourself into the sea,' and does not doubt in their heart but believes that what they say will happen, it will be done for them. 24 Therefore I tell you, whatever you ask for in prayer, believe that you have received it, and it will be yours. 25 And when you stand praying, if you hold anything against anyone, forgive them, so that your Father in heaven may forgive you your sins."

Mark 11:22–25, NIV

It is difficult to do anything for other people when we have nothing left in our tanks. Faith dulls at times and the notion of helping someone else might feel scary or painful. However, through His strength and love, we can help someone else feel encouraged even when we are feeling discouraged.

Is this an easy task? No. Are we the only person God can ask for help? No. But, are we one of the people He has asked to help Him? Yes, we are. We can move mountains according to His Word. When we ask God to save the lost, He does it. It may take longer than we would like, but He is faithful.

There is one other distraction from praying for others and that is we cannot have issues with people while attempting to go to the throne. God is approachable, no matter what, but if we are mad at someone or they are mad at us, it becomes distracting and our prayers are not as genuine.

Actively Listening to God (Meditation)

Oh boy, this one is my weakness. How many of us are really good at praying? How many of us take the time to stop and listen after prayer? I am guilty of not stopping after every prayer to hear what He has to say. Slowing down is difficult, but necessary. We must hear what He has to say.

> May these words of my mouth and this meditation of my heart
> be pleasing in your sight,
> LORD, my Rock and my Redeemer.
> **Psalm 19:14, NIV**

We pray to the Lord and He answers. Remember that when He seems to have no direct answer, it is usually the answer of maybe or even wait. We pray for loved ones who do not know Him or who have walked away from their faith. However, when we pray for their salvation, we must also be patient with the Lord's actions. He does not ask 'how high' when we say 'jump.' He does listen to our cries. He does not make super gestures all the time. We need to listen to His still small voice.

11 Then He said, "Go out, and stand on the mountain before the LORD." And behold, the LORD passed by, and a great and strong wind tore into the mountains and broke the rocks in pieces before the LORD, but the LORD was not in the wind; and after the wind an earthquake, but the LORD was not in the earthquake; 12 and after the earthquake a fire, but the LORD was not in the fire; and after the fire a still small voice.

1 Kings 19:11–12, NKJV

His still small voice is bigger than anything in the world. He will talk to us, but we must be ready to hear Him. Actively listening means that we must be quiet and know that He is God (see Psalm 46:10). This might seem difficult, and we may not know that we are hearing His voice, but He is talking to us through His voice, other people, and His Word.

Encouragement from Prayer

Have you ever heard someone say that they are still here because of mom, dad, sister, brother, grandmother, grandfather, or a friend's prayers? Well, that is because it's true.

For me, it was my grandmother. She would pray for me even when I noticeably walked away from our Quaker faith. I would tell her not to bother and that I was a lost cause. She continued even though I tried to discourage her from doing this for me. Boy, I sure am glad she listened to Him instead of me.

The most encouraging thing about her continued prayer is that I will one day see her next to the Lord in heaven. I could have continued through my destructive road, but with the help of my grandmother, the Lord caught my attention again and here we are. I hope that you will use the email at the end of this book to share with me stories of your prayerfully, lifesaving angels. I will not use them in a book unless you want me to, so please mention whether that would be all right with you in the email.

The Importance of Fasting

Fasting does not always mean from food. However, this is the most popular way to fast. Fasting means that we abstain from something to devote time to listening to God. When we fast, we are to remain productive so that it is not obvious that we are fasting.

> 16 "When you fast, do not look somber as the hypocrites do, for they disfigure their faces to show others they are fasting. Truly I tell you, they have received their reward in full. 17 But when you fast, put oil on your head and wash your face, 18 so that it will not be obvious to others that you are fasting, but only to your Father, who is unseen; and your Father, who sees what is done in secret, will reward you."
> **Matthew 6:16–18, NIV**

The reward for fasting should not come from something that people can give us. The reward is from God instead. His rewards are far greater than the rewards of human beings. We are to remain happy, content, and focused when we fast. When we fast from food, it is especially rewarding to be able to talk to God every time our stomach growls.

When we fast from other things, it is rewarding to stop and listen to what He has to say during these time periods. We must remain engaged in our daily activities and honor God by remembering to hear His still small voice while we are fasting. He is with us and His grace, mercy, and comfort are all that we need.

Whether in prayer, meditation, or fasting, we will encourage each other daily. Our encouragement comes from Him. Our sharing of this encouragement honors Him. It is a blessing to remain focused upon the Lord and His Kingdom.

PART 3: Family Encouragement

1 If I speak in the tongues of men or of angels, but do not have love, I am only a resounding gong or a clanging cymbal. 2 If I have the gift of prophecy and can fathom all mysteries and all knowledge, and if I have a faith that can move mountains, but do not have love, I am nothing. 3 If I give all I possess to the poor and give over my body to hardship that I may boast, but do not have love, I gain nothing.

4 Love is patient, love is kind. It does not envy, it does not boast, it is not proud. 5 It does not dishonor others, it is not self-seeking, it is not easily angered, it keeps no record of wrongs. 6 Love does not delight in evil but rejoices with the truth. 7 It always protects, always trusts, always hopes, always perseveres.

8 Love never fails. But where there are prophecies, they will cease; where there are tongues, they will be stilled;

where there is knowledge, it will pass away. 9 For we know in part and we prophesy in part, 10 but when completeness comes, what is in part disappears. 11 When I was a child, I talked like a child, I thought like a child, I reasoned like a child. When I became a man, I put the ways of childhood behind me. 12 For now we see only a reflection as in a mirror; then we shall see face to face. Now I know in part; then I shall know fully, even as I am fully known.

13 And now these three remain: faith, hope and love. But the greatest of these is love.

1 Corinthians 13, NIV

"Honor your father and your mother, so that you may live long in the land the LORD your God is giving you."
Exodus 20:12, NIV

Remember that even our 'friends' are family. We are all related through the blood of Jesus Christ. God's love never fails. We are to love each other with the love that God has gifted each of us with.

*****

Encouraging family members is a reward for them and us; let's encourage our family members today and always!

Chapter 10: Spousal Encouragement (Unevenly Yoked)

22 Then the LORD God made a woman from the rib he had taken out of the man, and he brought her to the man. 23 The man said,

"This is now bone of my bones
    and flesh of my flesh;
she shall be called 'woman,'
    for she was taken out of man."

24 That is why a man leaves his father and mother and is united to his wife, and they become one flesh.
Genesis 2:22–24, NIV

Since God chose you to be the holy people he loves, you must clothe yourselves with tenderhearted mercy, kindness, humility, gentleness, and patience.
Colossians 3:12, NLT

21 Submit to one another out of reverence for Christ.

22 Wives, submit yourselves to your own husbands as you do to the Lord. 23 For the husband is the head of the wife as Christ is the head of the church, his body, of which he is the Savior. 24 Now as the church submits to Christ, so also wives should submit to their husbands in everything.

25 Husbands, love your wives, just as Christ loved the church and gave himself up for her 26 to make her holy, cleansing her by the washing with water through the word, 27 and to present her to himself as a radiant church, without stain or wrinkle or any other blemish, but holy and blameless. 28 In this same way, husbands ought to love their wives as their own bodies. He who loves his wife loves himself. 29 After all, no one ever hated their own

body, but they feed and care for their body, just as Christ does the church—30 for we are members of his body. 31 "For this reason a man will leave his father and mother and be united to his wife, and the two will become one flesh." 32 This is a profound mystery—but I am talking about Christ and the church. 33 However, each one of you also must love his wife as he loves himself, and the wife must respect her husband.

Ephesians 5:21–33, NIV

Husbands and wives are to love each other, build each other up, and encourage each other. There are times when we do not feel loved, built up, or encouraged. However, God has called us to help each other to feel loved by Him and this includes building each other up and encouraging each other. Woman was taken from the rib of man. Therefore, we are to work together to glorify God.

There are times when our spouse does not believe in the same way that we do. We are to continue to encourage them through our love and actions to allow the Holy Spirit to work in their heart. We must remain humble and work for the glory of God until our spouse realizes that He is our strength, and He can certainly be their strength also; they simply need to believe.

*****

Go! Encourage your spouse today. Make him or her see the love that God has for them through your actions toward them! Blessings and honor to you all!

Flesh of His Flesh

Many women are not satisfied with being an 'obeying spouse.' However, this does not mean that our husbands can abuse this hierarchy. He is to love us as Christ loves him. Christ does not believe that women are lower than men. During His return to earth, after His resurrection, who did Christ visit first? It was Mary.

Women are not necessarily the weaker gender. For goodness sake, do you think that a man could give birth to a baby? Not a chance, even if he had the same plumbing (tee-hee-hee). Therefore, when we read the Scripture which reads,

> Then the LORD God said, "It is not good that the man
> should be alone; I will make him a helper fit for him."
> **Genesis 2:18, ESV**

God made 'man' a helper—not a slave, but a helper. Women are helpers to men (and other women, I hope).

Women are flesh of his (man) flesh and bone of his (man) bone. Women were made from his rib, not his tail bone or spine (below or behind). Therefore, women are made in His image as well as men. This does not mean that we try to figure out who wears the pants in the family. Men wear the pants, and they treat women with the love that the Lord treats them with.

Women are to submit to their husbands as they submit to the Lord. The husbands are to love their wives as they love the Lord. Where does it say that the man is the slave owner of the woman? Nowhere. However, man is the head of the wife (see 1 Corinthians 11:3). This still does not mean that the wife is a slave.

Would a man ask Christ the Lord to be a slave? Would he expect that the Lord would serve him? The Lord has already served us all with the only way to the Father, through His death on the Cross. Ephesians 5:22-33 reads that the husband is to love his wife as the Lord loves the church and that the wife is to respect her husband. All of this means that they are a stronger team if they submit to the Lord and follow His commands.

The man (husband) is to realize that his woman (wife) is a blessing and respond like this...

The man said,

"This is now bone of my bones
    and flesh of my flesh;
she shall be called 'woman,'
    for she was taken out of man."
Genesis 2:23, NIV

The man is filled with joy to have a woman he can love as much as the Lord loves him. He and the woman will communicate and be loved by the Lord in the same way. The Lord loves the man (husband) and the Lord loves the woman (wife). He blessed man with woman and woman is to be His blessing to man. I would also state that man is a blessing to woman.

Faith

Weddings are beautiful ways to show that we love each other and honor the Lord with the celebration of having faith in His love for each of us. The wedding is only the beginning. Do we really know our spouse on our wedding day? Not usually. There are things we have not shared with each other and this can cause some stress in the beginning.

There are many things that we already know about our spouse though. S/he is an unbeliever. Remember that we are to remain faithful to our spouse. It will be a difficult journey when we are bound to an unbelieving spouse. We are to remain righteous and love them unconditionally. We must remain faithful in our prayer for their salvation. We must wait for His work that will be done in their heart.

14 Do not be yoked together with unbelievers. For what do righteousness and wickedness have in common? Or what fellowship can light have with darkness? 15 What harmony is there between Christ and Belial? Or what does a believer have in common with an unbeliever? 16 What agreement is there between the temple of God and idols? For we are the temple of the living God. As God has said:

"I will live with them
    and walk among them,
and I will be their God,

and they will be my people."

17 Therefore,

"Come out from them
and be separate,
says the Lord.
Touch no unclean thing,
and I will receive you."

18 And,

"I will be a Father to you,
and you will be my sons and daughters,
says the Lord Almighty."
2 Corinthians 6:14–18, NIV

If we connect ourselves with an unbeliever, we are bound to have stress and anguish throughout the marriage. Choosing to bind ourselves to an unbeliever will cause us discouragement. However, if we are already married to an unbeliever, we are not to leave them unless they desire for us to leave. When we remain and love them with His love, they will see the love of God through these acts of loving kindness.

12 To the rest I say this (I, not the Lord): If any brother has a wife who is not a believer and she is willing to live with him, he must not divorce her. 13 And if a woman has a husband who is not a believer and he is willing to live with her, she must not divorce him. 14 For the unbelieving husband has been sanctified through his wife, and the unbelieving wife has been sanctified through her believing husband. Otherwise your children would be unclean, but as it is, they are holy.

15 But if the unbeliever leaves, let it be so. The brother or the sister is not bound in such circumstances; God has called us to live in peace. 16 How do you know, wife, whether you will save your husband? Or, how do you know, husband, whether you will save your wife?
1 Corinthians 7:12–16, NIV

We are to pray for our spouse, no matter the marriage circumstances. We are to be the light in the darkness of an unbelieving spouse. Also, we are to obey and honor our spouse (unless abuse is present) to show them the light. Our faith will be present, and our spouse will eventually realize where this faith stems from—our Lord and Savior, Jesus Christ.

Our faith will pull us through until our spouse is saved also. Our faith is strong enough to wait upon the Lord and He promises to bring salvation to those who wait. Our pride and our fears cannot allow us to become impatient with the Lord's timing. His timing is all that matters. Prayer, meditation and fasting will bring us near to Him while we wait upon His perfect timing.

Our faithfulness will be noticed by the unsaved spouse and God is always at work in us all. This includes our unsaved spouse. Our righteous living will eventually move our spouse to notice why we have faith and why they see the light through us. He is working right now with all the unsaved spouses. How exciting!

Faithfulness to Righteous Living

Our righteous living will be an honor to God and cause our spouse to desire His love for them. While we are pursuing righteous living, our spouse is watching us and noticing that we love them with unconditional love. There will be questions. Such as, "Why are you so good to me?" and "Why do you put up with me?" etc. We answer that we love them as God loves us.

> "He himself bore our sins" in his body on the cross, so that we might die to sins and live for righteousness; "by his wounds you have been healed."
> **1 Peter 2:24, NIV**

> Whoever pursues righteousness and unfailing love will find life, righteousness, and honor.
> **Proverbs 21:21, NLT**

Christ took our sins, and our spouses' sins to the Cross and this sinful life we used to live has died. We might be struggling in this life, but we have all eternity to look forward to, with Him. By His stripes we are healed means that since He was beaten, battered, and torn, we are saved through the healing power of the Cross. We must pursue righteousness to understand His unfailing love for us. We share this same love with our spouse, our children, our parents, and the community.

Our righteousness does not stem from how wonderful we are; no, this righteous living we have comes from Christ's sacrifice at the Cross. His righteousness is what we strive for to become more Christlike so that we can share His love with others. His righteousness lives inside of us, but we are to pursue this righteousness to truly live in it.

Hope

We share our hope with our spouse daily. When they do not understand how we find joy in the struggles of life, we are to gently remind them that God is the source of our joy and He can be their source also. We find joy in His hope, and our spouse can also. They simply need to believe.

> 1 Therefore, since we have been justified through faith, we have peace with God through our Lord Jesus Christ, 2 through whom we have gained access by faith into this grace in which we now stand. And we boast in the hope of the glory of God. 3 Not only so, but we also glory in our sufferings, because we know that suffering produces perseverance; 4 perseverance, character; and character, hope. 5 And hope does not put us to shame, because God's love has been poured out into our hearts through the Holy Spirit, who has been given to us.
> **Romans 5:1–5, NIV**

> Be joyful in hope, patient in affliction, faithful in prayer.
> **Romans 12:12, NIV**

> May the God of hope fill you with all joy and peace as you trust in him, so that you may overflow with hope by the power of the Holy Spirit.
> **Romans 15:13, NIV**

Christine C. Sponsler

We are justified through our faith in Christ Jesus, our Lord and Savior. We might stand inside of this hope through our faith, but we must remember that our faith is a gift from God, and He is the author of our salvation.

He is also the author of our spouse's salvation and continued prayer will allow the Holy Spirit to work inside of them. We must only boast in the glory of God and not in our own deeds. This means, when our spouse finally does come around, it is not because of our actions, but the actions of Christ through us.

There will be suffering. When we think of suffering, how many of us go directly to rejoicing? Probably not too many of us. Our spouse might be lost, and we are frustrated with the results of our prayers. However, we must use our faith to continue to pray for them.

I know that it takes me a minute to understand that suffering is what Christ did for me. This means that suffering produces true joy. When we suffer, we learn to persevere and remain in the Lord. We can then share this revelation with our spouse and watch the Holy Spirit move in them. This is perseverance.

When we persevere, He is better able to build our character, and this means we are more Christlike. When we get through character building, He gives us hope. Hope that our lost spouse will turn to Him. This hope is built into us through the Holy Spirit, and we are not to be ashamed of this Spirit because it is the core part of our life.

We are finally joyful in hope when we are capable of being patient in affliction and faithful to prayer. Our prayer lives must surround our hearts so that we can share His hope and love. When He brings us His hope, we find His love also. When we share this love with our spouse, trust and believe that God is doing a work in their heart also.

Love

God's love is for everyone. They simply must believe in Him and His Word. Sharing this love with an unbelieving spouse will cause the Holy Spirit to work in their heart and redesign the way they think. We must urge, but not push, our spouse toward the love of God.

1 Therefore, I urge you, brothers and sisters, in view of God's mercy, to offer your bodies as a living sacrifice, holy

96

and pleasing to God—this is your true and proper worship. 2 Do not conform to the pattern of this world, but be transformed by the renewing of your mind. Then you will be able to test and approve what God's will is—his good, pleasing and perfect will.
Romans 12:1–2, NIV

And…

9 Love must be sincere. Hate what is evil; cling to what is good. 10 Be devoted to one another in love. Honor one another above yourselves. 11 Never be lacking in zeal, but keep your spiritual fervor, serving the Lord. 12 Be joyful in hope, patient in affliction, faithful in prayer. 13 Share with the Lord's people who are in need. Practice hospitality.
Romans 12:9–13, NIV

I like to read such things in the Bible as I urge you to. When Paul wrote Romans, he truly wanted them to understand that he desired to urge them toward the Lord. He loved them because he was one of them.

As they stretched him out to flog him, Paul said to the centurion standing there, "Is it legal for you to flog a Roman citizen who hasn't even been found guilty?"

26 When the centurion heard this, he went to the commander and reported it. "What are you going to do?" he asked. "This man is a Roman citizen."

27 The commander went to Paul and asked, "Tell me, are you a Roman citizen?"

"Yes, I am," he answered.

28 Then the commander said, "I had to pay a lot of money for my citizenship."

"But I was born a citizen," Paul replied.

29 Those who were about to interrogate him withdrew immediately. The commander himself was alarmed when he realized that he had put Paul, a Roman citizen, in chains.
Acts 22:25–29, NIV

His love knew no boundaries. He attempted to get them to realize their mistakes and come to know Jesus as their Lord and Savior. Paul's love for the Romans is like our love for a lost spouse. We must share the Lord's love with them.

We offer our bodies as a sacrifice to God because of our love for Him. However, He showed His love even more intently than we ever could. He died in our place. He also died in the place of our spouse. When we are weak, He is strong.

> 6 For while we were still weak, at the right time Christ died for the ungodly. 7 For one will scarcely die for a righteous person—though perhaps for a good person one would dare even to die— 8 but God shows his love for us in that while we were still sinners, Christ died for us. 9 Since, therefore, we have now been justified by his blood, much more shall we be saved by him from the wrath of God. 10 For if while we were enemies we were reconciled to God by the death of his Son, much more, now that we are reconciled, shall we be saved by his life. 11 More than that, we also rejoice in God through our Lord Jesus Christ, through whom we have now received reconciliation.
> **Romans 5:6–11, ESV**

We are still called to show our love to the Lord as best as we can. When we do, others might emulate this love and find their salvation. Encouraging our spouse to love God is our one true calling. Together, we can show the love of God to the world.

When we decide to invite Jesus into our lives and rely on the Holy Spirit's guidance, we are transformed into the creation for which God desires us to be. We are to present the Lord to our spouse through the love and kindness of our actions. This is how Christ loves the church.

He loves us, yes, but we must share this love with our spouse to demonstrate what His love looks like. We can only do this if we allow Him to transform our entire life. We must die to ourselves (see Ephesians 4:22-24). Dying to ourselves does not mean death, it means no longer living by the flesh, but by His Spirit of love.

We are also called to love each other, sincerely. When someone pretends to love another person, they are cheating themselves and the other person out of true love. God desires that we truly love Him and show this sincere love to our spouse and others through encouraging words and other kind actions.

Being devoted to each other in love and honoring each other above ourselves is another encouraging way to bring His love to our spouse. Christ did not wait until we were 'good' to die for our sins. He died for us while we were still sinners. We all fall short of the glory of God (see Romans 3:23) and He still would have died for each of us, individually. This means that if you or I were the only person on earth, Christ still would have gone to the Cross and suffered the crucifixion.

Really think about that for a moment.

Wow, that is love!

Another act of love is hospitality. When we are hospitable, we might be serving an angel (see Hebrews 13:2). Also, we must not wait until we think Christ is returning to live by the Spirit. When He returns, we are to be righteously living and loving our spouse as Christ loves us.

> 36 "But of that day and hour no one knows, not even the angels of heaven, but My Father only. 37 But as the days of Noah were, so also will the coming of the Son of Man be. 38 For as in the days before the flood, they were eating and drinking, marrying and giving in marriage, until the day that Noah entered the ark, 39 and did not know until the flood came and took them all away, so also will the coming of the Son of Man be. 40 Then two men will be in the field: one will be taken and the other left. 41 Two women will be grinding at the mill: one will be taken and the other left. 42 Watch therefore, for you do not know what hour your Lord is coming. 43 But know this, that if the master of the house had known what hour the thief would come, he would have watched and not allowed his house to be broken into. 44 Therefore you also be ready, for the Son of Man is coming at an hour you do not expect."
> **Matthew 24:36–44, NKJV**

Christine C. Sponsler

(See also 1 Thessalonians 5:2; 2 Peter 3:10; Revelation 16:15.)

We do not know the time or day or anything about exactly when the Lord will return. Let's not get caught with our hand in the cookie jar, per se. he will be here and come as a thief does, when we least expect it. let us be prepared now, even if He does not come until after our earthly death.

The Lord does not desire for us to show insincere love. We must live life as though we are ready for His triumphant return (see 1 Thessalonians 4:16-17). Let us show true love toward our spouses so that they might come to know Him through these acts of love. Love is not fake. Love is truth. God is truth. By His grace, we are loved!

Grace

We live by the gift of faith from the Lord. He gives us His grace when we fall short in our faith. However, this does not mean that we commit sins simply to activate His grace. We are to live as righteously as we can and share His love with our spouses as often as possible.

> 1 Well then, should we keep on sinning so that God can show us more and more of his wonderful grace? 2 Of course not! Since we have died to sin, how can we continue to live in it? 3 Or have you forgotten that when we were joined with Christ Jesus in baptism, we joined him in his death? 4 For we died and were buried with Christ by baptism. And just as Christ was raised from the dead by the glorious power of the Father, now we also may live new lives.
> **Romans 6:1–4, NLT**

And…

> 15 Well then, since God's grace has set us free from the law, does that mean we can go on sinning? Of course not! 16 Don't you realize that you become the slave of whatever you choose to obey? You can be a slave to sin, which leads to death, or you can choose to obey God, which leads to righteous living. 17 Thank God! Once you were slaves of sin, but now you wholeheartedly obey this

teaching we have given you. 18 Now you are free from your slavery to sin, and you have become slaves to righteous living.

Romans 6:15–18, NLT

Even though we were given the gift of grace, we are not to continue sinning to test this grace. We have been called to live righteous lives instead—encouraging others, including our spouses, to do the same. We are His royal priesthood (see 1 Peter 2:9) and He will call upon us to share His love and the hope of His grace and mercy.

We have been joined to Christ and find this encouraging. How can we not encourage others with this Good News? We must be ready for whatever He calls us to do for others. His grace is sufficient for all that He calls us to do and we are made strong in our weaknesses through this grace.

1 I must go on boasting. Though there is nothing to be gained by it, I will go on to visions and revelations of the Lord. 2 I know a man in Christ who fourteen years ago was caught up to the third heaven—whether in the body or out of the body I do not know, God knows. 3 And I know that this man was caught up into paradise—whether in the body or out of the body I do not know, God knows— 4 and he heard things that cannot be told, which man may not utter. 5 On behalf of this man I will boast, but on my own behalf I will not boast, except of my weaknesses— 6 though if I should wish to boast, I would not be a fool, for I would be speaking the truth; but I refrain from it, so that no one may think more of me than he sees in me or hears from me. 7 So to keep me from becoming conceited because of the surpassing greatness of the revelations, a thorn was given me in the flesh, a messenger of Satan to harass me, to keep me from becoming conceited. 8 Three times I pleaded with the Lord about this, that it should leave me. 9 But he said to me, "My grace is sufficient for you, for my power is made perfect in weakness." Therefore I will boast all the more gladly of my weaknesses, so that the power of Christ may rest upon me. 10 For the sake of Christ, then, I am content with weaknesses, insults,

hardships, persecutions, and calamities. For when I am weak, then I am strong.
2 Corinthians 12:1–10, ESV

God is not made strong by our actions. We are made strong by His grace. His grace and His mercy are gifts from heaven which we must share with our spouses, and we are to use these gifts to encourage others also to come to know this powerful and peaceful grace and mercy.

We have become slaves to a righteous life, rather than a sinful life because of His grace. We are to encourage our spouses with this Good News and share the hope of His grace with everyone. We obey His teaching when we encourage others to live new lives inside of His grace.

Our baptism into His family has given us the strength and courage of His grace and mercy. This courage might be used to prayerfully bring our spouses to a relationship with Christ. We were given new lives through baptism. We died with Christ and were then raised again to live the righteous lives He set forth for us to live. His death means our life through His gift of grace!

The Power of His Death

When we think of death, we do not automatically think of strength. We think of the end or the loss of a battle. However, Christ's death is the strength that we cling to because it means that death is conquered for us. We may still be sinners, but His death makes it so that we can approach God and will be with God throughout all of eternity.

> 5 Since we have been united with him in his death, we will also be raised to life as he was. 6 We know that our old sinful selves were crucified with Christ so that sin might lose its power in our lives. We are no longer slaves to sin. 7 For when we died with Christ we were set free from the power of sin. 8 And since we died with Christ, we know we will also live with him. 9 We are sure of this because Christ was raised from the dead, and he will never die again. Death no longer has any power over him. 10 When he died, he died once to break the power of sin. But now that he lives, he lives for the glory of God. 11 So you also

should consider yourselves to be dead to the power of sin and alive to God through Christ Jesus.
Romans 6:5–11, NLT

19 "For through the law I died to the law so that I might live for God. 20 I have been crucified with Christ and I no longer live, but Christ lives in me. The life I now live in the body, I live by faith in the Son of God, who loved me and gave himself for me. 21 I do not set aside the grace of God, for if righteousness could be gained through the law, Christ died for nothing!"
Galatians 2:19–21, NIV

He has not left us in the realm of death. Through the baptism into His family, we have also been raised to righteous living through Christ's ultimate sacrifice and the death on the Cross. This righteous living also includes respecting and loving our spouse. Christ was not left in the realm of death. His resurrection has become our hope for an eternity spent with Him. This same hope is meant to be shared with our spouses also.

The sinfulness of our flesh was crucified with Christ so that we can live in righteousness and encourage each other to remember His love. The power of sin no longer lives in our spirit. We will continue to struggle with our fleshly selves. However, we have His resurrection power to fight through the struggles.

Death no longer has power over Christ which means that death has no power over us. Death will be broken for our spouses also, even if s/he is not yet a believer, we must continue to pray for their salvation. His death broke the power that sin had on our lives and we are to encourage our spouses with this Good News. We are alive to God through Christ's sacrificial death and we have all eternity to thank Him for this.

We must begin to live for God. Encouraging our spouses, the lost, and each other will demonstrate His love to them and they can be saved from their death. Christ lives in us and we encourage the lost to find this hope through how we live, righteously.

Our righteousness, which includes sharing His love with our spouses, does not come from our actions. If it did, then Christ died for no reason. Our actions could not have saved us. It is through His death on the Cross that we share the hope of eternity with Him. Remember that the law has shown us that we are sinners and that we need a Savior, and His name is Jesus Christ, our Lord and Savior. We are to encourage each other to live in love and joy.

The power of His death includes how we feel and act toward our spouse. We are not perfect, and we must not expect perfection from our spouses. Our husband or wife might not yet know that God loves them, but when we are obedient to God, they cannot help but ask how we are so obedient to Him while things are such a mess. And what we say is that His death on the Cross brought us to a faithful response to any circumstance.

The Fruit of the Spirit

God gives each of us the fruit of the Spirit to help others come to know Him. We are called to produce the fruit which best glorifies God. Our spouses will not see God in us if we are cruel to them. We must always be in prayer that His fruit will show through to our spouse.

> 22 But the fruit of the Spirit is love, joy, peace, forbearance, kindness, goodness, faithfulness, 23 gentleness and self-control. Against such things there is no law. 24 Those who belong to Christ Jesus have crucified the flesh with its passions and desires. 25 Since we live by the Spirit, let us keep in step with the Spirit.
> **Galatians 5:22–25, NIV**

The fruit of the Spirit—notice that it is not the fruits, but the fruit. The fruit pertains to what we share with others. Our fruit used to be sinful, in nature. Now our fruit is spiritual, and encouraging people is part of this spiritual component. We are to encourage our spouses, each other, and the lost through our actions (the fruit) and demonstrate His love for them (another facet of the fruit) because He first loved us.

Love is the first component of the fruit. It appears that love is first in many things, according to the Bible (see 1 Corinthians 13 again)—love of our spouse and mostly, the love of the Lord. Love is why we are saved—not so much our love for God, but His love for us, first. We share this love with our spouses so they will come to know His love for them.

7 Beloved, let us love one another, for love is of God; and everyone who loves is born of God and knows God. 8 He who does not love does not know God, for God is love. 9 In this the love of God was manifested toward us, that God has sent His only begotten Son into the world, that we might live through Him. 10 In this is love, not that we loved God, but that He loved us and sent His Son to be the propitiation for our sins. 11 Beloved, if God so loved us, we also ought to love one another.

1 John 4:7–11, NKJV

God desires for us to use His love to encourage others to come to know this love for them too. This love will bring about many feelings. One of these feelings is joy.

Joy is the next component of the fruit. When we find joy in our spouses, saved or not, s/he can see the light of the Lord shine through this joy. We are not filled with joy because of what we see. We are filled with joy because of what we know. We know that God is love and He fills us with His joy. This brings our marriage peace.

Next, we have peace. Peace is not the kind of peace that the world understands, but the peace from God that surpasses all worldly understanding. Has anyone ever prayed for world peace? I have, but this is futile when we know that there will be wars and famine in the end times.

2 Be watchful, and strengthen the things which remain, that are ready to die, for I have not found your works perfect before God. 3 Remember therefore how you have received and heard; hold fast and repent. Therefore if you will not watch, I will come upon you as a thief, and you will not know what hour I will come upon you.

Revelation 3:2–3, NKJV

Peace is not mentioned here because there will be no more war or death. We have the knowledge that our Savior has kept us from death, and we will only die to be reunited with Him. Our spouses need to know about this peace—the peace that passes all understanding (see Philippians 4:7) moves through us into our spouse so that they are promised His peace of eternity. We must tolerate the circumstances of this world to live in heaven through eternity.

Next is forbearance. What is forbearance? It is tolerance and restraint. We must restrain ourselves from treating our spouses with contempt or disrespect, even when this is how they treat us. We do this by using His strength to tolerate such actions. However, no abuse is allowed.

When we treat our spouses with the forbearance that only the Lord can give us, they can see His light shining through these acts. These acts of forbearance can only lead to kindness, both to and from our spouses.

Kindness is difficult to use through our frustrations. When our spouse is lost, it is hard to change our attitude toward them and even sometimes toward God. Why is s/he so mean? Why do I have to take this or that? Who is going to save me and my spouse? Only God has this power. Through His kindness, our spouse will not be able to look to the left or to the right anymore (see Proverbs 4:25-27; Isaiah 30:21). His kindness will save us and our spouses because of His goodness.

Goodness gracious! Have we ever used this term? I have...and I just did. His goodness is declared by the death of His Son for our sins. Our spouse must learn that God's Son died for his or her sins also. Christ will return and when He does, we need to be able to approach Him with no shame. No shame means that we share His love with our spouses.

> 5 Now the LORD descended in the cloud and stood with him there, and proclaimed the name of the LORD. 6 And the LORD passed before him and proclaimed, "The LORD, the LORD God, merciful and gracious, longsuffering, and abounding in goodness and truth, 7 keeping mercy for thousands, forgiving iniquity and transgression and sin, by no means clearing the guilty, visiting the iniquity of the fathers upon the children and the children's children to the third and the fourth generation."
> **Exodus 34:5–7, NKJV**

The Lord is good, we are not. Let me explain. Our hearts try to become more and more like Christ. However, Christ was and is the only human who never sinned. Think about that for a minute. We have all sinned and fallen short of the glory of God (see Romans 3:23). Therefore, He is good, and we are not.

We are, however, capable of His goodness when we are striving to become more Christlike. Goodness is not simply an act of good. It includes our intentions. Our intentions are only 'good' if they are not selfish. His goodness has never been selfish, and we must strive to allow His goodness to shine through to our spouses. This shares with them the power of gentleness.

Gentleness might not automatically be associated with power. However, His power is gentle, strong, and kind. True gentleness shown to our spouses will create a softened heart that the Holy Spirit will work with to create a clean heart in them.

> Create in me a pure heart, O God,
>   and renew a steadfast spirit within me.
> 11 Do not cast me from your presence
>   or take your Holy Spirit from me.
> 12 Restore to me the joy of your salvation
>   and grant me a willing spirit, to sustain me.
>
> 13 Then I will teach transgressors your ways,
>   so that sinners will turn back to you.
> 14 Deliver me from the guilt of bloodshed, O God,
>   you who are God my Savior,
>   and my tongue will sing of your righteousness.
> 15 Open my lips, Lord,
>   and my mouth will declare your praise.
> 16 You do not delight in sacrifice, or I would bring it;
>   you do not take pleasure in burnt offerings.
> 17 My sacrifice, O God, is a broken spirit;
>   a broken and contrite heart
>   you, God, will not despise.
>
> 18 May it please you to prosper Zion,
>   to build up the walls of Jerusalem.
> 19 Then you will delight in the sacrifices of the righteous,
>   in burnt offerings offered whole;
>   then bulls will be offered on your altar.

Christine C. Sponsler

Psalm 51:10–19, NIV

We must show gentleness toward our spouse. Then expect the Lord to work in their heart. His gentleness in our hearts creates the self-control that we need to continue praying for our spouses.

Self-control does not sound biblical. However, anarchy is opposite of biblical and self-control is opposite of anarchy. We are not to create anarchy of any type. Not in our marriage or the rest of our lives. Therefore, obtaining self-control is biblical and necessary to allow the Lord to work in us and our spouses.

When we allow self-control to rule our thoughts, we become patient and this is necessary to pray for our spouses, even when they are mean to us. Patience is a virtuous facet of being human.

Patience

Patience needs another section. As you know, love has already been elaborated upon. Therefore, I will elaborate on patience and loving kindness further in the next two sections. Without His patience, we are not able to watch as our spouses ruin their lives, while truly believing He will help. We would expect things to change in our own timing, instead of His timing. And His timing is perfect.

29 Whoever is patient has great understanding,
    but one who is quick-tempered displays folly.

30 A heart at peace gives life to the body,
    but envy rots the bones.
Proverbs 14:29–30, NIV

1 I therefore, a prisoner for the Lord, urge you to walk in a manner worthy of the calling to which you have been called, 2 with all humility and gentleness, with patience, bearing with one another in love, 3 eager to maintain the unity of the Spirit in the bond of peace. 4 There is one body and one Spirit—just as you were called to the one hope that belongs to your call— 5 one Lord, one faith, one

baptism, 6 one God and Father of all, who is over all and through all and in all.
Ephesians 4:1–6, ESV

Patience does not mean that we are perfect. Only God is perfect. It does mean that we can understand how faithful we must remain as we pray for our spouses. The peace in our hearts might be the only God-gifted life our spouses will see. S/he will notice the life-giving changes in us and be drawn toward the Lord because of it.

Whether we are literal prisoners or prisoners of this world, the Lord gives us His patience to endure that time it will take to share His love with our spouses. We have vowed to be 'one' with our spouse. Therefore, we must vow to pray for their salvation. If they are already saved and our marriage still feels difficult, we must have patience with the Lord in creating a new heart in both of us.

As mentioned before, gentleness is a strength like no other. God grants us His gentleness toward others, including our spouse and we are to wait upon the Lord's timing humbly and patiently. God is in us and He works through us to share His encouraging words with our loved ones. We are eagerly waiting for His peace in our relationship. Through His loving kindness, we find the strength of His patience.

Loving Kindness

Elaborating upon loving kindness is necessary so that we can share this with our spouse. What does lovingkindness mean? How will we know if we are practicing it? Why do we practice it anyway? Who says it's necessary? What does it look like when practiced properly?

All these questions are often on our minds. Especially when we are trying to share this loving kindness with our spouse. It is not easy to share this with someone who either does not accept it or does not even notice it. Therefore, patience along with loving kindness will help to get us through these steps.

Loving kindness is to show love and kindness even when it is most difficult. We were shown this through Christ's love for us and His sacrifice on the Cross. It means that even when we feel hurt and disappointed, we show kindness that comes from God to whomever has hurt us.

Yikes! Sounds impossible.

We are practicing loving kindness when we pray for our spouse. Demonstrating true love, we have for them but mostly demonstrating the love that the Lord has placed upon us. The reason that we practice loving kindness is to prove to our spouse and others that God is with us and they can benefit from this truth also. God says that we must act with loving kindness and lay down our lives for others which does include our spouse…

> There is no greater love than to lay down one's life for one's friends.
> **John 15:13, NLT**

> This is how we know what love is: Jesus Christ laid down his life for us. And we ought to lay down our lives for our brothers and sisters.
> **1 John 3:16, NIV**

> So encourage each other and build each other up, just as you are already doing.
> **1 Thessalonians 5:11, NLT**

We encourage each other to be the godly man or woman that He created us to be. When we build up our spouses, they are more likely to desire the same love that we share with them and seek after God. So, keep it up. God is with us and for us, and our spouses. It is humbling just how much He loves us.

Humility

Humility does not need to be humiliating. It is a word that demonstrates Christ's love for the world. He humbly came to earth to save our butts. Without this act of humility, we would not be able to approach God with our prayers for our spouse. This would be devastating.

> 3 Do nothing out of selfish ambition or vain conceit. Rather, in humility value others above yourselves, 4 not looking to your own interests but each of you to the interests of the others.

Philippians 2:3–4, NIV

We must value our spouse above our self. What this means is that we must value our spouse over and above the fear of rejection from them. We must humbly understand that God is not done with any of us until the day He returns or the day that we join Him in heaven. Therefore, He is still working on our spouse also.

> 1 Wives, in the same way submit yourselves to your own husbands so that, if any of them do not believe the word, they may be won over without words by the behavior of their wives, 2 when they see the purity and reverence of your lives. 3 Your beauty should not come from outward adornment, such as elaborate hairstyles and the wearing of gold jewelry or fine clothes. 4 Rather, it should be that of your inner self, the unfading beauty of a gentle and quiet spirit, which is of great worth in God's sight. 5 For this is the way the holy women of the past who put their hope in God used to adorn themselves. They submitted themselves to their own husbands, 6 like Sarah, who obeyed Abraham and called him her lord. You are her daughters if you do what is right and do not give way to fear.
> 7 Husbands, in the same way be considerate as you live with your wives, and treat them with respect as the weaker partner and as heirs with you of the gracious gift of life, so that nothing will hinder your prayers.
> **1 Peter 3:1–7, NIV**

When we practice arrogance, vanity, or are conceited, the Lord does not shine through our actions. Therefore, as mentioned before, we must humbly call upon Him for strength to continue praying for our spouses or any lost loved one. He hears us (see 1 John 5:14-15). We are like-minded and have compassion for others, including our unbelieving spouse.

> 8 Finally, all of you, be like-minded, be sympathetic, love one another, be compassionate and humble. 9 Do not repay evil with evil or insult with insult. On the contrary,

repay evil with blessing, because to this you were called so that you may inherit a blessing. 10 For,

> "Whoever would love life
>> and see good days
> must keep their tongue from evil
>> and their lips from deceitful speech.
> 11 They must turn from evil and do good;
>> they must seek peace and pursue it.
> 12 For the eyes of the Lord are on the righteous
>> and his ears are attentive to their prayer,
> but the face of the Lord is against those who do evil."

13 Who is going to harm you if you are eager to do good? 14 But even if you should suffer for what is right, you are blessed. "Do not fear their threats; do not be frightened." 15 But in your hearts revere Christ as Lord. Always be prepared to give an answer to everyone who asks you to give the reason for the hope that you have. But do this with gentleness and respect, 16 keeping a clear conscience, so that those who speak maliciously against your good behavior in Christ may be ashamed of their slander. 17 For it is better, if it is God's will, to suffer for doing good than for doing evil. 18 For Christ also suffered once for sins, the righteous for the unrighteous, to bring you to God. He was put to death in the body but made alive in the Spirit.

1 Peter 3:8–18, NIV

Our humility will bring about the desire, in our unbelieving spouse, to seek God. Keeping our tongue from evil and allowing the Spirit to work in our loved ones is necessary. We are not to fear threats and must be prepared to answer our spouses when they ask why we are so faithful. It is an honor to suffer with Christ. It means that we are doing something right. His love will shine through.

The Lord is to always be trusted. His promises are true. He is faithful. We can, and should, stand firm on this because we know that He is trustworthy, even when we do not see immediate results from our prayers.

Our spouses will come to know God and we must show that we believe this to be His Truth.

Always Trustworthy

God is always trustworthy. Does that mean because we believe in Him that we are always trustworthy? No, it does not. It means that as we strive to become more like Christ, we become more trustworthy. We also become surer of His answers to our prayers. His trustworthiness creates an even stronger bond between us and our spouse. Whether there is obvious or not so obvious trouble in our marriage, He will answer our prayers. We can trust Him.

1 May the LORD answer you in the day of trouble!
    May the name of the God of Jacob protect you!
2 May he send you help from the sanctuary
    and give you support from Zion!
3 May he remember all your offerings
    and regard with favor your burnt sacrifices! Selah

4 May he grant you your heart's desire
    and fulfill all your plans!
5 May we shout for joy over your salvation,
    and in the name of our God set up our banners!
May the LORD fulfill all your petitions!

6 Now I know that the LORD saves his anointed;
    he will answer him from his holy heaven
    with the saving might of his right hand.
7 Some trust in chariots and some in horses,
    but we trust in the name of the LORD our God.
8 They collapse and fall,
    but we rise and stand upright.

9 O LORD, save the king!
    May he answer us when we call.
    Psalm 20, ESV

We might not be kings (or queens), but God, who talks to us in His Word today, is the same as He was during the writings of the Psalms. He remains trustworthy. And we remain trusting of His promises to us and our spouses. God answers prayers. It might not be the answer that we had hoped for, but it is the righteous answer.

The Lord protects us. He protects us from ourselves, our spouses, and from other people. He also knows when to answer our prayers and with what answer to protect us. Our sacrifices are worthy of His answers and He promises to answer those who seek His righteousness. His love is present, no matter His answer.

The desires of our heart are protected by His love. We can rest assured that when we seek His truth, He will hear our cries for ourselves and for our loved ones which include our spouses. His love shines through us as we encourage our spouses with kindness and love.

No matter His answers, we can shout for joy over our salvation— eventually over our spouses' salvation too. We trust in the name of the Lord and expect great things from Him. He does not desire to disappoint His anointed. Therefore, He is working in us right now and will be ready, willing, and able to shine through our spouses as soon as they turn to Him and find their faith in Him and His love and protection.

Thank You Lord for your answer! Amen!

Always Protects

We are truly protected. Maybe not protected from someone trying to harm or kill us, but our spirit is protected which means that we will be in eternity with Him. Since His promise includes protection, we must be willing to risk our comfort to encourage others to come to know Him and His divine power.

> By his divine power, God has given us everything we need for living a godly life. We have received all of this by coming to know him, the one who called us to himself by means of his marvelous glory and excellence.
> **2 Peter 1:3, NLT**

> For I am the LORD your God
>   who takes hold of your right hand

and says to you, Do not fear;
    I will help you.
    Isaiah 41:13, NIV

Living a godly life might seem too difficult. However, we have been called to live such a life. What does this mean? It means that we seek first the Kingdom of God and love others as ourselves. It also means that we encourage others to know Him and His love. Even if our spouse is an unbeliever, we are to remember His promises and continue praying for their salvation.

He has called us to Himself. Therefore, we are to listen and draw others toward Him. We cannot accomplish this by being negative or discouraging. Therefore, we must find encouragement in His Word and then share it as much as possible. He promises to hold our hands as we struggle to figure out how to live godly lives for Him. This should create an obedient heart toward God.

Obedience…Not Abuse

God desires that a marriage honor Him. His Word states that women are to submit to their husbands and men are to love their wives. Does this mean that there is a slave relationship? No, it does not. However, obedience to each other must be dedicated to the Lord. Honoring the Lord in our marriage builds the strongest foundation for any marriage.

With God at the center of a marriage, the marriage is stronger. Building the strength of the Lord intertwined into the healthiest of marriages. Does this mean there will be no troubles? No, it does not. It means that there will be blessings anyway. Blessings will abound in the marriage.

> 1 If you fully obey the LORD your God and carefully follow all his commands I give you today, the LORD your God will set you high above all the nations on earth. 2 All these blessings will come on you and accompany you if you obey the LORD your God:
> 3 You will be blessed in the city and blessed in the country.
> **Deuteronomy 28:1–3, NIV**

There is no more slavery to wrongdoing and a sinful nature. Our spouse is one, we are two, and God is our third cord in our marriage (see Ecclesiastes 4:12). He is the light for our spouse as well as ours.

> Now you are free from your slavery to sin, and you have
> become slaves to righteous living.
> **Romans 6:18, NLT**

God does not desire that we honor Him without a joyful heart. He desires that we are consumed with His love and strive to serve Him. Encouraging each other is a form of service to the Lord. Through our encouraging words, the Lord shines His light upon our lives. Serving Him helps to create a stronger barrier between sin and our hearts. This is exciting! We serve out of obedience and He protects us from abuse. Therefore, with abuse, comes separation. Stay safe and encouraged! God is with us always.

Chapter 11: Spousal Encouragement (Evenly Yoked)

1 You, God, are my God,
  earnestly I seek you;
I thirst for you,
  my whole being longs for you,
in a dry and parched land
  where there is no water.

2 I have seen you in the sanctuary
  and beheld your power and your glory.
3 Because your love is better than life,
  my lips will glorify you.
4 I will praise you as long as I live,
  and in your name I will lift up my hands.
5 I will be fully satisfied as with the richest of foods;
  with singing lips my mouth will praise you.

6 On my bed I remember you;
  I think of you through the watches of the night.
7 Because you are my help,
  I sing in the shadow of your wings.
8 I cling to you;
  your right hand upholds me.

9 Those who want to kill me will be destroyed;
  they will go down to the depths of the earth.
10 They will be given over to the sword
  and become food for jackals.

11 But the king will rejoice in God;
  all who swear by God will glory in him,
  while the mouths of liars will be silenced.
Psalm 63, NIV

Christine C. Sponsler

When we seek God and find Him, we are to share His love with our loved ones. Our spouse knows Him, and we are blessed with a believing spouse. He upholds us in His mighty righteous right hand. Our enemies will not triumph over us any longer. We are to glorify the Lord with our faith in Him.

*****

Blessings to those whose spouse is a believer. Evenly yoked is strong and His love will shine through the relationship also!

Faith

Faith, hope, and love are an integral part of any successful marriage. God-centered marriages have trouble and trials, just as any other marriage does. However, the way through those issues is with God at the center of the marriage. Prayer is one of the main ways to keep God at the center of our marriage.

> 4 Rejoice in the Lord always. I will say it again: Rejoice! 5 Let your gentleness be evident to all. The Lord is near. 6 Do not be anxious about anything, but in every situation, by prayer and petition, with thanksgiving, present your requests to God. 7 And the peace of God, which transcends all understanding, will guard your hearts and your minds in Christ Jesus.
>
> 8 Finally, brothers and sisters, whatever is true, whatever is noble, whatever is right, whatever is pure, whatever is lovely, whatever is admirable—if anything is excellent or praiseworthy—think about such things. 9 Whatever you have learned or received or heard from me, or seen in me—put it into practice. And the God of peace will be with you.
>
> **Philippians 4:4–9, NIV**

Our love for each other begins with a right and strong relationship with the Lord. We must find it in our hearts to rejoice in everything. Let nothing draw us away from His love and then nothing will be able to separate us from each other.

> What, then, shall we say in response to these things? If God is for us, who can be against us? 32 He who did not spare his own Son, but gave him up for us all—how will he not also, along with him, graciously give us all things? 33 Who will bring any charge against those whom God has chosen? It is God who justifies. 34 Who then is the one who condemns? No one. Christ Jesus who died—more than that, who was raised to life—is at the right hand of God and is also interceding for us. 35 Who shall separate

119

us from the love of Christ? Shall trouble or hardship or persecution or famine or nakedness or danger or sword? 36 As it is written:

"For your sake we face death all day long;
    we are considered as sheep to be slaughtered."

37 No, in all these things we are more than conquerors through him who loved us. 38 For I am convinced that neither death nor life, neither angels nor demons, neither the present nor the future, nor any powers, 39 neither height nor depth, nor anything else in all creation, will be able to separate us from the love of God that is in Christ Jesus our Lord.
Romans 8:31–39, NIV

There is nothing that can separate us from His love, and this means that our spousal love will grow even stronger. Keeping everything true, noble, right, pure, lovely, and admirable makes us willing and able to praise God.

2 Consider it pure joy, my brothers and sisters, whenever you face trials of many kinds, 3 because you know that the testing of your faith produces perseverance. 4 Let perseverance finish its work so that you may be mature and complete, not lacking anything.
James 1:2–4, NIV

How many of us find 'joy' while we are inside of a trial? I know that this is difficult to do. However, the apostle Paul demonstrates the love of God when he shows us how and why we must find pure joy in the trials of life. He found joy in the fact that Jesus was the Messiah, which means that we have salvation in His pure death.

Hallelujah!

We are saved!

Therefore, even when we struggle here, we have eternity to look forward to, because of Christ's sacrifice for our sins. Share this 'joy' with your spouse and watch the wheels turn in their heads as we both praise God for our marriage. Our salvation is shared with one another and we must find encouragement from this truth. Perseverance is encouraging.

120

Jesus died for our sins. Jesus died for our spouse's sins. We have eternity to look forward to together meaning we can praise God together and encourage each other with this Good News. We will know Christ in heaven, and He is already there advocating for our place in heaven. Encouraging our spouses shows faithfulness to each other and prayer shows faithfulness toward God.

Faithfulness

To be faithful to God is the most important aspect of anybody's life. However, another important faithfulness is to yourself and your spouse. Suffering will come; we all lose loved ones, and this is challenging. The grieving process is only made easier knowing that we will see this loved one again, in Heaven.

10 Brothers and sisters, as an example of patience in the face of suffering, take the prophets who spoke in the name of the Lord. 11 As you know, we count as blessed those who have persevered. You have heard of Job's perseverance and have seen what the Lord finally brought about. The Lord is full of compassion and mercy.

12 Above all, my brothers and sisters, do not swear—not by heaven or by earth or by anything else. All you need to say is a simple "Yes" or "No." Otherwise you will be condemned.

13 Is anyone among you in trouble? Let them pray. Is anyone happy? Let them sing songs of praise. 14 Is anyone among you sick? Let them call the elders of the church to pray over them and anoint them with oil in the name of the Lord. 15 And the prayer offered in faith will make the sick person well; the Lord will raise them up. If they have sinned, they will be forgiven. 16 Therefore confess your sins to each other and pray for each other so that you may be healed. The prayer of a righteous person is powerful and effective.

17 Elijah was a human being, even as we are. He prayed earnestly that it would not rain, and it did not rain on the

land for three and a half years. 18 Again he prayed, and the heavens gave rain, and the earth produced its crops.

19 My brothers and sisters, if one of you should wander from the truth and someone should bring that person back, 20 remember this: Whoever turns a sinner from the error of their way will save them from death and cover over a multitude of sins.

James 5:10–20, NIV

Many prophets have shared the encouraging words that God provided them with while they suffered ridicule and other struggles. Through perseverance and patience these prophets were able to share the encouraging words that God gave them so that we would be encouraged through the Word of God.

Praying for each other brings encouragement to people who are struggling with trouble or sickness. Encouragement must be brought to people who are struggling or who are ill so that they can see the 'joy' of the Lord. The prayers of a righteous person can make a difference in another person's life. Therefore, to encourage each other, we must find His strength and then bring our prayers for each other to God.

Wandering from His truth can be deadly. When we notice that one of us is wandering, we are to draw them back into His graces through prayer, meditating, and loving kindness. Encouraging the wanderer to return to God will save their lives. This act is not of us, but God working through us to be the encourager He created us to be. The newfound encouragement will bring hope back into the wanderer's life.

Hope

Hope generates the courage we need to be the encouragers that God designed us to be. He built 'hope' into the very core of marriage. When we are struggling to find hope, God delivers the hope, in His own way. Recall 1 Peter 3:8-18 that we looked at before.

8 Finally, all of you, be like-minded, be sympathetic, love one another, be compassionate and humble. 9 Do not repay evil with evil or insult with insult. On the contrary,

repay evil with blessing, because to this you were called so that you may inherit a blessing. 10 For,

> "Whoever would love life
> and see good days
> must keep their tongue from evil
> and their lips from deceitful speech.
> 11 They must turn from evil and do good;
> they must seek peace and pursue it.
> 12 For the eyes of the Lord are on the righteous
> and his ears are attentive to their prayer,
> but the face of the Lord is against those who do evil."

13 Who is going to harm you if you are eager to do good? 14 But even if you should suffer for what is right, you are blessed. "Do not fear their threats; do not be frightened." 15 But in your hearts revere Christ as Lord. Always be prepared to give an answer to everyone who asks you to give the reason for the hope that you have. But do this with gentleness and respect, 16 keeping a clear conscience, so that those who speak maliciously against your good behavior in Christ may be ashamed of their slander. 17 For it is better, if it is God's will, to suffer for doing good than for doing evil. 18 For Christ also suffered once for sins, the righteous for the unrighteous, to bring you to God. He was put to death in the body but made alive in the Spirit.

1 Peter 3:8–18, NIV

What does 'likeminded' mean? Does it mean that we will always agree with each other? Will we always have the same opinions? No, it does not! It means we are to love each other as Christ first loved us. It means that we are all in agreement that His salvation is what we need to share with others to help encourage their life-changing decisions.

We are to sympathize with each other and demonstrate the same type of love that Christ has demonstrated toward us. We lay down our lives for others and encourage them to do the same. Finding ways to show His love through encouraging words must remain an integral focal point in our lives.

Demonstrating what it means to turn from evil, doing good for others, seeking His peace, pursuing Him without deceit on our lips, and encouraging each other to refrain from evil is another part of encouragement. God is encouraging His people (us) to share this hope with others.

We must remain eager to do good, even though people might try to do us harm. They cannot harm our soul (see Matthew10:28). Therefore, we are truly safe from eternal harm. Fear is no longer a part of our lives. We are to revere Christ in our hearts and encourage each other with this reverence. As Christ was put to death in the body and brought to life in the Spirit, so too are we. We must encourage others with this promise and demonstrate His love for all through our actions and words.

Love

Love does not envy or boast (see 1 Corinthians 13). Therefore, when our spouses find success, so do we. We love them with our heart and soul and share this love with the world through encouraging other married people with the truth of His love and joy in their marriage.

The joy of the Lord will give us the strength to share His love with others. Your family, friends, and community are waiting for the encouraging news of the Lord's salvation. We must be ready to share this news without reservation because the truth is liberating. We are guarded by His love, grace, and mercy. Encourage another person today!

> 12 Now about our brother Apollos: I strongly urged him to go to you with the brothers. He was quite unwilling to go now, but he will go when he has the opportunity.
> 13 Be on your guard; stand firm in the faith; be courageous; be strong.
> **1 Corinthians 16:12–13, NIV**

> 23 The grace of the Lord Jesus be with you.
> 24 My love to all of you in Christ Jesus. Amen.
> **1 Corinthians 16:23–24, NIV**

Being on our guard does not mean that we are to guard ourselves against other believers. We are to love and encourage each other as often as possible. We stand firm in our faith that Christ died for our salvation. We can approach God because of Christ's sacrifice. He created the pathway to the Father because He loves us and desires to spend eternity with us.

By the grace of God, and through the sacrifice of Christ, we can encourage others to find this truth. Christ died for each of us! I may not know each of you, but I can honestly say that I love you all, because Christ first loved me. God's grace shines in our lives; let it shine!

Grace

Grace might appear as something that we can 'work' for. However, His grace is a free gift to all (see Ephesians 2:8). Since this is a gift, it is up to us to encourage others with this gift from God. There are several gifts and promises that Paul draws believers to remember...

> 1 Paul, an apostle of Christ Jesus by the will of God, in keeping with the promise of life that is in Christ Jesus,
>
> 2 To Timothy, my dear son:
> Grace, mercy and peace from God the Father and Christ Jesus our Lord.
> 3 I thank God, whom I serve, as my ancestors did, with a clear conscience, as night and day I constantly remember you in my prayers. 4 Recalling your tears, I long to see you, so that I may be filled with joy. 5 I am reminded of your sincere faith, which first lived in your grandmother Lois and in your mother Eunice and, I am persuaded, now lives in you also.
> 6 For this reason I remind you to fan into flame the gift of God, which is in you through the laying on of my hands. 7 For the Spirit God gave us does not make us timid, but gives us power, love and self-discipline. 8 So do not be ashamed of the testimony about our Lord or of me his prisoner. Rather, join with me in suffering for the gospel, by the power of God. 9 He has saved us and called us to a holy life—not because of anything we have done

but because of his own purpose and grace. This grace was given us in Christ Jesus before the beginning of time, 10 but it has now been revealed through the appearing of our Savior, Christ Jesus, who has destroyed death and has brought life and immortality to light through the gospel.

2 Timothy 1:1–10, NIV

Paul sends grace, mercy, and peace to the believers because he desires that they be encouraged by the Word of God. The Good News is how Paul shares God's love for His people. Believers can be encouraged by this truth and it could also bring not-yet-believers to the realization that they are included in this truth.

I thank God for my husband every single day. I might be upset with him, here and there, but I could never love anyone this way because of Christ's love for me and for him. We talk about how we long to see the Lord and then remember that we are here, for such a time as this. Our flames toward each other are fanned by the love of the Lord.

We no longer live in fear of what we can do to achieve salvation because Christ already died for our sins. He died for yours and your spouse's sins also. Rejoice in the holy name of Jesus. Christ destroyed death, for good. We are saved by His sacrifice and so are our spouses.

Hallelujah!

LORD, be gracious to us;
   we long for you.
Be our strength every morning,
   our salvation in time of distress.
Isaiah 33:2, NIV

God's grace is sufficient for anything (see 2 Corinthians 12:9). When we find His hope, His love, and His faithfulness, we are present in His grace also. His grace and strength are renewed every morning and they remind us of our salvation. He left us His Holy Spirit to be our guide. Let's be guided toward encouraging many people today and tomorrow.

Guidance

We have the ultimate 'guide.' The Holy Spirit is our guide. He serves as a compass in our marriage also. We get the strength and are encouraged through the Holy Spirit and He guides us when we are encouraging others.

> 1 Blessed is the one
>   whose transgressions are forgiven,
>   whose sins are covered.
> 2 Blessed is the one
>   whose sin the LORD does not count against them
>   and in whose spirit is no deceit.
>
> 3 When I kept silent,
>   my bones wasted away
>   through my groaning all day long.
> 4 For day and night
>   your hand was heavy on me;
> my strength was sapped
>   as in the heat of summer.
>
> 5 Then I acknowledged my sin to you
>   and did not cover up my iniquity.
> I said, "I will confess
>   my transgressions to the LORD."
> And you forgave
>   the guilt of my sin.
>
> 6 Therefore let all the faithful pray to you
>   while you may be found;
> surely the rising of the mighty waters
>   will not reach them.
> 7 You are my hiding place;
>   you will protect me from trouble
>   and surround me with songs of deliverance.
> **Psalm 32:1–7, NIV**

We are blessed to be forgiven of our sins. Our sins became covered, once and for all, by Christ's sacrifice. He died to cover our sins and those of our spouses. Therefore, we must allow His Spirit to guide us toward others who need to be encouraged. We are not to keep silent anymore.

When we keep silent, we struggle against the Word of God. Therefore, circumstances appear to be worse than they are. We forget that we are covered by His blood and then neglect to share encouragement with others. Have you ever felt truly drained from the heat? This is what it feels like to work against the Word of God, only multiply it by infinity.

He has forgiven our sins. Christ died to prove this and to make it more realistic. His sacrifice should have been ours, but His love for us and our spouse is the ultimate sacrifice to cover sin. We must be in the spirit of repentance, always. He only covers the repentant hearts. Prayers to Him bring us back into His hiding place and we are ready to encourage others again. It is completely by His strength that we can encourage our spouse, others, and ourselves.

His Strength

God's strength is all we can truly rely upon. Even if you are only in your twenties or thirties, you will notice that these bodies are beginning to give out. God's strength never gives out. His promises are new every single day. Jesus gave us the hope for a future with Him and we are to encourage others with this Good News.

His strength brings us encouragement in our hearts. We must share this encouragement with our spouses. They will see His love and strive to remain inside of His strength and encouragement. His grace has given us and our spouse eternal life and we get to spend eternity with Him.

> 16 May our Lord Jesus Christ himself and God our Father, who loved us and by his grace gave us eternal encouragement and good hope, 17 encourage your hearts and strengthen you in every good deed and word.
> **2 Thessalonians 2:16–17, NIV**

His mercy is made new every day. How do we remain inside of His mercy? We encourage each other to live righteous lives for His glory. We are currently living new lives. In these new lives, we are asked, by our loving Father, to encourage each other in His love and demonstrate the love of Christ to our spouse. People will try to tempt us away from Him. However, through His strength and encouraging words, we can stand strong and not be wavered.

Hallelujah!

We no longer are to hide His Good News and discourage each other. We are to encourage each other so that His Good News is preached to everybody. The god of this world cannot be given the strength to waver us unless we allow him to have our strength.

> In their case the god of this world has blinded the minds of the unbelievers, to keep them from seeing the light of the gospel of the glory of Christ, who is the image of God.
> **2 Corinthians 4:4, ESV**

When we feel ourselves or suspect that our spouse's strength is wavering, we immediately pray for each other and encourage each other with the reminder of repentance. The enemy has no power over our prayer. This is why he is trying to keep unbelievers away from God's Truth.

There is no boasting of ourselves when demonstrating His strength and encouragement to others. Only His strength shines through any circumstance. Jesus Christ is all that we are to boast and preach about. He is the Way, the Truth, and the Life. There is no other Way to the Father, and this is encouraging because we and our spouses are not expected to 'work' our way to the Lord. We simply believe in Christ as our Lord and Savior and find grace and mercy waiting for us.

> 1 Therefore, since through God's mercy we have this ministry, we do not lose heart. 2 Rather, we have renounced secret and shameful ways; we do not use deception, nor do we distort the word of God. On the contrary, by setting forth the truth plainly we commend ourselves to everyone's conscience in the sight of God. 3 And even if our gospel is veiled, it is veiled to those who are perishing. 4 The god of this age has blinded the minds of unbelievers, so that they cannot see the light of the gospel that displays the glory of Christ, who is the image of God. 5 For what we preach is not ourselves, but Jesus Christ as Lord, and ourselves as your servants for Jesus' sake. 6 For God, who said, "Let light shine out of darkness," made his light shine in our hearts to give us the

light of the knowledge of God's glory displayed in the face of Christ.

7 But we have this treasure in jars of clay to show that this all-surpassing power is from God and not from us. 8 We are hard pressed on every side, but not crushed; perplexed, but not in despair; 9 persecuted, but not abandoned; struck down, but not destroyed. 10 We always carry around in our body the death of Jesus, so that the life of Jesus may also be revealed in our body. 11 For we who are alive are always being given over to death for Jesus' sake, so that his life may also be revealed in our mortal body. 12 So then, death is at work in us, but life is at work in you.

13 It is written: "I believed; therefore I have spoken." Since we have that same spirit of faith, we also believe and therefore speak, 14 because we know that the one who raised the Lord Jesus from the dead will also raise us with Jesus and present us with you to himself. 15 All this is for your benefit, so that the grace that is reaching more and more people may cause thanksgiving to overflow to the glory of God.

16 Therefore we do not lose heart. Though outwardly we are wasting away, yet inwardly we are being renewed day by day. 17 For our light and momentary troubles are achieving for us an eternal glory that far outweighs them all. 18 So we fix our eyes not on what is seen, but on what is unseen, since what is seen is temporary, but what is unseen is eternal.

2 Corinthians 4, NIV

When we are encouraging to others, we can see the light better. The power that we receive from this light is all God. His glory shines through our actions toward ourselves, our spouse, our family, our friends, and others in the communities where we reside.

We will have trouble and be pressed down with the pressures of this life. However, His strength will guide us through these troubles so that His glorious light will shine. When we struggle with despair, His grace allows us to encourage each other and work through the troubles and struggles of this life. God is good, all the time.

He will never abandon us. How many of us have struggled with abandonment? I know this is one of the things that marriages struggle with. Is s/he going to leave me? Am I going to be alone again? How can I keep him/her from leaving? And this list goes on.

Remember, God is always with us and will never forsake or abandon us. This should be encouraging enough to allow us to feel joy in our marriage. How many times have we been knocked down? That does not matter half as much as how many times we get back up again. His strength will allow us to get back up and then to help our spouse back up when s/he needs it. How encouraging!

Death surrounds us, but if you read Psalm 91, you will notice that we are not defined or touched by death. Yes, we will all die eventually. However, we have the encouragement to know that our eternity has been paid for and we are going to spend it with Him. Our eternity does not include the struggles we work through here in this life. Thank the Lord for this encouraging news.

We are to continue to encourage others because we believe in God. We will be raised into the eternal arms of our Lord and we know this because He raised Jesus also. God will receive more glory when we are willing to share His love and encouragement through our words toward others and our actions. Since God's grace is what we rely upon, we are to encourage others to do the same, rely upon the strength of the Lord.

We must never give up on each other. Do not give up on ourselves, our spouse, our family, our friends, our communities, our nation, and even on the world. We must share His encouragement with as many people as we can so that they can share it with even more people and so on.

Let's face the truth, our bodies are decaying and dying. However, our spirit is being renewed daily, hourly, and even by the minute. His glory shines through the trouble that we struggle with because we end up showing others that we rely upon His strength. The trouble that we can see is nothing compared to the things which we cannot yet see—His glory and our eternity with Him.

His Beauty

There is beauty all around us. Look up into the sky…beauty. Look into the forests…beauty. See the seas and the mountains…beauty. Watch birds fly and soar above us…beauty. Catch a glimpse of beauty in the bees, butterflies, and hummingbirds. Can you all tell that I love bees, butterflies, and hummingbirds? Anything that I plant must attract at least one of these beautiful creatures of God.

Hopefully, we all consider our spouses as part of His beauty. As I mentioned before, I believe that God gifted me with my husband. Therefore, I see His beauty in my husband. He makes things and people beautiful, inside and out. However, everything that He makes beautiful is for His timing. This means that when things wilt, they are supposed to wilt.

Along with the beauty which He allows us to enjoy, He places the yearning and desires of eternity in our hearts. Think about that for a moment. God our Father created beautiful things for our (and His) enjoyment. We are not yet aware of what the beginning of time looked like.

He created time and space. He created us and our spouses. He also created beautiful things and people for our lives to be encouraging.

> 11 He has made everything beautiful in its time. He has also set eternity in the human heart; yet no one can fathom what God has done from beginning to end. 12 I know that there is nothing better for people than to be happy and to do good while they live. 13 That each of them may eat and drink, and find satisfaction in all their toil—this is the gift of God. 14 I know that everything God does will endure forever; nothing can be added to it and nothing taken from it. God does it so that people will fear him.
> **Ecclesiastes 3:11–14, NIV**

It is good for His people to be happy. However, happiness does not fill us up as well as His joy does. The difference between happiness and joy is that happiness is at the surface and joy is in our core. Joy is less about ourselves and more about others, including our beautiful spouse.

Happiness is fleeting. God's beautiful gifts to us allow us to find some happiness in circumstances, as we find true joy in knowing and loving the Lord. Even when our circumstances are grim, we can find His joy.

God has given us beauty to enjoy. He has fed us and allowed us to enjoy food and drink. Nothing can be added to what God has done for us. We cannot add to what God does for us. We can get remarkably close though. We can share His love and encourage others, so they are privy to His beauty also.

Fear of the Lord is not the same as being afraid of the Lord. When we are afraid of the Lord, we tend to hide and feel ashamed of ourselves. When we fear the Lord, we revere Him for Who He is, our Savior, our Abba Father, our God. Therefore, it is a gift to have 'fear' of the Lord and we share this with our spouse to find His beauty in our marriage.

> 1 As for you, you were dead in your transgressions and sins, 2 in which you used to live when you followed the ways of this world and of the ruler of the kingdom of the air, the spirit who is now at work in those who are disobedient. 3 All of us also lived among them at one time, gratifying the cravings of our flesh and following its desires and thoughts. Like the rest, we were by nature deserving of wrath. 4 But because of his great love for us, God, who is rich in mercy, 5 made us alive with Christ even when we were dead in transgressions—it is by grace you have been saved. 6 And God raised us up with Christ and seated us with him in the heavenly realms in Christ Jesus, 7 in order that in the coming ages he might show the incomparable riches of his grace, expressed in his kindness to us in Christ Jesus. 8 For it is by grace you have been saved, through faith—and this is not from yourselves, it is the gift of God—9 not by works, so that no one can boast. 10 For we are God's handiwork, created in Christ Jesus to do good works, which God prepared in advance for us to do.
> **Ephesians 2:1–10, NIV**

Have we heard of the saying that we are dead in our sins? What this is referring to is that

> …the wages of sin is death, but the gift of God is eternal life in Christ Jesus our Lord.
> **Romans 6:23, NIV**

When we were focused on our fleshly (non-spirit) ways and thoughts, we were not only living in sin, we were living in death. I don't know about any of you, but my life went from darkness into light as soon as He came back into my life. Things became beautiful again and I became filled with joy, no matter the circumstances. That's all God!

We became alive with Christ as soon as we repented and turned back toward Him. This is beyond beautiful; it is life-transforming and we must praise God for this. His mercy is anew every single day. Therefore, if we are upset or unhappy about today, we remember that tomorrow brings new life.

Marriage can be difficult. Our lives go from being an individual to sharing everything with another person. Our spouse becomes a part of us (see Genesis 2:24). It is by His grace that we are saved and so is our spouse. Christ died for our sin and He loves each of us. We are saved from eternal damnation by His gift of grace and mercy which strengthens our faith in Him.

Thankfully, we cannot work our way into heaven. We are not beautiful without Christ. His sacrifice made us holy, righteous, and beautiful enough to approach God our Father. We are God's handiwork. Do you realize what this means? It means that since He made us in His image (see Genesis 1:27) and He is beautiful, we are beautiful too.

13 For you created my inmost being;
    you knit me together in my mother's womb.
14 I praise you because I am fearfully and wonderfully made;
    your works are wonderful,
    I know that full well.
15 My frame was not hidden from you
    when I was made in the secret place,
    when I was woven together in the depths of the earth.
16 Your eyes saw my unformed body;
    all the days ordained for me were written in your book
    before one of them came to be.
17 How precious to me are your thoughts, God!
    How vast is the sum of them!
18 Were I to count them,
    they would outnumber the grains of sand—

when I awake, I am still with you.
Psalm 139:13–18, NIV

His beauty only shines through us when we are in a right relationship with Him. He created us and made us beautiful. What we do with this knowledge is our free will that everybody talks about. Free will is not to allow us to live in sin…although that is a choice that we all have made. It is meant so that we can choose the Lord and live with Him throughout eternity. Daily and sometimes even more often, we need to remember that our spouse is human. Therefore, s/he is made in His image also.

We are all fearfully and wonderfully made in His image. Really grasp ahold of the meaning behind the last sentence. Read it again and think about what that means. The image of God lives inside of us. We are encouraged every day to share this with as many people as we can.

His precious thoughts are to be an encouragement toward us and to the ones that we love—to the ones we do not know and our enemies. We must share His love with the world. Trusting relationships are only made when we share His love!

Relationships

There are so many types of relationships. There are parents, children, husbands, wives, and our relationship with our Lord and Savior. Sometimes relationships are not what they appear to be. We are betrayed by people often and trust becomes difficult when we are scorned. However, God will not betray or disappoint us.

We are children of God and our spouses are also. He guides us through trouble and pain. He meets us where we are to comfort and encourage us. He also demonstrated the ultimate act of love by sending His only Son to die for our sins (see John 3:16). We are His children which is a wonderfully beautiful relationship with God the Father.

He desires us to live inside of our relationship with Him while we are on earth so that we have an even better relationship with Him in heaven. We must try and test any spirit which appears contrary to His loving and righteous Spirit so as not to fall into a life of sin again.

1 Dear friends, do not believe every spirit, but test the spirits to see whether they are from God, because many

false prophets have gone out into the world. 2 This is how you can recognize the Spirit of God: Every spirit that acknowledges that Jesus Christ has come in the flesh is from God, 3 but every spirit that does not acknowledge Jesus is not from God. This is the spirit of the antichrist, which you have heard is coming and even now is already in the world.

4 You, dear children, are from God and have overcome them, because the one who is in you is greater than the one who is in the world. 5 They are from the world and therefore speak from the viewpoint of the world, and the world listens to them. 6 We are from God, and whoever knows God listens to us; but whoever is not from God does not listen to us. This is how we recognize the Spirit of truth and the spirit of falsehood.

7 Dear friends, let us love one another, for love comes from God. Everyone who loves has been born of God and knows God. 8 Whoever does not love does not know God, because God is love. 9 This is how God showed his love among us: He sent his one and only Son into the world that we might live through him. 10 This is love: not that we loved God, but that he loved us and sent his Son as an atoning sacrifice for our sins. 11 Dear friends, since God so loved us, we also ought to love one another. 12 No one has ever seen God; but if we love one another, God lives in us and his love is made complete in us.

13 This is how we know that we live in him and he in us: He has given us of his Spirit. 14 And we have seen and testify that the Father has sent his Son to be the Savior of the world. 15 If anyone acknowledges that Jesus is the Son of God, God lives in them and they in God. 16 And so we know and rely on the love God has for us.

God is love. Whoever lives in love lives in God, and God in them. 17 This is how love is made complete among us so that we will have confidence on the day of judgment: In this world we are like Jesus. 18 There is no fear in love. But perfect love drives out fear, because fear has to do with punishment. The one who fears is not made perfect in love.

19 We love because he first loved us. 20 Whoever claims to love God yet hates a brother or sister is a liar. For whoever does not love their brother and sister, whom they have seen, cannot love God, whom they have not seen. 21 And he has given us this command: Anyone who loves God must also love their brother and sister.

1 John 4, NIV

We have heard about people who are taking 'God' out of everything these days. Those people, though they might seem nice or right, are false prophets and antichrists. People who believe that Jesus is not the Way to God the Father are also antichrists. We must not believe a word they have to say. They are only professing another god…Satan! No spirit is of God which believes that Jesus is not the Way. We must test each spiritual encounter so that we can remain the encouragers which God has made us to be.

A right relationship with God might not make it so that every relationship here on earth is perfect, but we know that we can rely on the Lord for His joy. Just because someone states that we are being closed-minded and unjust because we know that the only Way to God is Jesus, do not listen. We do not have to argue with these people either.

Pray for them. Let them know that Christ died for their sins too. Bless them, do not curse them. But do not believe what they are saying. Our spouse must also know that these spirits exist. To be sure, sit down with him/her and talk about what it takes to get into heaven. Make sure they are 'on the same page,' and nothing is distracting their beliefs.

Our spouses might believe that leaders of this great nation are always right. However, we must help them to realize that only God is always right. Yes, we are to obey the law of this nation, but we are not to allow that law to define our beliefs. Our spouse will listen to us and we should also listen to them. Our relationship depends on hearing each other as we listen to God.

Remember that judging and testing a spirit is not the same as judging each other. Jesus is the only judge. We are to show each other what love looks like so that we are more capable of judging spirits.

God is love. He desires to have a relationship with us all. Therefore, we must know His spirit and listen only to Him. Notice I did not print 'it' when speaking of God's spirit. The Holy Spirit is one with the Father and the Son. Therefore, He is not an 'it.'

God sent His one and only Son to save us all. When we hear His Spirit, we know Him better. We must encourage everyone that we know with this knowledge, without shoving it down their throats. Forcing Him on people is not what He desires.

How many times did someone try to get us to hear them by demanding that we listen? Did we bother listening? No, we did not. Therefore, we must graciously remind people that God is our Father, whether they choose to believe it or not.

A right relationship with God begins with knowing that He is love and that His love conquers all fear. People might try to sway us from His truth but remember that Jesus is the only Way to the Father and that if a person believes this, they are of God too.

Even though we are to fear (revere) the Lord, there is no fear in His perfect love. A right relationship with Him will demonstrate this so that we do not live in fear, but in reverence for our Father. We are not the ones who first loved.

God first loved us. Therefore, we must love Him back through loving and encouraging others. We cannot love God and hate our brother or sister. This means that even though our relationship with our relatives might be difficult, we must show them love, even when they show us hate, loathing, or disdain. Remember, we have His strength to accomplish this… so let's use it to love others so that they can trust what we have to say about the Lord.

Trust

Putting our trust in another person is difficult. Putting our trust in the Lord is always safe. Most of us have either been betrayed, seen a loved one get betrayed, or betrayed someone else. Therefore, our trust levels are not as high as they can be for the Lord. Not even our spouse can say that their love will endure forever because they will die, eventually. His love endures forever.

> 7 But the LORD shall endure forever;
>   He has prepared His throne for judgment.
> 8 He shall judge the world in righteousness,

And He shall administer judgment for the peoples in
uprightness.

9 The LORD also will be a refuge for the oppressed,
A refuge in times of trouble.
10 And those who know Your name will put their trust in You;
For You, LORD, have not forsaken those who seek You.
Psalm 9:7–10, NKJV

The only judge we can trust is the Lord. He is trustworthy, true, and
will not abandon us. I am not saying that our spouse is abandoning us
when they die, but it does feel like an abandonment when they are gone.
The Lord judges the righteous and questions why we are not encouraging
each other. He is our safe place and we can trust Him to help us trust our
spouse.

When we call upon the name of the Lord, we will be heard and saved.
Since He will never forsake or abandon us, we can always put our trust in
Him. Even though He is the judge, He will not judge us unfairly. He is to
be trusted because He is truth! We are human and will have our doubts,
but this does not make us evil or cursed by God. Turn around and
repent...He is there!

5 This is what the LORD says:

"Cursed is the one who trusts in man,
who draws strength from mere flesh
and whose heart turns away from the LORD.
6 That person will be like a bush in the wastelands;
they will not see prosperity when it comes.
They will dwell in the parched places of the desert,
in a salt land where no one lives.

7 "But blessed is the one who trusts in the LORD,
whose confidence is in him.
8 They will be like a tree planted by the water
that sends out its roots by the stream.
It does not fear when heat comes;
its leaves are always green.
It has no worries in a year of drought

and never fails to bear fruit."

9 The heart is deceitful above all things
and beyond cure.
Who can understand it?

10 "I the LORD search the heart
and examine the mind,
to reward each person according to their conduct,
according to what their deeds deserve."
Jeremiah 17:5–10, NIV

Our flesh is strong. However, our spirit is even stronger. His power is found in His spirit which is in us. When we trust in the Lord, the encouragement of His truth helps guide us. We are then able to help our spouse see His truth more clearly. His guidance helps us to guide others toward Him.

We have all turned away from the Lord. This is not our ultimate demise. We can turn back to Him and trust that He will save us from ourselves. This hope is found at the center of our marriage also.

God is the center of righteous marriages. Therefore, our spouse must be willing to trust in the Lord also. Otherwise, we need to encourage them to return to the Lord and be loved.

We have the blessing of being able to trust in the only one who is called Truth. Other gods are not real and are not to be trusted. We find the confidence to encourage each other when we realize that God is to be trusted, no matter the circumstance.

I enjoy the tree references because I have been known to have a green thumb. My green thumb comes from trusting in the Lord to allow us to watch things and people grow. It's pure joy to watch as trees, plants, and especially people grow.

Growth in the garden comes from the beginning of the Bible. The setting is in the Garden of Eden and Adam and Eve are enjoying communication with the Lord. However, since they (and we) have flesh hearts, they were deceived by the enemy. The Lord searches our hearts and examines our minds to assure us that we are righteous and that we believe that Christ is our Savior. Our deeds are an integral part of what He examines in our hearts. He desires a giving, caring, and encouraging heart. We are treasured by the Lord.

Amen!

There are certainly times when we feel horrible and even in a state of distress. However, when these feelings arise, it is best to remain encouraged by getting into the Word of God and listening to what He has to say. Even though it is simple to fall into a state of discouragement, we must remember that He is with us. Discouraging another person is not right. It might feel right for the moment, but it is never right or righteous.

Discouraging

Again, this is my least favorite section to discuss. However, without a better understanding of discouragement, it is difficult to understand what encouragement is. We live in a world where 'dog-eat-dog' is praised and lifting each other up is booed. We must be the change that the world needs to see His glory, here on earth.

Bringing shame to our spouse and/or family and friends is not good. Bringing the discouraging words to any other person can cause them to move even further away from God. This is not righteous, and God needs us to be righteous.

> …but she who brings shame is like rottenness in his bones.
> **Proverbs 12:4b, ESV**

His love for us must be shared with our spouse, our family and friends, strangers, and even our enemies. I know the last thing on that list is difficult, especially when we feel discouraged. We can remember that His love never leaves us though and we must share this hope with others.

Our love must be drawn from His love on a minute-by-minute basis. This means that when we feel discouraged, we find ways to pray, read the Bible, and meditate on His Word to fill up our encouragement tank. There is hope for our future. Therefore, we are to share this hope and watch the Lord work His blessings through the people we share this with.

> 4 Love is patient, love is kind. It does not envy, it does not boast, it is not proud. 5 It does not dishonor others, it is not self-seeking, it is not easily angered, it keeps no record of wrongs. 6 Love does not delight in evil but

141

rejoices with the truth. 7 It always protects, always trusts, always hopes, always perseveres.
1 Corinthians 13:4–7, NIV

We read that love is patient. Have you ever prayed for patience? I always tell people, "When you pray for patience, duck," because something to test our patience is about to happen.

His patience is so much purer than what we imagine patience to be. Therefore, we are not always ready for how He will deliver patience to us. He might allow us to be tried by other people. But do not be discouraged. He only does this to His children whom He loves so much.

Have you ever thought to yourself, "I wish I had the abilities that—insert a person's name here—has?" Or "I wish I knew how to do the things that—insert a person's name here—can do?" This is envy.

When we envy another person, we are stuck inside of discouragement. We must find ways to get out so that we do not discourage another person. It is not easy to remain an encourager, but it is required so that the Lord can work in the minds and hearts of others and we get to watch this growth and transformation.

We must be willing to protect each other from the enemy's falsehoods. We must rejoice in the hope of our future with the Lord and share His encouragement with others. Avoiding discouragement will not always be simple, but it is necessary, and we have His strength to use so that we dig our way out of discouragement. It is wise not to remain inside discouragement.

> 1 Listen as Wisdom calls out!
>   Hear as understanding raises her voice!
> 2 On the hilltop along the road,
>   she takes her stand at the crossroads.
> 3 By the gates at the entrance to the town,
>   on the road leading in, she cries aloud,
> 4 "I call to you, to all of you!
>   I raise my voice to all people.
> 5 You simple people, use good judgment.
>   You foolish people, show some understanding.
> 6 Listen to me! For I have important things to tell you.
>   Everything I say is right,

7 for I speak the truth
   and detest every kind of deception.
8 My advice is wholesome.
   There is nothing devious or crooked in it.
9 My words are plain to anyone with understanding,
   clear to those with knowledge.
10 Choose my instruction rather than silver,
   and knowledge rather than pure gold.
11 For wisdom is far more valuable than rubies.
   Nothing you desire can compare with it.

12 "I, Wisdom, live together with good judgment.
   I know where to discover knowledge and discernment.
13 All who fear the LORD will hate evil.
   Therefore, I hate pride and arrogance,
   corruption and perverse speech.
14 Common sense and success belong to me.
   Insight and strength are mine.
15 Because of me, kings reign,
   and rulers make just decrees.
16 Rulers lead with my help,
   and nobles make righteous judgments.

17 "I love all who love me.
   Those who search will surely find me.
18 I have riches and honor,
   as well as enduring wealth and justice.
19 My gifts are better than gold, even the purest gold,
   my wages better than sterling silver!
20 I walk in righteousness,
   in paths of justice.
21 Those who love me inherit wealth.
   I will fill their treasuries.

22 "The LORD formed me from the beginning,
   before he created anything else.
23 I was appointed in ages past,
   at the very first, before the earth began.
24 I was born before the oceans were created,

before the springs bubbled forth their waters.
25 Before the mountains were formed,
before the hills, I was born—
26 before he had made the earth and fields
and the first handfuls of soil.
27 I was there when he established the heavens,
when he drew the horizon on the oceans.
28 I was there when he set the clouds above,
when he established springs deep in the earth.
29 I was there when he set the limits of the seas,
so they would not spread beyond their boundaries.
And when he marked off the earth's foundations,
30 I was the architect at his side.
I was his constant delight,
rejoicing always in his presence.
31 And how happy I was with the world he created;
how I rejoiced with the human family!

32 "And so, my children, listen to me,
for all who follow my ways are joyful.
33 Listen to my instruction and be wise.
Don't ignore it.
34 Joyful are those who listen to me,
watching for me daily at my gates,
waiting for me outside my home!
35 For whoever finds me finds life
and receives favor from the LORD.
36 But those who miss me injure themselves.
All who hate me love death."
Proverbs 8, NLT

In Proverbs 8, we read about many discouraging things. There are unwise ways to handle this life and most of the Proverbs of the Bible share ways not to do things along with ways to do things. We are called to raise our voice to God and all mankind. We are expected to encourage each other to share His hope with the world.

The foolish and simpletons must be made aware of His Word to help them achieve His wisdom and truths. Everything that the Lord says is just, fair, and righteous; we must encourage others to find these truths also.

His words are true and upright, how can we read this and then discourage another? We discourage others because we are simply human beings. However, we must strive to not be discouragers and we must help our spouses to do the same. They must understand His love for them, so they are not discouragers either.

His instruction is worth more than any silver or gold. What this means is that we are to find wisdom, seek Him, and then share His love with all the people that we can. Encouragement must become an integral part of our value system.

Encouraging, huh?!

Prudence is the ability to govern yourself enough not to lack wisdom. It means that we use reason instead of feelings to work with others. Since we use reason, we can encourage others. We do not discourage others simply because of our feelings, toward them, or our circumstances. It is not the other person's fault that we feel yucky. There is mostly no fault for feeling this way. It just happens from time to time.

Our pride cannot be a part of encouragement. Maybe our spouse is occasionally wrong, but our pride must not address this wrong, we must address it with encouragement instead. We read that wisdom and prudence carry sound judgment and good counsel. Why do we use these truths to discourage others? We should not do this. But we are human.

The Lord calls His people to live inside of His love. We are not to discourage others from this same love. Our words can be harmful and the Lord desires for us to find His encouraging words to use toward others.

The Lord loves those who love Him. Therefore, drawing people toward His love is not a part of discouragement. Encouraging words are more likely to draw people into His love.

God is righteous and He calls us to become more righteous. This means that we must seek wisdom to become more righteous. Wisdom walks in righteousness and so must we. Our treasuries (future in heaven) are full and the Lord desires that we share this fullness through encouragement.

Some extra encouraging words are included in verses 23-31. It can be said that these verses are speaking of the up-and-coming visit by Jesus. He was there in the beginning...

> 1 In the beginning was the Word, and the Word was with God, and the Word was God. 2 He was with God in the beginning. 3 Through him all things were made;

without him nothing was made that has been made. 4 In
him was life, and that life was the light of all mankind.
John 1:1–4, NIV

He was there when the heavens, the seas, and land were created. He
was there to rejoice in the making of all things, including mankind. This is
encouraging because we know that Christ comes to save us all.

Wisdom is necessary so that our words encourage others to follow God.
We cannot ignore His words of wisdom and this includes the wisdom to
know how to encourage others.

Our spouse may not appear to be 'wise' all the time, but neither are we.
We must be reading His Word daily to find the wisdom to encourage each
other. The alternative is death. We live in His light, now share it.

> 1 A gentle answer deflects anger,
>   but harsh words make tempers flare.
>
> 2 The tongue of the wise makes knowledge appealing,
>   but the mouth of a fool belches out foolishness.
>
> 3 The LORD is watching everywhere,
>   keeping his eye on both the evil and the good.
>
> 4 Gentle words are a tree of life;
>   a deceitful tongue crushes the spirit.
> **Proverbs 15:1–4, NLT**

Sometimes it is so difficult to hold our tongue. I have a saying that I
may have mentioned before. It is a prayer that goes like this, "Lord, please
bite my tongue because I do not know how, and I feel some discouraging
words coming on." It usually works if I do not fall right back into my flesh.

It is discouraging to be hit with someone's harsh words. Therefore, I
try not to use these words with anyone. I slip just as much as the next
person and then feel discouraged by my actions and words. I pray for a
tongue of the wise so as not to be discouraging. I despise looking foolish
and hope to share His righteousness instead.

The Lord knows when we mess up. He loves us anyway. Therefore, this
should make us want to be more encouraging because we are encouraged
by His love. God watches over us. We simply need to ask for His help

146

when encouraging others. Discouraging words are not of the Lord. Therefore, we must use gentle words to not crush a person's spirit.

Our God is an awesome God who reigns from heaven and shares His strength with us to encourage others. Discouragement is not godly. It is worldly and we are no longer of this world (see John 15:19). We are treasured by the 'Most High,' let's encourage others with this truth.

Treasured

Again, as mentioned before, we love because He first loved us. What a tremendous example that Christ gave to us.

> 19 We love because he first loved us. 20 Whoever claims to love God yet hates a brother or sister is a liar. For whoever does not love their brother and sister, whom they have seen, cannot love God, whom they have not seen. 21 And he has given us this command: Anyone who loves God must also love their brother and sister.
> **1 John 4:19–21, NIV**

He first loved us. How does that make us feel? It makes me want to dance around like David did...

> Wearing a linen ephod, David was dancing before the LORD with all his might, 15 while he and all Israel were bringing up the ark of the LORD with shouts and the sound of trumpets.
> 16 As the ark of the LORD was entering the City of David, Michal daughter of Saul watched from a window. And when she saw King David leaping and dancing before the LORD, she despised him in her heart.
> 17 They brought the ark of the LORD and set it in its place inside the tent that David had pitched for it, and David sacrificed burnt offerings and fellowship offerings before the LORD. 18 After he had finished sacrificing the burnt offerings and fellowship offerings, he blessed the people in the name of the LORD Almighty. 19 Then he gave a loaf of bread, a cake of dates and a cake of raisins to

each person in the whole crowd of Israelites, both men and women. And all the people went to their homes.

20 When David returned home to bless his household, Michal daughter of Saul came out to meet him and said, "How the king of Israel has distinguished himself today, going around half-naked in full view of the slave girls of his servants as any vulgar fellow would!"

21 David said to Michal, "It was before the LORD, who chose me rather than your father or anyone from his house when he appointed me ruler over the LORD's people Israel—I will celebrate before the LORD. 22 I will become even more undignified than this, and I will be humiliated in my own eyes. But by these slave girls you spoke of, I will be held in honor."

2 Samuel 6:14–22, NIV

Again, we cannot hate our brother or sister and then claim that we love the Lord; this makes us liars. God treasures us and our brother and sister. He desires that we encourage each other to love as He loves us.

His desire also includes us finding the wisdom to encourage our spouse. He treasures our spouse as much as He treasures us. We are all encouraged by His love for us all. It is wise to share this love with other people as much as possible and as often as possible. Christ was not only crucified for us, but for our loved ones, strangers, and enemies. God's glory shines through our encouraging words to others.

6 We do, however, speak a message of wisdom among the mature, but not the wisdom of this age or of the rulers of this age, who are coming to nothing. 7 No, we declare God's wisdom, a mystery that has been hidden and that God destined for our glory before time began. 8 None of the rulers of this age understood it, for if they had, they would not have crucified the Lord of glory. 9 However, as it is written:

"What no eye has seen,
what no ear has heard,
and what no human mind has conceived"—
the things God has prepared for those who love him—

10 these are the things God has revealed to us by his Spirit.

The Spirit searches all things, even the deep things of God. 11 For who knows a person's thoughts except their own spirit within them? In the same way no one knows the thoughts of God except the Spirit of God. 12 What we have received is not the spirit of the world, but the Spirit who is from God, so that we may understand what God has freely given us. 13 This is what we speak, not in words taught us by human wisdom but in words taught by the Spirit, explaining spiritual realities with Spirit-taught words. 14 The person without the Spirit does not accept the things that come from the Spirit of God but considers them foolishness, and cannot understand them because they are discerned only through the Spirit. 15 The person with the Spirit makes judgments about all things, but such a person is not subject to merely human judgments, 16 for,

> "Who has known the mind of the Lord
> so as to instruct him?"

But we have the mind of Christ.
1 Corinthians 2:6–16, NIV

God's wisdom is considered our treasure. Have we ever been on a treasure or scavenger hunt? It's like that. We hunt and find reassurance, or the thing of the scavenger hunt, and this treasure might be a clue to the next treasure we are going to find. God's wisdom is the same idea. We hunt for Him and find His treasures of love, peace, joy, and hope which produces the wisdom we need to be encouragers.

Just because we have not seen the treasure of the scavenger hunt item yet, does not mean that it is not there. Just because we do not see God's wisdom with our eyes does not mean that it is not there either. God is preparing the ultimate treasure in heaven for those who love Him. Encouragement stems from these truths...let's go on and share this with as many people as we can.

We do not know another person's thoughts. God does. We do not know God's thoughts, except through the Spirit of God. We no longer rely upon the spirit of this world, but on the Spirit of God. Since we understand what God has given to us, we must get out there and encourage others to better understand what God can, and will, give them; His Spirit.

Human wisdom is no longer what we rely upon because God has given us His Spirit to hear and to see Him. We are to encourage our spouse with this revelation also. Encourage our spouse with our joy.

People might not understand how we still find joy when we struggle, but we do. It's from listening to His Spirit and rejoicing in all things. We have the mind of Christ now…let's get out there and share this with the world.

Encouraging

Truth is found in the Word of The Lord. The Lord praises lovely women and encourages righteous men. Our spouse will not always feel that we are a blessing, and we may not always feel they are a blessing. However, when all is said and done, we all know that a righteous spouse is a gift from God, and we are to be encouraged while encouraging our spouse.

> A wife of noble character who can find?
> She is worth far more than rubies.
> **Proverbs 31:10, NIV**

> Her children stand and bless her.
> Her husband praises her:
> **Proverbs 31:28, NLT**

> An excellent wife is the crown of her husband…
> **Proverbs 12:4, ESV**

The above verses are not simply to prove that women are loved, but that they are to love their spouse because God does. There are evil people in this world, and we need our spouse to remind us that all people are not evil. Encouraging words from a spouse can go a long way to help us through the trials and tribulations of this world.

It goes both ways though. We must also encourage our spouse through the trials of life. Encouragement might take courage, but our courage is found in the Lord, and that makes it all powerful.

Fear does not rule our lives anymore because we have His Spirit living inside of us. What this means is that even though we are struggling, hurting, and trying to stay afloat, God's promises, grace, mercy, and hope are an encouragement during these times.

Sharing these truths with our spouse will generate a blessing which will cause the struggles and pain to feel a little bit less devastating. True joy is found inside struggles which we work through because of His strength in our hearts. Do not fret anymore…He is always with us!

Let's dive into Psalm 37. This Psalm presents the troubles we might have with finding His strength to conquer such troubles…

1 Do not fret because of those who are evil
    or be envious of those who do wrong;
2 for like the grass they will soon wither,
    like green plants they will soon die away.

3 Trust in the LORD and do good;
    dwell in the land and enjoy safe pasture.
4 Take delight in the LORD,
    and he will give you the desires of your heart.

5 Commit your way to the LORD;
    trust in him and he will do this:
6 He will make your righteous reward shine like the dawn,
    your vindication like the noonday sun.

7 Be still before the LORD
    and wait patiently for him;
do not fret when people succeed in their ways,
    when they carry out their wicked schemes.

8 Refrain from anger and turn from wrath;
    do not fret—it leads only to evil.
9 For those who are evil will be destroyed,
    but those who hope in the LORD will inherit the land.

10 A little while, and the wicked will be no more;
    though you look for them, they will not be found.
11 But the meek will inherit the land
    and enjoy peace and prosperity.

12 The wicked plot against the righteous
    and gnash their teeth at them;
13 but the Lord laughs at the wicked,
    for he knows their day is coming.

14 The wicked draw the sword
    and bend the bow
to bring down the poor and needy,
    to slay those whose ways are upright.
15 But their swords will pierce their own hearts,
    and their bows will be broken.

16 Better the little that the righteous have
    than the wealth of many wicked;
17 for the power of the wicked will be broken,
    but the LORD upholds the righteous.

18 The blameless spend their days under the LORD's care,
    and their inheritance will endure forever.
19 In times of disaster they will not wither;
    in days of famine they will enjoy plenty.

20 But the wicked will perish:
    Though the LORD's enemies are like the flowers of the
        field,
    they will be consumed, they will go up in smoke.

21 The wicked borrow and do not repay,
    but the righteous give generously;
22 those the LORD blesses will inherit the land,
    but those he curses will be destroyed.

23 The LORD makes firm the steps
    of the one who delights in him;
24 though he may stumble, he will not fall,
    for the LORD upholds him with his hand.

25 I was young and now I am old,
  yet I have never seen the righteous forsaken
  or their children begging bread.
26 They are always generous and lend freely;
  their children will be a blessing.

27 Turn from evil and do good;
  then you will dwell in the land forever.
28 For the LORD loves the just
  and will not forsake his faithful ones.

Wrongdoers will be completely destroyed;
  the offspring of the wicked will perish.
29 The righteous will inherit the land
  and dwell in it forever.

30 The mouths of the righteous utter wisdom,
  and their tongues speak what is just.
31 The law of their God is in their hearts;
  their feet do not slip.

32 The wicked lie in wait for the righteous,
  intent on putting them to death;
33 but the LORD will not leave them in the power of the wicked
  or let them be condemned when brought to trial.

34 Hope in the LORD
  and keep his way.
He will exalt you to inherit the land;
  when the wicked are destroyed, you will see it.

35 I have seen a wicked and ruthless man
  flourishing like a luxuriant native tree,
36 but he soon passed away and was no more;
  though I looked for him, he could not be found.

37 Consider the blameless, observe the upright;
  a future awaits those who seek peace.
38 But all sinners will be destroyed;
  there will be no future for the wicked.

39 The salvation of the righteous comes from the LORD;
  he is their stronghold in time of trouble.
40 The LORD helps them and delivers them;
  he delivers them from the wicked and saves them,
  because they take refuge in him.
Psalm 37, NIV

Watch for evil-doers and either avoid them when temptation appears too near or remind them that the Lord loves them too. They are withering away, but only God knows who He can use to touch their hearts. Let's make ourselves available for Him to use us to touch the hearts of others. This is a strong form of encouragement.

Committing our lives to the Lord will help Him to demonstrate His love toward the lost and outcast of our lives and neighborhoods. We must be patient when He uses us to encourage others. Sometimes, they are not responsive to the encouraging words until later and we must be all right with this. When approaching another person, even a struggling spouse, we are not to show anger or resentment toward them, we are not the judges!

It might appear that someone who is practicing evil ways is finding success. Or, they appear wealthy, etc. However, our wealth comes from the promise of eternity with God. Our spouse knows this; let's share it beyond our perimeters too.

People might appear to have the upper hand when we know they are harming others. They might be utilizing the 'dog-eat-dog' attitude with the innocent. However, we are not to harm them with our words or actions but show them His love through the words He gives us and the actions which Christ demonstrated long ago, and still does today.

People may appear to be our enemies, but I like to think that we have no enemies, simply people who do not know that they are our friends/family yet. God is calling us to encourage others so that they are aware of Him. How can someone be aware of God if we treat them with the same unkindness that they treat us or other people with? We can't!

He has made our steps firm and solid. We must allow Him to use us to do the same for others. We might stumble or fall at times, but we have the encouragement that His love never fails. Turning from evil and being generous with His love for others is encouraging for all.

Be as generous with sharing His love as He has been with His forgiving love toward us. Sharing His love with our spouse and then with others.

The ultimate encouragement is to love others as God has loved us. It might not be easy. But do we honestly believe that being crucified for our sins was easy?

36 Then Jesus went with his disciples to a place called Gethsemane, and he said to them, "Sit here while I go over there and pray." 37 He took Peter and the two sons of Zebedee along with him, and he began to be sorrowful and troubled. 38 Then he said to them, "My soul is overwhelmed with sorrow to the point of death. Stay here and keep watch with me."

39 Going a little farther, he fell with his face to the ground and prayed, "My Father, if it is possible, may this cup be taken from me. Yet not as I will, but as you will."

40 Then he returned to his disciples and found them sleeping. "Couldn't you men keep watch with me for one hour?" he asked Peter. 41 "Watch and pray so that you will not fall into temptation. The spirit is willing, but the flesh is weak."

42 He went away a second time and prayed, "My Father, if it is not possible for this cup to be taken away unless I drink it, may your will be done."

43 When he came back, he again found them sleeping, because their eyes were heavy. 44 So he left them and went away once more and prayed the third time, saying the same thing.

45 Then he returned to the disciples and said to them, "Are you still sleeping and resting? Look, the hour has come, and the Son of Man is delivered into the hands of sinners. 46 Rise! Let us go! Here comes my betrayer!"

Matthew 26:36–46, NIV

And being in anguish, he prayed more earnestly, and his sweat was like drops of blood falling to the ground.

Luke 22:44, NIV

It was Christ's choice to die for us, but it does not make it easy. Using wisdom to encourage others is the best remedy for evil actions.

He has encouraged us, now we must encourage others. Our future is with God. Let's encourage others, including our spouse, to find this same truth and allow them to hear from and to see God on their own terms today, and always. This is all for the glory of God. His glory is what we must focus on when encouraging others.

His Glory

Have any of us been glorified and it felt nice? Have we been glorified, and it felt awkward? How about this, have we seen someone glorified when we know that they did not accomplish what they are getting glory for?

This probably has occurred at work the most. However, the only glory that matters is to glorify God. We are not the ones who suffered through crucifixion, even though we were innocent.

First, we are not innocent. Secondly, Christ is innocent and did suffer through crucifixion for us! Glorifying God makes it so that when we do receive human glory, we can point people to God to find where the true glory belongs.

How encouraging that we do not have to feel badly when we do not receive what we believe we deserve. People, we all deserve death (see Romans 6:23). However, through Christ's sacrifice, death has been conquered for all who believe that He is their Lord and Savior. As Romans 8 states, we will soon know His glory for all eternity.

Hallelujah!

> Yet what we suffer now is nothing compared to the glory he will reveal to us later.
> **Romans 8:18, NLT**

God is getting us ready for Him to reveal all His glory to us for all eternity. This is more than exciting, it is awesome! We will be with Him for eternity and get to praise Him forever. These facts, promises, and truths make me want to sing and dance again, like David.

Hey, do us all a favor right now…go over and dance with your spouse right now because s/he needs to be encouraged by His glory. Let's bless our spouse with some off-the-wall praises right now. God is love and He loves us!

1 I will praise You with my whole heart;
    Before the gods I will sing praises to You.
2 I will worship toward Your holy temple,
    And praise Your name
    For Your lovingkindness and Your truth;
    For You have magnified Your word above all Your name.
3 In the day when I cried out, You answered me,
    And made me bold with strength in my soul.

4 All the kings of the earth shall praise You, O LORD,
    When they hear the words of Your mouth.
5 Yes, they shall sing of the ways of the LORD,
    For great is the glory of the LORD.
6 Though the LORD is on high,
    Yet He regards the lowly;
    But the proud He knows from afar.

7 Though I walk in the midst of trouble, You will revive me;
    You will stretch out Your hand
    Against the wrath of my enemies,
    And Your right hand will save me.
8 The LORD will perfect that which concerns me;
    Your mercy, O LORD, endures forever;
    Do not forsake the works of Your hands.
    Psalm 138, NKJV

If we give God our whole hearts, He can use us to further His kingdom and to glorify His name. Singing and dancing to the Lord is not discouraged. It is encouraged because we are allowed to look like fools to people who do not understand Him (see 1 Corinthians 1:27). Have fun with the Lord. After all, the joy of the Lord is our strength (see Nehemiah 8:10). We are stronger when we sing and dance for the Lord.

When we struggle in this world, the Lord does not just leave amidst the trouble. He helps us work through the trouble. He does not allow us to go around, over, or under the trouble. He helps us work through it. His powerful right hand will save us from our enemies so that we can, in turn, encourage them to know Him too. He will not abandon nor will He forsake us. Therefore, we have His strength to encourage others.

Christine C. Sponsler

Reading through the Book of 1 Corinthians has been a favorite of mine. My husband is most pleased with the Book of Ephesians. This does not mean that I do not appreciate Ephesians or that he does not appreciate 1 Corinthians, it simply means that we have different 'life' books of the Bible.

To me, 1 Corinthians is extremely insightful and does not mince words. I appreciate this because I can be a bit dense when it comes to hearing God. (I am getting better, but still a little bit dense). Therefore, the following verses should shed some light on how we are to encourage each other...

> 23 "I have the right to do anything," you say—but not everything is beneficial. "I have the right to do anything"— but not everything is constructive. 24 No one should seek their own good, but the good of others.
>
> 25 Eat anything sold in the meat market without raising questions of conscience, 26 for, "The earth is the Lord's, and everything in it."
>
> 27 If an unbeliever invites you to a meal and you want to go, eat whatever is put before you without raising questions of conscience. 28 But if someone says to you, "This has been offered in sacrifice," then do not eat it, both for the sake of the one who told you and for the sake of conscience. 29 I am referring to the other person's conscience, not yours. For why is my freedom being judged by another's conscience? 30 If I take part in the meal with thankfulness, why am I denounced because of something I thank God for?
>
> 31 So whether you eat or drink or whatever you do, do it all for the glory of God. 32 Do not cause anyone to stumble, whether Jews, Greeks or the church of God—33 even as I try to please everyone in every way. For I am not seeking my own good but the good of many, so that they may be saved.
>
> **1 Corinthians 10:23–33, NIV**

When we glorify the Lord, we do not boast about ourselves, we boast about His love. I might have the 'right' to say anything or to do anything

158

(free will), but this does not lead to righteousness. Therefore, it makes better sense that I ask God for help to be constructive and beneficial for others. Encouraging others is what we need to strive to improve.

Entertaining is not always a welcome thing for my husband. He does not like all the work that is put into it. Therefore, when we 'entertain,' I do the work so that he might enjoy himself. I am a vegetarian, and he has kind of become one too. His mom makes special dishes for me so that I do not have to feel uncomfortable refusing the meat that she makes.

It is not because of my conscience that I do not eat meat; I simply am allergic to the hormones and antibiotics found in meat. However, if it hurt his mom's feelings not to eat what she prepared for us, I would do my best to eat it. It is encouraging for both his mom and me that we can share a meal without discomfort. We even say a prayer before each meal, and this is encouraging also.

Whenever we eat together, it is encouraging because we are doing so to His glory. The Lord is present at each of our meals together; this is encouraging because how many people can say they love their mother-in-law? I can!

Christine C. Sponsler

Chapter 12: Encouragement Toward Our In-Laws

Anyone who does not provide for their relatives, and especially for their own household, has denied the faith and is worse than an unbeliever.

1 Timothy 5:8, NIV

...a devout man who feared God with all his household, gave alms generously to the people, and prayed continually to God.

Acts 10:2, ESV

1 Since, then, you have been raised with Christ, set your hearts on things above, where Christ is, seated at the right hand of God. 2 Set your minds on things above, not on earthly things. 3 For you died, and your life is now hidden with Christ in God. 4 When Christ, who is your life, appears, then you also will appear with him in glory.

Colossians 3:1–4, NIV

11 Here there is no Gentile or Jew, circumcised or uncircumcised, barbarian, Scythian, slave or free, but Christ is all, and is in all.
12 Therefore, as God's chosen people, holy and dearly loved, clothe yourselves with compassion, kindness, humility, gentleness and patience. 13 Bear with each other and forgive one another if any of you has a grievance against someone. Forgive as the Lord forgave you. 14 And over all these virtues put on love, which binds them all together in perfect unity.

Colossians 3:11–14, NIV

Christine C. Sponsler

We have new relatives in our in-laws. They are now a part of our family. God is their Father as well as ours and He loves that we have more people to encourage in our lives.

Whether our in-laws are devout Christians or not, we are to encourage them with His love and share His truths with them always. His love for them does not stem from our relationship with them, but from His relationship with them.

Our in-laws are not the enemy. It might appear that they are, but they are not. We cherish them as much as Christ cherishes us. His love for them is as real as His love for us. We must encourage our in-laws and treat them with the kindness that Christ has shown us. We must be patient with our in-laws as much as God is patient with us.

*****

Share His love with your in-laws today! Bless them as He has blessed you!

Peace

Peacefulness is not usually associated with the word in-laws. However, for this blessed woman, the word rings true. I find peace in my mother-in-law, brother-in-law, sister-in-law, and the extended family members of these in-laws. We do not judge each other, and the gatherings are usually filled with the Lord's presence.

Does this mean that there is always peace during the gatherings or quiet dinners? No, it does not. It means that even when there are pressing issues, the family comes together, communicates, and then resolves things peacefully. This is extremely encouraging.

Prayer is a part of the communication which brings its own peacefulness to the room. We realize that we only have short spurts of time to gather, eat, socialize, and encourage each other. Therefore, we try to use this time to boost each other. I am fortunate to find peace and love in my extended family and I pray that anyone reading this finds this encouraging.

> 1 As for other matters, brothers and sisters, pray for us that the message of the Lord may spread rapidly and be honored, just as it was with you. 2 And pray that we may be delivered from wicked and evil people, for not everyone has faith. 3 But the Lord is faithful, and he will strengthen you and protect you from the evil one. 4 We have confidence in the Lord that you are doing and will continue to do the things we command. 5 May the Lord direct your hearts into God's love and Christ's perseverance.
> **2 Thessalonians 3:1–5, NIV**

> Now may the Lord of peace himself give you peace at all times and in every way. The Lord be with all of you.
> **2 Thessalonians 3:16, NIV**

> The grace of our Lord Jesus Christ be with you all.
> **2 Thessalonians 3:18, NIV**

When my husband's family gathers, we share new things which occur in our lives. God is at the center of these conversations, which makes His peace easier to find. He is honored as much as possible so that the gathering is fruitful. Even if we are struggling with issues that life brings, the family tries to help each other through these issues.

God is always faithful and during these dinners and/or gatherings, His love shines through. We even pray for family members who might not yet believe in God so that His faithfulness will cover them and work in their hearts, minds, and souls. His protection brings encouraging words to the family.

The Lord has been directing the hearts of my in-laws for some time now. It is encouraging to witness the breakthroughs and revelations that my in-laws share with us when we gather. Christ's sacrifice was meant for our salvation and watching this family live inside of that is encouraging.

God is peace and He shares this peace each time that we see each other. It might be months and it might be years before we gather again, but we always arrive with God in our hearts and this is extremely encouraging. By His grace and mercy, I wish for this same peace to be brought to all your families.

Joy

Another beautiful word that is not always associated with the word in-laws is joy. Again, I find joy along with the peace of the Lord when thinking about and visiting my in-laws. Our fleshly feelings are not filled with His joy, but the spiritual feelings we get from Him are filled with joy and love. These encouraging words are meant for anyone who adores their in-laws and for those who need to pray to find these feelings with their in-laws.

God designed 'family.' He is our Father, and He knows what family should look like. Families today are more complicated because it appears that the name 'God' has been taken out of integral parts of our nation, our communities, and our schools. However, nobody can take Him out of our families but us. Be encouraged to know that God is present in our families. Get to know each other through His love, peace, and joy.

Our strength to encourage each other still comes from the Lord, even when it concerns our in-laws. Can you imagine a world where we do not pray for our in-laws? Some people already do refuse to pray for their in-laws. I pray today, that anyone reading this finds pure joy in praying for their in-laws.

1 We who are strong ought to bear with the failings of the weak and not to please ourselves. 2 Each of us should please our neighbors for their good, to build them up. 3 For even Christ did not please himself but, as it is written: "The insults of those who insult you have fallen on me." 4 For everything that was written in the past was written to teach us, so that through the endurance taught in the Scriptures and the encouragement they provide we might have hope.

5 May the God who gives endurance and encouragement give you the same attitude of mind toward each other that Christ Jesus had, 6 so that with one mind and one voice you may glorify the God and Father of our Lord Jesus Christ.

7 Accept one another, then, just as Christ accepted you, in order to bring praise to God.
Romans 15:1–7, NIV

29 I know that when I come to you, I will come in the full measure of the blessing of Christ.

30 I urge you, brothers and sisters, by our Lord Jesus Christ and by the love of the Spirit, to join me in my struggle by praying to God for me. 31 Pray that I may be kept safe from the unbelievers in Judea and that the contribution I take to Jerusalem may be favorably received by the Lord's people there, 32 so that I may come to you with joy, by God's will, and in your company be refreshed. 33 The God of peace be with you all. Amen.
Romans 15:29–33, NIV

When we gather or have small dinners with our in-laws, we are blessed to have this time with them. We must remember this because joy is found in the feelings of thankfulness that we should have toward our in-laws. Pleasing our in-laws with sharing the Good News during these dinners and other gatherings encourages them to remain true to God's Word. Insulting each other does nothing but harm our spirits. Therefore, find pure joy in sharing His love with our in-laws.

His Word is here to teach all of us how to love, encourage, and find joy in each other. We find hope and joy in Scripture. Sharing this with our in-laws can save them from feelings of being alone. They will find His joy for their lives when we share the encouragement of us constantly praying for and with them.

Accepting our in-laws, as they are, shares the Lord's forgiveness so that they know they are also forgiven. Blessings from Christ bring His joy also. There will be struggles in any family, but God is ready, willing, and able to bring us through these struggles together. Prayers for the safety and health of our in-laws are necessary to realize His joy in our lives.

I pray right now that every single person reading this finds the endurance and encouragement of the Lord to love each other as Christ loves us and find joy inside His love. Blessings and honor to you, your family, including your in-laws, and your friends. May God bless and keep you all inside of His love.

Love

His love conquers all!

God's love is not meant only for the people we love and cherish. His love is for everyone. He desires that all His children love each other and share His love within their relationships. This does include our in-laws. I love my in-laws; however, there might be many of you who do not presently feel the same.

Here is the thing…too bad! I do not mean to sound harsh, but it is biblical to love God's children and to encourage unbelievers to share in His love. When we do not show love to our enemies, we limit His love in our lives and the lives of others.

> 43 "You have heard that it was said, 'Love your neighbor and hate your enemy.' 44 But I tell you, love your enemies and pray for those who persecute you, 45 that you may be children of your Father in heaven. He causes his sun to rise on the evil and the good, and sends rain on the righteous and the unrighteous. 46 If you love those who love you, what reward will you get? Are not even the tax collectors doing that? 47 And if you greet only your own people, what are you doing more than others? Do not even

pagans do that? 48 Be perfect, therefore, as your heavenly
Father is perfect."
Matthew 5:43–48, NIV

I pray that love for your in-laws comes soon. Since some of you might
feel as though our in-laws are the enemy: Good! We are taught to love our
enemies. Therefore, we must love our in-laws.

Wow, that was a difficult lesson. I had to pretend to not have a loving
relationship with my in-laws to write that. We all must realize that our in-
laws deserve His love, especially while they are still living in sin. They need
prayer to help them find their salvation.

We are God's children and so are the in-laws we might not get along
with. Therefore, encouraging each other to live inside of God's love is
necessary. The Bible states that even 'tax collectors' (usually lowly and evil
people) love people who love them. We must love people, even if they
have made it clear that they do not love us. Ouchy!

We are striving to be more Christlike. This means that we must love
everybody. God has placed our in-laws in our lives for such a time as this
and we must seriously love them.

Our heavenly Father is perfect. Our Father God is love. How do we
suppose that we could be made 'perfect' while showing anyone hatred? We
cannot do it! Listen to the Lord. Love our in-laws as ourselves.

27 "But to you who are listening I say: Love your
enemies, do good to those who hate you, 28 bless those
who curse you, pray for those who mistreat you. 29 If
someone slaps you on one cheek, turn to them the other
also. If someone takes your coat, do not withhold your
shirt from them. 30 Give to everyone who asks you, and if
anyone takes what belongs to you, do not demand it back.
31 Do to others as you would have them do to you.

32 "If you love those who love you, what credit is that
to you? Even sinners love those who love them. 33 And if
you do good to those who are good to you, what credit is
that to you? Even sinners do that. 34 And if you lend to
those from whom you expect repayment, what credit is
that to you? Even sinners lend to sinners, expecting to be
repaid in full. 35 But love your enemies, do good to them,

and lend to them without expecting to get anything back. Then your reward will be great, and you will be children of the Most High, because he is kind to the ungrateful and wicked. 36 Be merciful, just as your Father is merciful."
Luke 6:27–36, NIV

The power and love of the Most High will penetrate the lives of our in-laws so that we all realize that we are family. God is our Father. He loves us all. We understand feelings better than wisdom at times. We must find His wisdom to create a new and right heart inside of us.

People, including our in-laws, might hate us. However, we are to show God's love to them and pray constantly for His strength to do so. Turning the other cheek is not a metaphor which allows or condones abuse. However, we are not to return anger with more anger. We are to lovingly allow them to get whatever they need to off of their chest.

Helping our in-laws when they are struggling is another way to show God's love for them. The Golden Rule is "…do to others what you would have them do to you…" (Matthew 7:12, NIV). What this means is that we are not to harm someone, we are to show them His love. Loving only people who love us is useless. Even evil people care for others who care for them. We are to be as merciful as God has been to us, and this includes our in-laws.

When people are weak, the world desires to kick them. "Kick 'em when they're down," is the saying. There is no biblical basis to harm people, at all.

When our in-laws are struggling, in any way, we are to at least pray for their success in finding encouragement. Sometimes, when we are mad at an in-law, it is difficult to know how to pray for them. The Holy Spirit will help us pray for them. It is the will of God for us to love our in-laws, as much as He has loved us.

26 In the same way, the Spirit helps us in our weakness. We do not know what we ought to pray for, but the Spirit himself intercedes for us through wordless groans. 27 And he who searches our hearts knows the mind of the Spirit, because the Spirit intercedes for God's people in accordance with the will of God.

28 And we know that in all things God works for the good of those who love him, who have been called according to his purpose. 29 For those God foreknew he also predestined to be conformed to the image of his Son, that he might be the firstborn among many brothers and sisters. 30 And those he predestined, he also called; those he called, he also justified; those he justified, he also glorified.

31 What, then, shall we say in response to these things? If God is for us, who can be against us? 32 He who did not spare his own Son, but gave him up for us all—how will he not also, along with him, graciously give us all things? 33 Who will bring any charge against those whom God has chosen? It is God who justifies. 34 Who then is the one who condemns? No one. Christ Jesus who died—more than that, who was raised to life—is at the right hand of God and is also interceding for us. 35 Who shall separate us from the love of Christ? Shall trouble or hardship or persecution or famine or nakedness or danger or sword? 36 As it is written:

"For your sake we face death all day long;
    we are considered as sheep to be slaughtered."

37 No, in all these things we are more than conquerors through him who loved us. 38 For I am convinced that neither death nor life, neither angels nor demons, neither the present nor the future, nor any powers, 39 neither height nor depth, nor anything else in all creation, will be able to separate us from the love of God that is in Christ Jesus our Lord.
Romans 8:26–39, NIV

We know that God is at work in all of us. Why not ask God to help our in-laws through their struggles? They need prayer too.

Who are we that we would say no to God? We have all been called to be in His family. Therefore, encouraging each other, especially when we are struggling, is showing His love to each other.

Christine C. Sponsler

Here's the thing, if God is for us, who can be against us? What this means is that since God is faithfully with us, no one can harm us permanently. God sent His Son to save us and our in-laws. He is love and we must share this love constantly. To be more Christlike we must pray for our family. Christ is interceding for all of us to the Father, this does include our in-laws.

We face the looming death which every person feels. However, we also have the hope of knowing that we will be present with God when this death occurs. This same hope is for our in-laws as well.

We are all more than conquerors which means that since Christ died for our sins, we know death is conquered. Nothing will separate us from God. Nothing will separate our in-laws from God. When we all believe in Christ Jesus as our Lord and Savior, He can bless us and the people we are encouraging.

Blessings

I enjoy using a signature which includes, "May the Lord bless and keep you, always!" I never truly realized it, but it is named a priestly blessing; it's from Moses and Aaron to the Israelites. It is a signature that I use because I desire that people I write to are blessed and kept by God.

> 22 Then the LORD said to Moses, 23 "Tell Aaron and his sons to bless the people of Israel with this special blessing:
>
>> 24 'May the LORD bless you
>> and protect you.
>> 25 May the LORD smile on you
>> and be gracious to you.
>> 26 May the LORD show you his favor
>> and give you his peace.'
>
> 27 Whenever Aaron and his sons bless the people of Israel in my name, I myself will bless them."
> **Numbers 6:22–27, NLT**

Sending blessings just like this one to our in-laws creates a strong relationship and God is honored by this. When the Lord smiles on us, we are blessed. I can only hope and pray this for all my family which includes my in-laws. His grace and mercy are not just for us, it is for all members of our family, He desires that we include our in-laws.

There is hope for us to find the Lord and share His love and blessings with others. Encouragement includes sharing the Lord with our in-laws. When they can see the Lord's love for them, they are truly blessed.

> 11 For I know the plans I have for you," declares the LORD, "plans to prosper you and not to harm you, plans to give you hope and a future. 12 Then you will call on me and come and pray to me, and I will listen to you. 13 You will seek me and find me when you seek me with all your heart.
> **Jeremiah 29:11–13, NIV**

God's plans for us are not to harm us, but to fill us with the hope of His future for us. These same words are true for our in-laws. When we pray to God, He will hear us and bless us with spiritual communication and communion with Him. His blessings are not only for us but for our entire family. When we seek Him, we will find Him? Therefore, when we are truly seeking Him, we include our in-laws in our prayers and blessings.

I have been discouraged and encouraged by the same person. Sometimes within minutes of being encouraged, a person has discouraged me. However, when this happens, we are to encourage this same person. We are to bless and not curse this person so that they will be encouraged and notice His miracles.

Miracles

It is a miracle when we, human beings, get along together. Several things distinguish us from other beings and that is that we can be mean to each other, just because. Praise to the Lord that He comes down and does miracles in our lives so that we know Him and His love.

> 1 Praise the LORD!
> Give thanks to the LORD, for he is good!
>   His faithful love endures forever.
> 2 Who can list the glorious miracles of the LORD?

> Who can ever praise him enough?
> 3 There is joy for those who deal justly with others
>   and always do what is right.
>
> 4 Remember me, LORD, when you show favor to your people;
>   come near and rescue me.
> 5 Let me share in the prosperity of your chosen ones.
>   Let me rejoice in the joy of your people;
>   let me praise you with those who are your heritage.

Psalm 106:1–5, NLT

Will wonders never cease? The Lord works in mysterious ways. Have we ever truly seen a miracle? The answer to the last question is yes. We witness miracles daily. The Lord works in us so that we can even get along with our in-laws—so that we can love our in-laws.

God is faithful and He shows us how to be faithful to each other. The faithfulness of God is shared with our in-laws when we love them, even if they appear to be unlovable. God is great and He encourages us to share His greatness with our in-laws. He shares His greatness by giving us His miracles daily. It is a miracle that we are awake today. No day is promised, but God woke us up.

Hallelujah!

I have a challenge for all of us here…can we list all of God's miracles in our lives? Ready, set, go!

My Miracle List Page 1

My Miracle List Page 2

My Miracle List Page 3

How did we do? I know that I missed some, how about you? His miracles are many more than we can even list on our paper. He is constantly performing miracles.

His glory and miraculous deeds outweigh anything we are struggling with in this life. He is faithful to share these miracles, do we ever miss them? Yes, we do.

Can we ask Him to reveal them? Yes, we can and should! Praise be to God our Father. We ask and He delivers…yet another miracle.

His miracles include loving people that we are not sure we can, safely. Our in-laws are not our enemy, if we pray for them, love them, and watch, with joy, all the miracles occurring in their lives. Does this make us righteous? It makes us closer to it. God makes us righteous, through His Son and this is another miracle. Therefore, sharing these miracles with our in-laws will demonstrate to them that His love is true.

Prosperity does not mean riches and fame. It means prospering in the Lord's treasures. Our treasures are from the Lord. Let's share these treasures with our in-laws and watch them prosper in His Kingdom.

We are to rejoice for the people that Lord has placed in our lives. They are miracles and the relationship we have with them is also a miracle.

We are His heirs. Our in-laws are His heirs. We can share this miracle together, in this life. Why wait until He takes us home to get along? It would always feel like it was too late… because it was. We must love our in-laws and encourage them whenever we see them.

Encouragement

Encouraging words are a blessing for those who receive them and to those who present them as well.

Encouragement for our in-laws might feel awkward if it is not real. However, it must be real. Genuine love comes directly from the Lord.

What has the Lord done for us today? He has given us breath for yet another day. This is encouragement. We are to share it with our in-laws. We are not to keep this revelation from them. They must find His encouragement in the fact that each new day is a miraculous gift, for us all.

Condemnation might be present if we attempt to keep the Good News from our in-laws. How can we condemn someone that the Lord does not condemn? We cannot do it! Encourage them instead.

1 There is therefore now no condemnation to those who are in Christ Jesus, who do not walk according to the flesh, but according to the Spirit. 2 For the law of the Spirit of life in Christ Jesus has made me free from the law of sin and death. 3 For what the law could not do in that it was weak through the flesh, God did by sending His own Son in the likeness of sinful flesh, on account of sin: He condemned sin in the flesh, 4 that the righteous requirement of the law might be fulfilled in us who do not walk according to the flesh but according to the Spirit. 5 For those who live according to the flesh set their minds on the things of the flesh, but those who live according to the Spirit, the things of the Spirit. 6 For to be carnally minded is death, but to be spiritually minded is life and peace. 7 Because the carnal mind is enmity against God; for it is not subject to the law of God, nor indeed can be. 8 So then, those who are in the flesh cannot please God.

9 But you are not in the flesh but in the Spirit, if indeed the Spirit of God dwells in you. Now if anyone does not have the Spirit of Christ, he is not His. 10 And if Christ is in you, the body is dead because of sin, but the Spirit is life because of righteousness. 11 But if the Spirit of Him who raised Jesus from the dead dwells in you, He who raised Christ from the dead will also give life to your mortal bodies through His Spirit who dwells in you.

Romans 8:1–11, NKJV

When we condemn someone, it is like we are saying that God is wrong, and we are right. This is far from the truth—His truth. Our in-laws might not be 'in Christ' right now, but how will they ever be in Christ with our anger or hatred in the way? Therefore, God has asked that we love them as much as He has loved us. I don't know about any of you, but I don't even want to say 'no' to God.

Loving our in-laws might not come naturally, but it is necessary. People in our lives do not simply fall into our laps. God's hand is in it. We no longer live by the laws of the land, but by the Spirit of God. This world believes that in-laws are a curse, etc. I disagree, strongly. They are a blessing from God. Challenging? Maybe, but none the less, a blessing.

When people lived by the Law of God, they did not live up to the standards. Nor would we. The law demonstrates what is sin in our lives and Christ demonstrates grace and mercy for the repentance of these sins. Therefore, we are to love as God loves us.

Our minds can also be discouraging. We must be careful with what we are thinking, right? What we think sometimes falls out of our mouths and can cause major harm. When we are thinking with our flesh, we are not pleasing God. Therefore, loving our in-laws is pleasing to God and will not cause harm.

Creating a loving relationship with our in-laws may appear to be impossible. However, God will make it possible, in His timing. Be patient, He is at work right now. Since Christ dwells in our hearts, we must share His love with our in-laws. God, our Father has shown us that we have more than our biological parents to shape us. We have our mom and dad, our grandparents (if we are blessed enough to have them still), our in-laws, and Him!

Chapter 13: Parental Encouragement

9 We accept human testimony, but God's testimony is greater because it is the testimony of God, which he has given about his Son. 10 Whoever believes in the Son of God accepts this testimony. Whoever does not believe God has made him out to be a liar, because they have not believed the testimony God has given about his Son. 11 And this is the testimony: God has given us eternal life, and this life is in his Son. 12 Whoever has the Son has life; whoever does not have the Son of God does not have life.

1 John 5:9–12, NIV

Remember the story of the little boy who felt alone when his mommy took him to preschool? And then, how he felt encouraged when she returned to pick him up? That mommy obviously left her encouraging mark on her son. He, in turn, encourages others with his story. Vicarious encouragement is also known as testimonies.

Testimonies can help people find hope in this hopeless world. Jesus came to earth to bring hope and has given each of us His Spirit to continue encouraging each other with the same hope. Parents are blessed to have children and children can be blessed with loving parents. The boy in this story obviously had loving parents while growing up. However, not all of us have been this blessed.

*****

(See the Epilog of this book for my short testimony.)

Christine C. Sponsler

Truth and Love

Honoring our father and mother can come at what appears to be a high cost. There are times when our earthly parents seem wrong. However, God has placed them in our lives for such a time as this. His truth and His love are the encouraging factors to our obedience to our parents.

Honoring our parents shows that we honor and trust God. Even when the circumstances feel wrong and overwhelming, we can still trust God. The truth is, He is our Father and the Father of our parents also. Therefore, He is to be trusted in all circumstances. Is this simple? No way, but it is a blessing to honor our parents.

God is our Father. He expects us to honor Him and the parents that He provided for us. Is it God's fault that our parents are abusive? No. Is God going to simply sit back and watch the abuse? No. But He does provide us with His strength to pray for our abusive parents. God desires that no one will perish. He hopes to change our parents' hearts. When this does occur, He will be glorified, and we will find even more encouragement.

> 1 The elder,
> To the lady chosen by God and to her children, whom I love in the truth—and not I only, but also all who know the truth—2 because of the truth, which lives in us and will be with us forever:
> 3 Grace, mercy and peace from God the Father and from Jesus Christ, the Father's Son, will be with us in truth and love.
> 4 It has given me great joy to find some of your children walking in the truth, just as the Father commanded us. 5 And now, dear lady, I am not writing you a new command but one we have had from the beginning. I ask that we love one another. 6 And this is love: that we walk in obedience to his commands. As you have heard from the beginning, his command is that you walk in love.
> **2 John 1–6, NIV**

Most parents try their best to love, support, and care for their children. However, life has a way of becoming overwhelming for even the most caring parent alive. Therefore, we must remember who our Spiritual Father is and take parenting lessons from Him. God is our parental example, and it blesses and encourages children to do the same for their own children, eventually.

Christ Jesus is with each of us during our childhood and throughout our adult lives, but we must invite Him. God's grace and mercy in our lives were only made possible because of what Christ did for us. Remember that He sacrificed Himself for our parents also. They are to find salvation in Him.

There will be many generations of Christ believers in our lives when we remain focused on what the Lord is doing in our lives and the lives of our parents. Walking in His love will show our parents, abusive or not, that God's love is true, pure, and filled with His hopeful promises. There might be a parent who still finds it hard to believe…keep praying for them!

Still Questioning Salvation

When we put our profound devotion toward the Lord, His faithful love will shine through us. The Holy Spirit can use this so that our parents see His love and hope. It is difficult to watch our parents struggle with their faith. However, we struggled at one time or another and must continuously encourage our parents that the Bible is filled with His truths and promises.

> 2 Devote yourselves to prayer, being watchful and thankful. 3 And pray for us, too, that God may open a door for our message, so that we may proclaim the mystery of Christ, for which I am in chains. 4 Pray that I may proclaim it clearly, as I should. 5 Be wise in the way you act toward outsiders; make the most of every opportunity. 6 Let your conversation be always full of grace, seasoned with salt, so that you may know how to answer everyone.
> **Colossians 4:2–6, NIV**

Our devotion is to the Lord. His request of us is to share His love and encourage our parents with the actions which demonstrate His love for them. We must remain watchful and thankful for each step they take that brings them closer to God. Prayerfully relaying His message to them.

Christine C. Sponsler

Christ is a mystery. He desires that all God's children seek the answers to His mystery. We might feel as though we are stuck or unable to reach people with His messages. However, when we share the messages with our parents, He is pleased. Proclaiming His love for them encourages them and He is pleased.

We are to make the most of every opportunity that we have with our parents and others. Our answers to their questions about God must honor Him and be filled with His Truth. God is with us when we make these gestures and will supply us with His words to encourage our parents and others. This is a merciful servitude for our family.

Merciful Servitude

We cry out to the Lord—for ourselves, our families, and our friends. Hear us, oh Lord, for we are struggling to be heard. Our parents need you right now. Let them be heard by you and answer their prayers. You are the ultimate parent, Father God, and our earthly parents need your guidance and mercy. You are faithful and we could all use your guidance and strength. Thank you, Lord, for your guidance.

> 1 Hear me, LORD, and answer me,
>   for I am poor and needy.
> 2 Guard my life, for I am faithful to you;
>   save your servant who trusts in you.
> You are my God; 3 have mercy on me, Lord,
>   for I call to you all day long.
> 4 Bring joy to your servant, Lord,
>   for I put my trust in you.
>
> 5 You, Lord, are forgiving and good,
>   abounding in love to all who call to you.
> 6 Hear my prayer, LORD;
>   listen to my cry for mercy.
> 7 When I am in distress, I call to you,
>   because you answer me.
>
> 8 Among the gods there is none like you, Lord;
>   no deeds can compare with yours.

9 All the nations you have made
    will come and worship before you, Lord;
    they will bring glory to your name.
10 For you are great and do marvelous deeds;
    you alone are God.

11 Teach me your way, LORD,
    that I may rely on your faithfulness;
give me an undivided heart,
    that I may fear your name.
12 I will praise you, Lord my God, with all my heart;
    I will glorify your name forever.
13 For great is your love toward me;
    you have delivered me from the depths,
    from the realm of the dead.

14 Arrogant foes are attacking me, O God;
    ruthless people are trying to kill me—
    they have no regard for you.
15 But you, Lord, are a compassionate and gracious God,
    slow to anger, abounding in love and faithfulness.
16 Turn to me and have mercy on me;
    show your strength in behalf of your servant;
save me, because I serve you
    just as my mother did.
17 Give me a sign of your goodness,
    that my enemies may see it and be put to shame,
    for you, LORD, have helped me and comforted me.
Psalm 86, NIV

His strength will guide us. As we serve the Lord, it might mean that our parents need services also. He will have mercy on us and watch over us and our parents. He brings our heart joy when He touches the hearts of our parents. His forgiveness abounds through us and into the lives of our parents.

When we cry out for His mercy, He is merciful and hears our cries. Our distress might occur because we are not sure how the Lord will save our parents or other family members, but in His answers, we will find hope.

His joy lives inside of us and will shine through into our parents' hearts and those of our other family members as well.

His love for us must shine through us and demonstrate His love for our family members. No other god can show love which is alive in the believers. God is love and His love is the only truth. He has taught us His ways and they are to glorify Him and His Kingdom. He is our faithful Father, and our parents will see this in our actions toward them.

Our heart becomes divided when we ignore His love and calling on us. Showing Him reverence and sharing His love with our parents establishes a much better chance for them to have a right relationship with God. Praise God that He is faithful and shows us how to love our parents. Glorifying His name is a righteous goal for us and our parents to have.

His love is great and has delivered each of us from the power of death. There will be people who believe that they are better than us, and even better than God, but He will protect each of us from their wiles. Our struggles will help us to help our parents and others make it through the same struggles.

The Lord's compassion draws us nearer to him, our ultimate parent so that we can help our earthly parents understand His love for them. We have chosen to serve the Lord, and this might mean that we will be serving our parents. After all, they raised us the best they could, right?

Our enemies might be the same as our parents' enemies, but even if they are different, we can help them to better understand how to love their enemies too. The Lord will comfort us through these steps and will allow us to use His strength for these actions.

There is no shame in needing spiritual help from a child. After all, Christ said to use our childlikeness to approach the Lord (see Matthew 18:4; Ephesians 5:1-2). It is up to us to introduce our parents to the Lord, if they do not already know Him, or if they might have walked away from Him.

The Lord does great deeds in our nations. He also does great deeds in the hearts of our parents. If we love our parents, and we should, we need to introduce them to Him either again, or for the first time. He is their Savior also. Through prayer, we can find ways to get along with our parents again and watch them find their salvation—again or anew.

Prayerfulness

Our prayers for family members do not hit a ceiling. They are necessary and useful. The Lord desires for us to love and honor our parents. What better way to do this, than by praying for their salvation and/or renewed salvation? He will hear our cries.

1 O LORD, hear me as I pray;
  pay attention to my groaning.
2 Listen to my cry for help, my King and my God,
  for I pray to no one but you.
3 Listen to my voice in the morning, LORD.
  Each morning I bring my requests to you and wait expectantly.

4 O God, you take no pleasure in wickedness;
  you cannot tolerate the sins of the wicked.
5 Therefore, the proud may not stand in your presence,
  for you hate all who do evil.
6 You will destroy those who tell lies.
  The LORD detests murderers and deceivers.

7 Because of your unfailing love, I can enter your house;
  I will worship at your Temple with deepest awe.
8 Lead me in the right path, O LORD,
  or my enemies will conquer me.
Make your way plain for me to follow.

9 My enemies cannot speak a truthful word.
  Their deepest desire is to destroy others.
Their talk is foul, like the stench from an open grave.
  Their tongues are filled with flattery.
10 O God, declare them guilty.
  Let them be caught in their own traps.
Drive them away because of their many sins,
  for they have rebelled against you.

11 But let all who take refuge in you rejoice;
  let them sing joyful praises forever.
Spread your protection over them,
  that all who love your name may be filled with joy.

> 12 For you bless the godly, O LORD;
> you surround them with your shield of love.
> **Psalm 5, NLT**

When our parents are saved and we do not feel that we need to pray for them, it might be when they need it most. Therefore, it is always a good idea to pray for them. He will determine whether they need it for renewed or a newly found salvation. We simply keep on praying.

When morning comes, it is said to be a 'new day.' We must pray, at least, every new day. Our requests are not only important but necessary and heard. When we pray to the Lord, we are to wait for His answer, patiently. Do any of us struggle with patience? I know that I do, and often. However, we can find His patience through our prayers.

When we believe that we have accomplished something through our own strength, the Lord does not honor our wishes. Our parents do not understand that we love them with His love unless we keep them in our prayers. He will destroy our requests if we are not humble and ask for His blessings over our parents. We are deceiving ourselves if we believe that we can love the Lord and hate our parents. We must love our parents as the Lord loves us.

Our enemies like to tell us that if our parents fall short, and we all do (see Romans 3:23), we should just ignore that they exist. Can you imagine if the Lord ignored our existence? We would still be powerless to death. We must ignore our enemies and pray for our parents always. Our enemies speak lies and the Lord speaks only the Truth.

The Lord has made the way for us to approach Him. We must learn to approach Him daily, hourly, and sometimes minutely. We take refuge in Him and through our prayers for our parents, they can take refuge in Him in their time of need. He shields us with His love; we must share this with our parents. This will teach them that being grateful in all circumstances is godly.

Gratefulness

Being grateful in all circumstances does not mean that we must like what is happening. It simply means that we know that God is with us during these struggles. Our parents will not always be right, but they will always be our parents. Do we need to take abuse from them? No. Do we pray for them even when they are abusive? For sure! His love is what we can always be grateful for and share this with our parents.

> 1 I want you to know how hard I am contending for you and for those at Laodicea, and for all who have not met me personally. 2 My goal is that they may be encouraged in heart and united in love, so that they may have the full riches of complete understanding, in order that they may know the mystery of God, namely, Christ, 3 in whom are hidden all the treasures of wisdom and knowledge. 4 I tell you this so that no one may deceive you by fine-sounding arguments. 5 For though I am absent from you in body, I am present with you in spirit and delight to see how disciplined you are and how firm your faith in Christ is.
>
> 6 So then, just as you received Christ Jesus as Lord, continue to live your lives in him, 7 rooted and built up in him, strengthened in the faith as you were taught, and overflowing with thankfulness.
>
> 8 See to it that no one takes you captive through hollow and deceptive philosophy, which depends on human tradition and the elemental spiritual forces of this world rather than on Christ.
>
> 9 For in Christ all the fullness of the Deity lives in bodily form, 10 and in Christ you have been brought to fullness. He is the head over every power and authority.
>
> **Colossians 2:1–10, NIV**

Our parents might be in a place where they need us to contend for them and to prayerfully ask for His gratitude. We need to learn to be grateful. The love of God is what we need to show our family.

We must pray that our parents find His encouragement and understanding that Christ died for them too. He did not simply die so that we could be saved, but so that we could pray for our parents' salvation also.

We must test each spirit that speaks to us so that we do not go astray from His Truth. His Spirit lives inside of us and we need to pray for our parents to receive this very same gift from God. Our lives came from them.

They might be on our poop list, but they are still our parents. Pray for them, always!

We must share the overflow of thankfulness that we have received through His promises, to us and our parents. We must not allow our enemies to take us captive and allow us to ignore the needs of our parents. Christ is the head of our needs and the needs of our parents.

God is love. God is peace. God gives us all hope. His peace surpasses all understanding because it is something that surfaces even when we are down. His peace brings us hope for a new day. We must share this with our parents today, and every single day.

Peace

If we are unable to find peace with our parents, life feels rough. When they are negative and/or mean to us and/or our children, we tend to avoid them. However, this is when the Lord desires us to work with them as we can and attempt to help them find His love for them. Christ is our 'peace,' and we need to share this with our parents to encourage them to find His peace in their lives.

> 1 If then you were raised with Christ, seek those things which are above, where Christ is, sitting at the right hand of God. 2 Set your mind on things above, not on things on the earth. 3 For you died, and your life is hidden with Christ in God. 4 When Christ who is our life appears, then you also will appear with Him in glory.
>
> 5 Therefore put to death your members which are on the earth: fornication, uncleanness, passion, evil desire, and covetousness, which is idolatry. 6 Because of these things the wrath of God is coming upon the sons of disobedience, 7 in which you yourselves once walked when you lived in them.
>
> 8 But now you yourselves are to put off all these: anger, wrath, malice, blasphemy, filthy language out of your mouth. 9 Do not lie to one another, since you have put off the old man with his deeds, 10 and have put on the new man who is renewed in knowledge according to the image of Him who created him, 11 where there is neither Greek

nor Jew, circumcised nor uncircumcised, barbarian, Scythian, slave nor free, but Christ is all and in all.

12 Therefore, as the elect of God, holy and beloved, put on tender mercies, kindness, humility, meekness, longsuffering; 13 bearing with one another, and forgiving one another, if anyone has a complaint against another; even as Christ forgave you, so you also must do. 14 But above all these things put on love, which is the bond of perfection. 15 And let the peace of God rule in your hearts, to which also you were called in one body; and be thankful. 16 Let the word of Christ dwell in you richly in all wisdom, teaching and admonishing one another in psalms and hymns and spiritual songs, singing with grace in your hearts to the Lord. 17 And whatever you do in word or deed, do all in the name of the Lord Jesus, giving thanks to God the Father through Him.
   Colossians 3:1–17, NKJV

Jesus Christ is sitting next to God our Father and was raised to this position after His sacrifice on the Cross. Our parents might not know this or may not understand what this means. We must encourage them by helping them to grasp this promise and truth sent by God. Christ died for our sins and now we are saved and can approach God the Father without shame from our sins. This goes for our parents also.

Even though it is difficult to understand what it means to be 'saved,' we must read the Bible, pray, and meditate about this so that we can explain it to our parents. Since we will appear with Christ in His glory, encouraging our parents to realize this through reading the Bible, praying, and meditating is another request from God.

There are many ways to sin here on earth, but eventually, we will be in His presence, where there is no more sin. We must not glorify fornication, ungodly passions, evil desires, being unclean, coveting things or people, or idolizing anything or anyone, other than God. We are to look to God for guidance as to how to avoid such things while we are still here, on earth. Prayers for this same peacefulness in our parents are honorable and will encourage them to look to God for an answer also.

When we were still unbelievers, we struggled with the above list of sins. There are other sins that we struggled with and all these sins caused us to not know His peace. Our parents might be struggling with this right now…PRAY! Pray that they find His peace. Pray that they will know Him and His love and share it with others as encouragers too.

I know that some of us have truly struggled with anger issues. Some would say that their personality includes strong anger, but this does not have to remain true. God will guide us and our parents through the issues of our anger so that they are no longer a part of us. Sometimes this anger would cause us to use filthy language. Does anyone relate to this? I do!

His wrath is what we deserve. However, through the sacrifice of Christ, we no longer deserve His wrath as soon as we repent of these issues. Blasphemy might have been a part of our lives when we were lost, but His love and peace repaired the relationship with Him, and we must share this with our parents.

Lying to each other might have been part of 'family life' while growing up. However, we must encourage our families to no longer lie to each other. The 'old self' was a liar, but the 'new self' has no lies because God is the truth. It does not matter what race, ethnicity, or nationality we are, God is our Father, which makes us all the same in His eyes. We were all created in His image, including our parents.

He has called us to be holy because He is Holy. We are His beloved…let that truly sink in, we are His beloved. No matter what we have done in our lives, we are His beloved. There is nothing more peaceful than those words in our ears. We must share them with our parents now. His mercy is anew every single day.

We must love our parents in the name of the Lord. Forgiving them of all their shortcomings and allowing them to know that God is our Father as well as theirs. We must give thanks to God for the parents that He gave us so that they will see His love in our lives. Humbly introducing them to Him, through our kind and peaceful actions.

We must be humble, yet proud (to be His beloved), meek, yet strong (with His strength), kind, patient, forgive each other, and bear with each other. What this means is that even though our parents might have fallen short, they deserve to hear the Good News so they can choose the Lord also. Let's encourage our parents today.

God has given each of us His strength to accomplish anything He asks us to do. His strength is what we rely upon to encourage people, including our parents. Let's encourage our parents to rely upon God's strength and watch what He does in their lives, today and every day!

Strength

As we have read throughout this book, God's strength is all that we need. He gives us His strength to do the things He asks of us. Our parents might not know Him. Other parents might know Him. However, all of us are called to be encouraging to each other and not be bitter. If our parents do not know the Lord, our lives might have been troubled. However, we are called to submit to our elders and parents throughout the Bible.

> 5 In the same way, you who are younger, submit yourselves to your elders. All of you, clothe yourselves with humility toward one another, because,
>
> "God opposes the proud
>   but shows favor to the humble."
>
> 6 Humble yourselves, therefore, under God's mighty hand, that he may lift you up in due time. 7 Cast all your anxiety on him because he cares for you.
> 8 Be alert and of sober mind. Your enemy the devil prowls around like a roaring lion looking for someone to devour. 9 Resist him, standing firm in the faith, because you know that the family of believers throughout the world is undergoing the same kind of sufferings.
> 10 And the God of all grace, who called you to his eternal glory in Christ, after you have suffered a little while, will himself restore you and make you strong, firm and steadfast. 11 To him be the power for ever and ever. Amen.
> **1 Peter 5:5–11, NIV**

Humility toward each other does not give the other person permission to take advantage of your humility. However, there might be times when this does occur. It is all right to humbly remove yourself from this type of atmosphere, even when it comes from your parents. Remember that pride comes before the fall (see Proverbs 16:18) and humility will allow our parents to realize why we are removing ourselves from them for that moment.

When our parents make us anxious, we are to call upon God to guide us through the anxiety and use His strength to remove ourselves or to calmly discuss the reason behind our anxiety. He will guide us so that our parents might hear what we need to say to them; however, only if we humbly use His strength to do it.

His strength reminds us that when we rely upon it, He will show us the way out of the temptation (see 1 Corinthians 10:13) to continue arguing or become angry with our parents. We must remain alert because the enemy would love to use this anger so that we are not able to speak to our parents about God and His strength for them. He prowls around like a roaring lion ready to devour our family.

When we stand firm in our faith, our parents will notice that we use His strength to share Him with them. Other believers' families are suffering from the same things that we are, and we are to encourage each other to find His strength. The enemy desires that our families break apart, but the Lord's strength helps our family to stay strong. God's grace will give us the endurance to encourage each other and to share His Good News with our parents.

Endurance

How many times in life have we had to 'endure' something or someone? It seems like we are moving backward when we are 'enduring.' Patience has never been a virtue that I grasped too well. I try to remain patient and then I tend to lose sight of the patience.

It is when I forget to pray and meditate that this occurs. It appears that my enemies can make me upset at this time and it is all my fault. My parents tend to frustrate me, and I find that I am not as able to endure.

1 LORD, how many are my foes!
　How many rise up against me!
2 Many are saying of me,
　"God will not deliver him."

3 But you, LORD, are a shield around me,
　my glory, the One who lifts my head high.
4 I call out to the LORD,
　and he answers me from his holy mountain.

5 I lie down and sleep;
    I wake again, because the LORD sustains me.
6 I will not fear though tens of thousands
    assail me on every side.

7 Arise, LORD!
    Deliver me, my God!
Strike all my enemies on the jaw;
    break the teeth of the wicked.

8 From the LORD comes deliverance.
    May your blessing be on your people.
Psalm 3, NIV

God appears to be far away when I allow myself to get upset. However, it is me who is far away. Do you ever feel this way? It can be frightening.

The glory of God shines through when we remember to call upon Him in our times of trouble. Sharing this encouraging revelation with our parents can help them to better understand how much they can rely upon God.

He will shield us from our foes (enemies). When we call upon Him in our times of trouble, have you ever noticed that He is always there? This is encouraging news. His glory must be shared with our parents so they can find His encouragement. He will show us all how to hold our heads high because He is our Lord and Savior.

We must remember to be grateful for each day that He wakes us up. Our parents might have fewer days to be awakened by His love, so share this love with them now. Even when the times are tough and we feel as though there is no hope, the Lord will guide us into the next stage of our lives. People might be falling all around us, especially political leaders, but the Lord lifts our heads to the skies so that we can rely upon Him. Sharing this with our parents will encourage them.

The passage reads that the psalmist desires for his enemy's teeth to be broken. We desire that our enemies will learn to know who God is to them. His people, our parents and us, will be delivered from the evil things and people around us as soon as we cry out to Him.

Let's cry out to Him right now!

Christine C. Sponsler

Encouragement

I know, I know…this whole book is about encouragement. However, this section is where we learn how important it can be to encourage our parents. I am guilty of not being as encouraging as I should be toward my parents. However, I am still a work in progress. I do believe that my earthly father made it to heaven. At least I am hopeful about it.

My father passed away in 2014 at the age of 67. He had Chronic Obstructive Pulmonary Disease (COPD), cirrhosis of the liver, and simply did not live healthily. My husband and I had the gift of sharing Jesus with him before he passed. God used us to encourage him, and he accepted Christ into his heart several years before he passed.

I am working up to directly ask my mother and stepdad if they still believe. It appears that they do, but I am curious and would like to be sure that I will see them in heaven too. My grandparents were believers and I believe that my great-grandmother (my Mimi) was also. My younger sister and her husband are, and I hope that my youngest sister still believes. (I don't know where she lives anymore.) I pray that my family knows Him.

Do any of us have family members who frustrate us or upset us? I do, but I believe that God is still working on all our hearts. I am learning not to be so quick to become angry when I am frustrated, and it appears to be working. I do not throw my opinions around as I used to do, so I believe that we can get along much better these days.

> 19 Understand this, my dear brothers and sisters: You must all be quick to listen, slow to speak, and slow to get angry. 20 Human anger does not produce the righteousness God desires. 21 So get rid of all the filth and evil in your lives, and humbly accept the word God has planted in your hearts, for it has the power to save your souls.
>
> 22 But don't just listen to God's word. You must do what it says. Otherwise, you are only fooling yourselves. 23 For if you listen to the word and don't obey, it is like glancing at your face in a mirror. 24 You see yourself, walk away, and forget what you look like. 25 But if you look carefully into the perfect law that sets you free, and if you

do what it says and don't forget what you heard, then God will bless you for doing it.

26 If you claim to be religious but don't control your tongue, you are fooling yourself, and your religion is worthless. 27 Pure and genuine religion in the sight of God the Father means caring for orphans and widows in their distress and refusing to let the world corrupt you.
James 1:19–27, NLT

Enjoying the company of our parents does not have to be difficult. When we work together to get together, it usually becomes a fun visit. I enjoy listening to some of the things which occur with my parents (mom and stepdad) and especially their adventure in their trailer. They have lived in their trailer for some time now and love the freedom and open spaces.

I now know that when I am angry, it usually means that I need God to work on something inside of me. He is faithful when I ask for His guidance during these times, and it occurs less often now. I can get rid of my angry thoughts much sooner than I used to. I desire to read the Word of God instead of getting upset anymore. I pray for my readers to find the desire to read His Word instead of getting upset too.

When we read the Bible, we must be sure to hear what God is saying to us. We must abide by His word and share His love with others, including our parents. The righteousness of the Lord will only shine through His word and His encouragement which means that when we speak with our parents, He must be present also. We are fooling ourselves if we believe that we are the reason our parents find salvation. However, when we are faithful to His Word, He is present in the conversations.

How many of us travel far to see our parents? Some of us travel several states to see them again. This delights the Lord as we are continuing our relationship with our parents. His love will shine through the conversations and the entire visit. Some of us do not have to travel far to visit our parents, but still do not see them often. This could be simply because of busy schedules. However, it is good to visit when possible.

When we visit our parents, we might have even forgotten what they look like. Have you ever not seen them for several months and then when you see them again, they look so different? It could be that they have lost weight, had a drastic haircut, or they simply look more peaceful.

The Lord can do this to His followers. He can make them appear differently and we all know that it is most likely from the joy of the Lord. It is encouraging to see peaceful changes in our parents.

Hallelujah!

We are not necessarily 'religious' as the world defines religion. We are believers and this means that we know that Christ died to save us from our sins. We must remember that religion and spirituality can mean several different things. We must remind our parents of this too.

Some spiritual people believe that fortune-telling is all right; it is not. Some religious people believe that more than one wife is all right, it is not. Therefore, we call ourselves Christians and believers in Christ. Our 'religion' comes from the Holy Bible of God.

We must care for people who others might deem 'nothings.' Sharing His love with our parents is only the beginning. Sharing His love with others means that we are to go and tell it on the mountains and praise His name to many other people. We are to share His love with our friends, our parents and our siblings.

Chapter 14: Encouragement Toward Our Siblings

46 While Jesus was still talking to the crowd, his mother and brothers stood outside, wanting to speak to him. 47 Someone told him, "Your mother and brothers are standing outside, wanting to speak to you."

48 He replied to him, "Who is my mother, and who are my brothers?" 49 Pointing to his disciples, he said, "Here are my mother and my brothers. 50 For whoever does the will of my Father in heaven is my brother and sister and mother."

Matthew 12:46–50, NIV

It is both a blessing and a challenge to have siblings. There are times when we see eye to eye and other times that we do not even see each other at all. Even Jesus' siblings did not always understand or support Him. Jesus embraces us all as siblings to cherish.

His love for us is something that we are to encourage our siblings with. Share His love with them so that they can come to know him as Lord and Savior. We must also remember that we are all brothers and sisters in Christ. We are all related by His blood.

*****

Hallelujah! And Amen!

Christine C. Sponsler

God has either blessed us with or without siblings. Maybe we used to have a sibling and they are with the Lord now. Maybe, He blessed us as an only child for a reason unknown to us.

Either way, we have read some things about siblings throughout the Bible. Not everyone who has been blessed with siblings is happy with them and not every only child is happy to be without siblings. However, we must remember that either way we are now in the Lord's family and have many siblings, in Christ.

> 1 How wonderful and pleasant it is
>   when brothers live together in harmony!
> 2 For harmony is as precious as the anointing oil
>   that was poured over Aaron's head,
>   that ran down his beard
>   and onto the border of his robe.
> 3 Harmony is as refreshing as the dew from Mount Hermon
>   that falls on the mountains of Zion.
> And there the LORD has pronounced his blessing,
>   even life everlasting.
> **Psalm 133, NLT**

It is wonderful to find peace and comfort inside of our family units. Our siblings are both our best friends and our worst nightmares from time to time. When we have siblings, we are fortunate to share things with them, but do not always want to know what is happening in their lives. When we become adults and still have our siblings, it is sometimes a miracle.

How many of us have brothers and sisters? I have two sisters and had one brother. He overdosed in 2005, at age 26. It was hard to see my brother leave this world, but I prayed that he cried out to God to be saved before his death. He was alive in the hospital for three days, and I just know in my heart that he cried out to God.

Sometimes we live in harmony with our siblings and sometimes there are battles that only siblings understand. My sisters are far and near, both metaphorically and geographically. One sister lives around 30 miles from me and the other lives around 1,800 miles away. Both are dearly loved by me, but are also far away, both metaphorically and geographically. I am reminded of the story of Moses and Aaron.

198

Moses was not good at communicating and Aaron was. Both served God in their own ways. I believe this is something my sisters still do, in their own ways, they are serving our Lord. Aaron came to Moses' rescue and both served the Lord through this act. We may not be living in Zion, but we are currently living in the Lord's family alongside our siblings, I hope. The Lord's blessings are upon us and our siblings need to be encouraged to remain, or to come to, His family.

Getting Along with Our Siblings

We do not always get along. Brothers and sisters are known for their 'sibling rivalries.' When we think way back into biblical days, we remember Cain and Abel. Hopefully, none of us have known this drastic of sibling rivalry, but I guess it still occurs.

Siblings are amazing. However, some of us with siblings might wish to have been an only child at times. This is also natural. The blessing of having siblings is also godly.

> 2 Dear brothers and sisters, when troubles of any kind come your way, consider it an opportunity for great joy. 3 For you know that when your faith is tested, your endurance has a chance to grow. 4 So let it grow, for when your endurance is fully developed, you will be perfect and complete, needing nothing.
>
> 5 If you need wisdom, ask our generous God, and he will give it to you. He will not rebuke you for asking. 6 But when you ask him, be sure that your faith is in God alone. Do not waver, for a person with divided loyalty is as unsettled as a wave of the sea that is blown and tossed by the wind. 7 Such people should not expect to receive anything from the Lord. 8 Their loyalty is divided between God and the world, and they are unstable in everything they do.
>
> 9 Believers who are poor have something to boast about, for God has honored them. 10 And those who are rich should boast that God has humbled them. They will fade away like a little flower in the field. 11 The hot sun rises and the grass withers; the little flower droops and falls,

and its beauty fades away. In the same way, the rich will fade away with all of their achievements.

12 God blesses those who patiently endure testing and temptation. Afterward they will receive the crown of life that God has promised to those who love him. 13 And remember, when you are being tempted, do not say, "God is tempting me." God is never tempted to do wrong, and he never tempts anyone else. 14 Temptation comes from our own desires, which entice us and drag us away. 15 These desires give birth to sinful actions. And when sin is allowed to grow, it gives birth to death.

16 So don't be misled, my dear brothers and sisters. 17 Whatever is good and perfect is a gift coming down to us from God our Father, who created all the lights in the heavens. He never changes or casts a shifting shadow. 18 He chose to give birth to us by giving us his true word. And we, out of all creation, became his prized possession.

James 1:2–18, NLT

We are important to the Lord and our siblings are also important. God shares His love with us, and we are to share this same love with our siblings. We must help them to find great joy in the trials and tribulations of this world. Our joy is not to be hidden but shared. Endurance is built from the trials and tribulations that we face, sometimes daily, so that we can stand firm upon His strength to encourage each other.

How many of us have ever felt pure joy, even during the most horrendous storms of life? This is His joy. We are to share it with our siblings. God gives generously to those who ask Him. We must ask for His guidance and strength to encourage our siblings. His wisdom will also help us to know what to say and when to say it to each of our siblings. God is good!

Our faith is in God alone. He is the only one who can guide us, strengthen us, and encourage us so that we can encourage even our most lost siblings. God will never rebuke or snub us for asking for His help. He encourages this often. We are to expect His answer to our prayers, especially concerning our siblings' welfare and salvation.

God honors our sacrifices. He loves for us to share His glory through whatever we have sacrificed. His glory is our main concern. When our siblings are struggling and we can help them through His strength, He is glorified. We cannot boast about anything that we have done. For whatever we have done, it has been through His strength and guidance and the Lord is glorified.

When we set things straight with our siblings, He is glorified. When we admit that we are weak, He is glorified. When our siblings witness our glorification of God, they tend to want what we have and that is the love of God. Honoring the Lord with loving our siblings will glorify Him. He is to be glorified in all that we do and say.

None of us is going to live forever, here on earth. However, we are all going to live forever in His presence. We must share this and rejoice with our siblings. Everything on earth will fade away. Nothing headed for heaven fades away, especially God's love for us all. Our siblings must be encouraged to find and share His love.

Go look out your window right now. See the trees and flowers? They are beautiful and show us God's beauty. Those things will fade. Now Skype, Zoom, or Facetime your sibling(s). This person (or people) will not fade if they know God.

Achieving business savvy, acknowledgments, and fame will fade away. The Lord will never fade away and we are being prepared to share eternity with Him. Let's go share this encouragement with our siblings today.

Again, there will be testing and temptations to sin every single day until we leave this earth and are in His presence. Let's encourage our siblings today. Let's share our support with our siblings today.

Our siblings need to know what it means to wear the crown of life. It means that they are going to meet us in heaven and wear the crown of victory for all eternity.

God is not our tempter nor is He our siblings' tempter. He desires that when we are tempted, we call out to Him and retreat from our temptations. God desires that we not only get along with our siblings but that we participate in what He is going to do in their lives. We must be ready, willing, and able to share His love and promises with our siblings.

When we see that our sibling, or any believer for that matter, is being misled, we must call out to God and pray for their rapid return to Him. His love is a perfect gift that we use to encourage our families. He will never change, nor will He abandon us. We will always be able to cry out to Him. Whether we are crying out for our siblings, our parents, our children, our friends, or for ourselves, He is faithful and hears our cries.

Christine C. Sponsler

We and our families are His prized possession. Read that over and over and over again. He loves us so much that we are to remember that we are His prized possessions. He has given us many examples of how much He loves us and our families.

Hallelujah!

Biblical Examples of His Love

God does not tempt us. He gives us ways to work through our temptations (see 1 Corinthians 10:13). We all make choices daily to either give in to temptation or avoid the sin of giving in to it. Our ancestors have all been able to choose God or not. Our siblings must realize the dire need to choose to follow Christ.

Baptism is not simply dunking ourselves in water to 'feel better.' Baptism is a renewing of our souls. We were born sinners. Christ died for the sins committed by us and our siblings. His sacrifice has made it possible to approach God. When we approach God, He hears us now.

Communion is also not a 'symbol' of our love. It is a choice we make to remember what Christ did for us and our families. The ancestors of the Bible were met with death and wandering because they chose to wander away from God. We have the same choices to make as the Israelites did. Our families can either walk toward or away from God. However, when there is a praying family member, most family members get saved too.

> 1 For I do not want you to be ignorant of the fact, brothers and sisters, that our ancestors were all under the cloud and that they all passed through the sea. 2 They were all baptized into Moses in the cloud and in the sea. 3 They all ate the same spiritual food 4 and drank the same spiritual drink; for they drank from the spiritual rock that accompanied them, and that rock was Christ. 5 Nevertheless, God was not pleased with most of them; their bodies were scattered in the wilderness.
>
> 6 Now these things occurred as examples to keep us from setting our hearts on evil things as they did. 7 Do not be idolaters, as some of them were; as it is written: "The people sat down to eat and drink and got up to indulge in revelry." 8 We should not commit sexual immorality, as

some of them did—and in one day twenty-three thousand of them died. 9 We should not test Christ, as some of them did—and were killed by snakes. 10 And do not grumble, as some of them did—and were killed by the destroying angel.

11 These things happened to them as examples and were written down as warnings for us, on whom the culmination of the ages has come. 12 So, if you think you are standing firm, be careful that you don't fall! 13 No temptation has overtaken you except what is common to mankind. And God is faithful; he will not let you be tempted beyond what you can bear. But when you are tempted, he will also provide a way out so that you can endure it.

1 Corinthians 10:1–13, NIV

The examples that we receive from His Word are to help us to make the right choices. Our siblings can watch us make these choices and then either do the same or walk away. However, we are given the power of prayer to encourage us never to stop praying for the lost siblings or other family members.

We must not act as idolaters of anything other than God. His wrath is generational and can cause families to part from each other. However, as soon as they turn back to Him, He can forgive them and hear their prayers again.

Some of us idolize food. Some of us idolize other people. Some of us idolize money. Some of us idolize sex. All these things are what get in between us and God. His desire is for us to walk toward Him and have our families follow in our footsteps; really, they are His footsteps.

We are not to test the Lord. What this means is that when we know that we are 'saved,' it is not right to test the Lord by trying to jump off a building without harm. We will be harmed when we jump off a building. This does not mean that the Lord does not love us. He certainly does. It means that we are testing His love for us.

Biblical ancestors made certain choices which were recorded in the Bible. These are testimonies for us to learn from. His love for us shines through every testimony. His desire to be approached by us shines through also. His Word reminds us what to do and what not to do to please Him.

We must be aware of the temptations we face. We must learn our limits so that we do not walk into a temptation which is difficult to get out of. He is with us, but we must choose to call to Him during a tempting situation to find His strength. Our siblings will see this and realize that only God can help them too.

Our temptations are usually from us allowing certain things to get into our hearts. We know they are bad, but make excuses to allow these temptations in. When we realize that we have allowed temptation in, we must call on Him for His way out of the situation. Our siblings might appear to be allowing temptations in, pray for them as soon as possible…in other words, now. God provides for us all and His faithfulness shines through our reliance upon His promises. His truths are always just.

I enjoy reading about people of the Bible finding and adhering to God, especially the least likely people. Nicodemus was one of these people. He was a Pharisee and according to the Bible, they adhered to the old law too much. Plus, they would expect other people to be a certain way, and then hypocritically do things to make it difficult for these people to be that way…

> Then Jesus said to the crowds and to his disciples: 2 "The teachers of the law and the Pharisees sit in Moses' seat. 3 So you must be careful to do everything they tell you. But do not do what they do, for they do not practice what they preach. 4 They tie up heavy, cumbersome loads and put them on other people's shoulders, but they themselves are not willing to lift a finger to move them.
>
> 5 "Everything they do is done for people to see: They make their phylacteries wide and the tassels on their garments long; 6 they love the place of honor at banquets and the most important seats in the synagogues; 7 they love to be greeted with respect in the marketplaces and to be called 'Rabbi' by others.
>
> 8 "But you are not to be called 'Rabbi,' for you have one Teacher, and you are all brothers. 9 And do not call anyone on earth 'father,' for you have one Father, and he is in heaven. 10 Nor are you to be called instructors, for you have one Instructor, the Messiah. 11 The greatest among you will be your servant. 12 For those who exalt

themselves will be humbled, and those who humble themselves will be exalted.

13 "Woe to you, teachers of the law and Pharisees, you hypocrites! You shut the door of the kingdom of heaven in people's faces. You yourselves do not enter, nor will you let those enter who are trying to. 14

15 "Woe to you, teachers of the law and Pharisees, you hypocrites! You travel over land and sea to win a single convert, and when you have succeeded, you make them twice as much a child of hell as you are.

16 "Woe to you, blind guides! You say, 'If anyone swears by the temple, it means nothing; but anyone who swears by the gold of the temple is bound by that oath.' 17 You blind fools! Which is greater: the gold, or the temple that makes the gold sacred? 18 You also say, 'If anyone swears by the altar, it means nothing; but anyone who swears by the gift on the altar is bound by that oath.' 19 You blind men! Which is greater: the gift, or the altar that makes the gift sacred? 20 Therefore, anyone who swears by the altar swears by it and by everything on it. 21 And anyone who swears by the temple swears by it and by the one who dwells in it. 22 And anyone who swears by heaven swears by God's throne and by the one who sits on it.

23 "Woe to you, teachers of the law and Pharisees, you hypocrites! You give a tenth of your spices—mint, dill and cumin. But you have neglected the more important matters of the law—justice, mercy and faithfulness. You should have practiced the latter, without neglecting the former. 24 You blind guides! You strain out a gnat but swallow a camel.

25 "Woe to you, teachers of the law and Pharisees, you hypocrites! You clean the outside of the cup and dish, but inside they are full of greed and self-indulgence. 26 Blind Pharisee! First clean the inside of the cup and dish, and then the outside also will be clean.

27 "Woe to you, teachers of the law and Pharisees, you hypocrites! You are like whitewashed tombs, which look beautiful on the outside but on the inside are full of the

bones of the dead and everything unclean. 28 In the same way, on the outside you appear to people as righteous but on the inside you are full of hypocrisy and wickedness.

29 "Woe to you, teachers of the law and Pharisees, you hypocrites! You build tombs for the prophets and decorate the graves of the righteous. 30 And you say, 'If we had lived in the days of our ancestors, we would not have taken part with them in shedding the blood of the prophets.' 31 So you testify against yourselves that you are the descendants of those who murdered the prophets. 32 Go ahead, then, and complete what your ancestors started!

33 "You snakes! You brood of vipers! How will you escape being condemned to hell? 34 Therefore I am sending you prophets and sages and teachers. Some of them you will kill and crucify; others you will flog in your synagogues and pursue from town to town. 35 And so upon you will come all the righteous blood that has been shed on earth, from the blood of righteous Abel to the blood of Zechariah son of Berekiah, whom you murdered between the temple and the altar. 36 Truly I tell you, all this will come on this generation.

37 "Jerusalem, Jerusalem, you who kill the prophets and stone those sent to you, how often I have longed to gather your children together, as a hen gathers her chicks under her wings, and you were not willing. 38 Look, your house is left to you desolate. 39 For I tell you, you will not see me again until you say, 'Blessed is he who comes in the name of the Lord.'"
Matthew 23, NIV

Nicodemus understood the law. He was trying to better understand Christ through his questions. Therefore, when Jesus said that one must be born again, Nicodemus took it literally and then asked, how?

1 There was a man named Nicodemus, a Jewish religious leader who was a Pharisee. 2 After dark one evening, he came to speak with Jesus. "Rabbi," he said, "we

all know that God has sent you to teach us. Your miraculous signs are evidence that God is with you."

3 Jesus replied, "I tell you the truth, unless you are born again, you cannot see the Kingdom of God."

4 "What do you mean?" exclaimed Nicodemus. "How can an old man go back into his mother's womb and be born again?"

5 Jesus replied, "I assure you, no one can enter the Kingdom of God without being born of water and the Spirit. 6 Humans can reproduce only human life, but the Holy Spirit gives birth to spiritual life. 7 So don't be surprised when I say, 'You must be born again.' 8 The wind blows wherever it wants. Just as you can hear the wind but can't tell where it comes from or where it is going, so you can't explain how people are born of the Spirit."

9 "How are these things possible?" Nicodemus asked.

10 Jesus replied, "You are a respected Jewish teacher, and yet you don't understand these things? 11 I assure you, we tell you what we know and have seen, and yet you won't believe our testimony. 12 But if you don't believe me when I tell you about earthly things, how can you possibly believe if I tell you about heavenly things? 13 No one has ever gone to heaven and returned. But the Son of Man has come down from heaven. 14 And as Moses lifted up the bronze snake on a pole in the wilderness, so the Son of Man must be lifted up, 15 so that everyone who believes in him will have eternal life.

16 "For this is how God loved the world: He gave his one and only Son, so that everyone who believes in him will not perish but have eternal life. 17 God sent his Son into the world not to judge the world, but to save the world through him.

18 "There is no judgment against anyone who believes in him. But anyone who does not believe in him has already been judged for not believing in God's one and only Son. 19 And the judgment is based on this fact: God's light came into the world, but people loved the darkness more than the light, for their actions were evil. 20 All who do evil

hate the light and refuse to go near it for fear their sins will be exposed. 21 But those who do what is right come to the light so others can see that they are doing what God wants."

John 3:1–21, NLT

Literal birth is not what Jesus was talking about when He said we all need to be born again. Through our earthly parents, we were born of water. Through our heavenly Father and the guidance of the Holy Spirit, we are to be reborn of the Spirit. Nicodemus would later develop the Spiritual birth that Jesus was talking about if he chose to follow Christ. The Kingdom of God is only found through our Spiritual birth.

Jesus is the Way, the Truth, and the Life. Therefore, being born again of His Spirit is the most important decision anyone could make. One of the ways that God uses us is to show our siblings these truths. Challenges of our spirit might arise such as questioning how we are to be born again. However, we do not question whether it is true because God is Truth, and He promises a new birth for all believers.

Nicodemus is probably not the only one to ever question how we are to be born again. One of us might have thought the same thing. Do not worry. God does not judge when we question things pertaining to Him.

We are to believe through faith which is not always by sight. Therefore, Nicodemus was not wrong to question how this would be possible. Our siblings might have similar questions and we are to encourage them to find His answers in the Bible.

Even as believers we might have questions. Our siblings might also. We are not to worry when we have questions because God will work in our hearts to guide us to His answers.

The Bible is filled with our Father's truths. Moses parted the sea… or did he? God used him to glorify Himself by allowing the Israelites to cross the sea and the Egyptians were never their problem again.

As Pharaoh approached, the Israelites looked up, and there were the Egyptians, marching after them. They were terrified and cried out to the LORD. 11 They said to Moses, "Was it because there were no graves in Egypt that you brought us to the desert to die? What have you done to us by bringing us out of Egypt? 12 Didn't we say to you in

Egypt, 'Leave us alone; let us serve the Egyptians'? It would have been better for us to serve the Egyptians than to die in the desert!'"

13 Moses answered the people, "Do not be afraid. Stand firm and you will see the deliverance the LORD will bring you today. The Egyptians you see today you will never see again. 14 The LORD will fight for you; you need only to be still."

15 Then the LORD said to Moses, "Why are you crying out to me? Tell the Israelites to move on. 16 Raise your staff and stretch out your hand over the sea to divide the water so that the Israelites can go through the sea on dry ground. 17 I will harden the hearts of the Egyptians so that they will go in after them. And I will gain glory through Pharaoh and all his army, through his chariots and his horsemen. 18 The Egyptians will know that I am the LORD when I gain glory through Pharaoh, his chariots and his horsemen."

19 Then the angel of God, who had been traveling in front of Israel's army, withdrew and went behind them. The pillar of cloud also moved from in front and stood behind them, 20 coming between the armies of Egypt and Israel. Throughout the night the cloud brought darkness to the one side and light to the other side; so neither went near the other all night long.

21 Then Moses stretched out his hand over the sea, and all that night the LORD drove the sea back with a strong east wind and turned it into dry land. The waters were divided, 22 and the Israelites went through the sea on dry ground, with a wall of water on their right and on their left.

23 The Egyptians pursued them, and all Pharaoh's horses and chariots and horsemen followed them into the sea. 24 During the last watch of the night the LORD looked down from the pillar of fire and cloud at the Egyptian army and threw it into confusion. 25 He jammed the wheels of their chariots so that they had difficulty driving. And the

Egyptians said, "Let's get away from the Israelites! The LORD is fighting for them against Egypt."

26 Then the LORD said to Moses, "Stretch out your hand over the sea so that the waters may flow back over the Egyptians and their chariots and horsemen." 27 Moses stretched out his hand over the sea, and at daybreak the sea went back to its place. The Egyptians were fleeing toward it, and the LORD swept them into the sea. 28 The water flowed back and covered the chariots and horsemen—the entire army of Pharaoh that had followed the Israelites into the sea. Not one of them survived.

29 But the Israelites went through the sea on dry ground, with a wall of water on their right and on their left. 30 That day the LORD saved Israel from the hands of the Egyptians, and Israel saw the Egyptians lying dead on the shore. 31 And when the Israelites saw the mighty hand of the LORD displayed against the Egyptians, the people feared the LORD and put their trust in him and in Moses his servant.

Exodus 14:10–31, NIV

Our siblings might need us to sit with them teach them more about what the Bible says about believing and being born again. we might also need to share with them the glory that God received from the Israelites fleeing from the Egyptians. When we share these stories of the Bible with our siblings, we learn more from this too.

Now we come to the most ever quoted scripture in the Bible: John 3:16. God loved His creation so much that He sent Jesus as the sacrifice for our sins so that we can approach God without shame. But here is what we are to take away from this verse…God loves us enough to suffer for our salvation.

Wow!

I don't know about anyone else, but I feel special and loved. John goes on to inform us that Jesus was not sent to judge us, but to save us. He is the Judge, but that is not why He came to earth…He knew we needed to be saved and then saved us.

When we genuinely believe in Him, we will not be judged harshly. Thankfully, we never have to live in the proverbial darkness anymore. We are children of the Light. We are to share this light with our siblings so that they can come to His Light also.

God's glory reigns and our siblings need to hear and to see this in action. Our encouraging words to our siblings will shine His Light into any darkness they are struggling with and His love will conquer all.

Let's get out there and be the encouraging words that our siblings need today!

Christine C. Sponsler

Chapter 15: Encouragement Toward Our Child/ren

1 These are the commands, decrees and laws the LORD your God directed me to teach you to observe in the land that you are crossing the Jordan to possess, 2 so that you, your children and their children after them may fear the LORD your God as long as you live by keeping all his decrees and commands that I give you, and so that you may enjoy long life. 3 Hear, Israel, and be careful to obey so that it may go well with you and that you may increase greatly in a land flowing with milk and honey, just as the LORD, the God of your ancestors, promised you.

4 Hear, O Israel: The LORD our God, the LORD is one. 5 Love the LORD your God with all your heart and with all your soul and with all your strength. 6 These commandments that I give you today are to be on your hearts. 7 Impress them on your children. Talk about them when you sit at home and when you walk along the road, when you lie down and when you get up. 8 Tie them as symbols on your hands and bind them on your foreheads. 9 Write them on the doorframes of your houses and on your gates.
Deuteronomy 6:1–9, NIV

The Lord has either given us our own children, or we know people with children. Either way, we are to teach the children about God and allow the Holy Spirit to reside in their hearts. Did any of us attend Sunday school? I did. It was amazing. I was raised Quaker by my grandparents, and they instilled morals in me. I did stray for almost 25 years. However, my grandmother's prayers helped to save my life.

Christine C. Sponsler

I know that my parents tried to love me. All parents seem to try. However, our Father is the ultimate parent, and we must instill this into our children early on in their lives. We must help them to understand that God is with them always. Through the trouble and the pain, God is with them. Our children are dear to us…they are even dearer to God!

*****

Encourage your little (and big) kiddos today and always!

Sibling Rivalry

I do not know about any of you reading this, but my sons fought. They loved each other, but they fought often. It would be quiet one moment and the next minute, tables were turning and chairs falling over and yelling. However, they knew how to defend each other too. God's love is constant. Our love has hiccups in it. Thankfully, the love of brothers and sisters can be the best and worst thing in the world.

> 3 Children are a heritage from the LORD,
>   offspring a reward from him.
> 4 Like arrows in the hands of a warrior
>   are children born in one's youth.
> 5 Blessed is the man
>   whose quiver is full of them.
> They will not be put to shame
>   when they contend with their opponents in court.
> **Psalm 127:3–5, NIV**

> The LORD is like a father to his children,
>   tender and compassionate to those who fear him.
> **Psalm 103:13, NLT**

Children are a blessing. I find it amusing that parents ignore and/or refute their own parents' advice and then live to regret it when their children become as difficult to raise as they were. We must remember who we were, growing up, before we wish for our child/ren to be just like us.

It might not be the most sensible wish, because when they do become more like us, is it all good? Not usually. Sometimes it is. But usually, the characteristics our children inherit are the less desirable ones and this can be stressful…just like it was for our own parents.

Encouraging our children can be the most precious gift that we share with them. However, have any of us ever felt as though, they simply do not deserve our encouraging words right now? The easiest way to get back into the encouraging mode is to remember that we do not deserve God's encouraging words, but He gives them to us anyway. Therefore, it is up to us to make our children feel encouraged as much as possible.

Even though scripture reads that children are to obey their parents…

> 1 Children, obey your parents in the Lord, for this is right. 2 "Honor your father and mother"—which is the first commandment with a promise—3 "so that it may go well with you and that you may enjoy long life on the earth."
> **Ephesians 6:1–3, NIV**

This does not mean that parents can abuse this command. Scripture also reads…

> Fathers, do not exasperate your children; instead, bring them up in the training and instruction of the Lord.
> **Ephesians 6:4, NIV**

Children are to obey their parents because they belong to the Lord. Parents are not to cause them to stumble or struggle because they all belong to the Lord. Causing a little one to stumble is one of the worst things to do. It would mean…

> But if you cause one of these little ones who trusts in me to fall into sin, it would be better for you to have a large millstone tied around your neck and be drowned in the depths of the sea.
> **Matthew 18:6, NLT**

This is one of the worst sins we could commit. Therefore, we must take our guidance and encouragement from the Lord and share this love and hope with our children.

Will this be difficult? At times. Are we to fear what we say or do to our children? Not if we know that our actions are from the Lord. Can we mess up, at times? Of course. Are we forgiven? Yes, and so are our children. Repentance can be taught. Thank the Lord!

Rejoice Over Our Child/ren

God has gifted some of us with children and some of us with other people's children. We rejoice in either situation because we are all a part of

God's family. We can all give thanks to the Lord because of His gifts to us. His love is His ultimate gift to each of us and we must encourage others through this love.

> Give thanks to the LORD, for he is good;
>   his love endures forever.

Psalm 118:1, NIV

> 5 When hard pressed, I cried to the LORD;
>   he brought me into a spacious place.
> 6 The LORD is with me; I will not be afraid.
>   What can mere mortals do to me?
> 7 The LORD is with me; he is my helper.
>   I look in triumph on my enemies.
>
> 8 It is better to take refuge in the LORD
>   than to trust in humans.
> 9 It is better to take refuge in the LORD
>   than to trust in princes.
> 10 All the nations surrounded me,
>   but in the name of the LORD I cut them down.
> 11 They surrounded me on every side,
>   but in the name of the LORD I cut them down.
> 12 They swarmed around me like bees,
>   but they were consumed as quickly as burning thorns;
>   in the name of the LORD I cut them down.
> 13 I was pushed back and about to fall,
>   but the LORD helped me.
> 14 The LORD is my strength and my defense;
>   he has become my salvation.
>
> 15 Shouts of joy and victory
>   resound in the tents of the righteous:
> "The LORD's right hand has done mighty things!
> 16 The LORD's right hand is lifted high;
>   the LORD's right hand has done mighty things!"
> 17 I will not die but live,
>   and will proclaim what the LORD has done.
> 18 The LORD has chastened me severely,

217

but he has not given me over to death.
19 Open for me the gates of the righteous;
   I will enter and give thanks to the LORD.
20 This is the gate of the LORD
   through which the righteous may enter.
21 I will give you thanks, for you answered me;
   you have become my salvation.

22 The stone the builders rejected
   has become the cornerstone;
23 the LORD has done this,
   and it is marvelous in our eyes.
24 The LORD has done it this very day;
   let us rejoice today and be glad.

25 LORD, save us!
   LORD, grant us success!

26 Blessed is he who comes in the name of the LORD.
   From the house of the LORD we bless you.
27 The LORD is God,
   and he has made his light shine on us.
With boughs in hand, join in the festal procession
   up to the horns of the altar.

28 You are my God, and I will praise you;
   you are my God, and I will exalt you.

29 Give thanks to the LORD, for he is good;
   his love endures forever.
Psalm 118:5–29, NIV

His faithful love endures, especially through the toughest and most hard-pressed times in our lives. We might have enemies. Our children might have enemies. However, we all know that we can call upon God to be placed into His safety. We are not to fear what mere people can do to us because God has saved us.

Taking refuge in the Lord does not mean that we are to hide from people. We are to do our best to share His love and encourage as many people as we can. Our children are growing up in an unstable nation right now. However, they (and we) can all count on God for eternity. People who do not know God will approach our children, but we have the powerful weapon of prayer to guard their hearts from this world.

People will try to conquer us and our children. However, the Lord is with us and His strength defends us from their wiles and human strengthened powers. Our salvation is something that we are claiming for our children as well. His love is vast and will overthrow the enemies forever.

We are to make claims to our children and share the encouraging words of God with them that we will live in eternity with God. No matter what people around us say, we must remind our children that God is Truth, and they can rely upon His words and promises. The gates of righteousness are here for our children to open.

We, as parents, must encourage our children to listen to the Holy Spirit and ask for His guidance. The Lord has become our Savior and our children must know that this Savior is Jesus Christ our Lord. He is their Savior also. All they need to do is to believe in Him.

Many Old Testament verses allude to Christ. One of them is Psalm 118:22. Jesus was rejected, and our children might be feeling rejected right now. Therefore, knowing how Christ was rejected and that our Father embraced Him through His rejection could encourage our children to rely even more on God. This truth makes it so that we rejoice in Christ's suffering. Without His suffering, and the promise of this suffering, we would be doomed to death instead of eternity with Him. Our children will be successful and flourish with His strength.

We are blessed that Christ came in the name of the Lord. We also can approach God in the name of the Lord and so can our children.

Hallelujah!

Our rejoicing during tough times will encourage our children to do the same. His love is enough to get anyone to rejoice. We are to exalt God and encourage our children to do this too. His love will endure (and has endured) forever. Amen!

Teaching Our Child/ren the Way

Having our children trust only in us can be dangerous. We must show them what it means to trust in the Lord. There will be times when our hearts are troubled. However, we must intentionally rejoice during these times. God has called us, and our children, into His home which is heaven. It will be full of His glory and we will be blessed.

1 "Don't let your hearts be troubled. Trust in God, and trust also in me. 2 There is more than enough room in my Father's home. If this were not so, would I have told you that I am going to prepare a place for you? 3 When everything is ready, I will come and get you, so that you will always be with me where I am. 4 And you know the way to where I am going."

5 "No, we don't know, Lord," Thomas said. "We have no idea where you are going, so how can we know the way?"

6 Jesus told him, "I am the way, the truth, and the life. No one can come to the Father except through me. 7 If you had really known me, you would know who my Father is. From now on, you do know him and have seen him!"

8 Philip said, "Lord, show us the Father, and we will be satisfied."

9 Jesus replied, "Have I been with you all this time, Philip, and yet you still don't know who I am? Anyone who has seen me has seen the Father! So why are you asking me to show him to you? 10 Don't you believe that I am in the Father and the Father is in me? The words I speak are not my own, but my Father who lives in me does his work through me. 11 Just believe that I am in the Father and the Father is in me. Or at least believe because of the work you have seen me do.

12 "I tell you the truth, anyone who believes in me will do the same works I have done, and even greater works, because I am going to be with the Father. 13 You can ask for anything in my name, and I will do it, so that the Son can bring glory to the Father. 14 Yes, ask me for anything in my name, and I will do it!

John 14:1–14, NLT

Jesus is making the home ready for us all to join Him and the Father in heaven. The Holy Spirit guides us toward the pathway to Him. Jesus is the Way to the Father and the Holy Spirit is our guide here on earth.

Some of us doubt as Thomas did. However, our faith is not perfect, and we must be reminded that our doubt is something that God can work with. Our children must also know that doubt does not exclude us, or them, from eternity.

Thomas had to be reminded that Jesus is the Way to the Father and our children might need to be reminded also. There is no other way to heaven. Many religions claim there are many ways to get into heaven and this is false teaching. Our children might be lured by this type of teaching and we must fall on our knees to cry out to God for them to find their way back to His Truth.

Even Philip had to re-hear the Good News when he asked that Jesus show him the Father. Our children might need to see the Father and sometimes that means they need to see our actions align with His Truth. Sometimes they hear Him directly and other times they might need to feel His arms wrapped around them during their struggles. He is with us all, here, and now.

Jesus is in the Father and the Father is in Jesus. What this means is that they are different pieces of the same Person…our Lord and Savior. We must allow our children to question these things and not discourage them from questioning. God is already working in their hearts to show Himself to them. We must remain in prayer to be a part of what He is doing in their hearts. Ask, and you will receive. He has the same desire…for our children to realize that they are His children.

Reconciled through Christ

How many of us reading this book have ever felt abandoned or left out? I have many times in my life—some warranted and other times, not so much. However, I have never felt abandoned by God. I was a criminal and He never left me. He saved my life many times while I was on the streets. I had to turn around and say, "I need You, Lord," to find reconciliation with Him. No hesitation by Him, at all. I desire that every one of my children find this reconciliation too.

9 For this reason we also, since the day we heard it, do not cease to pray for you, and to ask that you may be filled with the knowledge of His will in all wisdom and spiritual understanding; 10 that you may walk worthy of the Lord, fully pleasing Him, being fruitful in every good work and increasing in the knowledge of God; 11 strengthened with all might, according to His glorious power, for all patience and longsuffering with joy; 12 giving thanks to the Father who has qualified us to be partakers of the inheritance of the saints in the light. 13 He has delivered us from the power of darkness and conveyed us into the kingdom of the Son of His love, 14 in whom we have redemption through His blood, the forgiveness of sins.

15 He is the image of the invisible God, the firstborn over all creation. 16 For by Him all things were created that are in heaven and that are on earth, visible and invisible, whether thrones or dominions or principalities or powers. All things were created through Him and for Him. 17 And He is before all things, and in Him all things consist. 18 And He is the head of the body, the church, who is the beginning, the firstborn from the dead, that in all things He may have the preeminence.

19 For it pleased the Father that in Him all the fullness should dwell, 20 and by Him to reconcile all things to Himself, by Him, whether things on earth or things in heaven, having made peace through the blood of His cross.

21 And you, who once were alienated and enemies in your mind by wicked works, yet now He has reconciled 22 in the body of His flesh through death, to present you holy, and blameless, and above reproach in His sight—23 if indeed you continue in the faith, grounded and steadfast, and are not moved away from the hope of the gospel which you heard, which was preached to every creature under heaven, of which I, Paul, became a minister.

24 I now rejoice in my sufferings for you, and fill up in my flesh what is lacking in the afflictions of Christ, for the sake of His body, which is the church, 25 of which I became a minister according to the stewardship from God

which was given to me for you, to fulfill the word of God, 26 the mystery which has been hidden from ages and from generations, but now has been revealed to His saints. 27 To them God willed to make known what are the riches of the glory of this mystery among the Gentiles: which is Christ in you, the hope of glory. 28 Him we preach, warning every man and teaching every man in all wisdom, that we may present every man perfect in Christ Jesus. 29 To this end I also labor, striving according to His working which works in me mightily.

Colossians 1:9–29, NKJV

God is good and His Word is the Truth that each of our children need in their lives. We must pray without ceasing for their salvation and a right relationship with Christ. Reconciliation is theirs for the taking, are they ready to take it? Maybe some of them are, but sometimes, just as we have, they walk away from God.

PRAY!

Walking in the way of the Lord takes commitment; we must pray for this for our children. His glorious power will guide them and heal their wounds. However, they do have to want it. Our young children might be saved through our salvation, but when they get old enough, they must decide to love and trust Him themselves. This is where prayer is most necessary. We must pray that our children become fruitful and knowledgeable in God.

We must have patience with our children as God has with us. Remember what I wrote about me walking away and being a criminal? God had patience with me and now I realize that I am nothing without Him. I know that my grandmother's prayers had a lot to do with His hand in my life. Our children need this too.

The power of darkness might appear to be strong at times but remember that God is stronger than any other 'power.' Christ died for our sins. He also died for the sins of our children.

He has given us His might and power by allowing us to approach Him. Christ made this all possible through His sacrifice. Our children must know this.

They might shrug it off, but they need to hear it from us often. We cannot stop telling them and sharing with them His love. His desire is that we encourage our children as He encourages His children.

We are not 'preaching' to them when we show them His love through our actions. We are to preach to them (not at them) when they will listen though. He is already working in their hearts. We are His vessel so they can hear His voice through the words He gives us to share with them. This is called, you guessed it, encouragement.

Christ is the image of God and we are created in this image. Therefore, our children must see Christ in our lives. The principalities and powers in this world might seem overwhelmingly strong but God is much stronger. Our children must know this, must hear this, and must see this.

Christ is the head of the body (church). If our children ask if there is another way to get to heaven, we must be ready to explain that Jesus is the only Way to heaven. Some churches (yeah, Christian churches) claim that there are other ways to heaven. Our children must hear what the Bible says, not what people say.

We have been reconciled to God through Christ's sacrifice and this is true for our children as well. God desires that we all be reconciled to Him.

Let's pray for this to happen!

I know that I was alienated from God through my criminal choices. However, He remained faithful to me and the prayers of my grandmother. Therefore, we must do the same for our children.

Our children need us to pray for them, especially in this world today. We have all become blessed with the knowledge that by our faith, we are saved. Salvation is meant for all.

We will endure suffering, especially with this nation's government which tries to eliminate God in everything. We did have a president who cared about what God wants for His people, so there might have been a chance for national redemption.

Keep praying for it. Our children are inheriting this national mess, pray that they can see the Light, and change the current direction of God's elimination. God will not be eliminated, but it has begun to seem as though He is not welcome in most places anymore.

We have all been called to nurture at least one child, here and there—our sons, daughters, nieces, nephews, cousins and/or neighbors. Pray that the children of this world are given the opportunities to know who God is to them, their Savior.

God might seem to be a mystery to us and our children. However, we are guaranteed His inheritance and will be in His presence for eternity. All we need to do is to remind our children (and ourselves) to turn around, repent, and be forgiven by God. Jesus has made us and our children perfect through His sacrifice. His love must shine through so that our children learn how to hear from the Holy Spirit of God.

Introducing them to the Holy Spirit

The Holy Spirit is our Guide while we are on earth. He is also the Guide for our children. They need to know what it means to hear the Holy Spirit. Through the reading of Scripture, there will be many revelations. We can read with our children just in case they have questions. We must learn to obey the Lord and encourage our children to do the same.

15 "If you love me, obey my commandments. 16 And I will ask the Father, and he will give you another Advocate, who will never leave you. 17 He is the Holy Spirit, who leads into all truth. The world cannot receive him, because it isn't looking for him and doesn't recognize him. But you know him, because he lives with you now and later will be in you. 18 No, I will not abandon you as orphans—I will come to you. 19 Soon the world will no longer see me, but you will see me. Since I live, you also will live. 20 When I am raised to life again, you will know that I am in my Father, and you are in me, and I am in you. 21 Those who accept my commandments and obey them are the ones who love me. And because they love me, my Father will love them. And I will love them and reveal myself to each of them."

22 Judas (not Judas Iscariot, but the other disciple with that name) said to him, "Lord, why are you going to reveal yourself only to us and not to the world at large?"

23 Jesus replied, "All who love me will do what I say. My Father will love them, and we will come and make our home with each of them. 24 Anyone who doesn't love me will not obey me. And remember, my words are not my own. What I am telling you is from the Father who sent

225

me. 25 I am telling you these things now while I am still with you. 26 But when the Father sends the Advocate as my representative—that is, the Holy Spirit—he will teach you everything and will remind you of everything I have told you.

27 "I am leaving you with a gift—peace of mind and heart. And the peace I give is a gift the world cannot give. So don't be troubled or afraid. 28 Remember what I told you: I am going away, but I will come back to you again. If you really loved me, you would be happy that I am going to the Father, who is greater than I am. 29 I have told you these things before they happen so that when they do happen, you will believe.

30 "I don't have much more time to talk to you, because the ruler of this world approaches. He has no power over me, 31 but I will do what the Father requires of me, so that the world will know that I love the Father. Come, let's be going.

John 14:15–31, NLT

Jesus asks His disciples to obey His commandments. He desires that we do also. Our children are watching our every move and they are encouraged when His light shines through us as we are struggling. We need the Holy Spirit to guide us as we help our children to better understand who the Holy Spirit is to them. The world does not know the Holy Spirit. Our children must not be discouraged by the ways of the world.

Easier said than done, right? Wrong. God shows us the way to guide our children every single day. We are to become more Christlike and share this Christlikeness with our children. This world is flailing, and the reason is that God is not at the center of decisions. God has not abandoned us, the nation, or the world. It is the other way around. We, they, the nation, the world has abandoned God. Drawing our children back toward God might seem impossible. But we must have faith and pray!

We all know the Bible story about Judas Iscariot, right? If not, he decided to betray Jesus to the Pharisees and Sadducees for money and ultimately regretted his decisions. How many of us have made poor decisions? We all have (see Romans 3:23), but not like Judas did. However, what is less known is that there is another Judas (not Iscariot) who wondered why Jesus would only reveal Himself to the disciples and not the world at large. It appears that this is occurring right now also. However, the world simply must turn around and repent to find His forgiveness.

Several things remind me of how we hear, feel, and see the Holy Spirit. One fun thing that reminds me of Him is Jiminy Cricket—Pinocchio's conscience. Our conscience is more than our mind…it includes our heart and soul. When we feel as though something is 'wrong,' we are probably hearing the Holy Spirit's guidance. Our children need to understand how this works. We can learn this together and share it with others too.

When we do not obey that feeling that the Holy Spirit puts upon our hearts, it is difficult for us to hear Him the next time also. We begin to ignore His nudges and still small voice. This is dangerous. Christ is attempting to share His gift of the Holy Spirit with us, and we need to be in a place where we can hear Him. This way, we can guide our children in this same direction.

Christ had to leave His disciples, in body. However, He left us all His Spirit so that we can hear Him. Our children must know that Christ left His Guide for them also. Christ will return for all His disciples (that includes us).

We are His disciples too. When He does return, we need to be ready and prayerfully know that our children are ready too. He has created hearts of gold inside of us and is ready, willing, and able to create hearts of gold inside of our children too.

Pray!

Hearts of Gold

God the Father and Christ our Lord have hearts of gold and created us and our children in His image. His kindness is not to be mistaken for weakness as He is the mightiest strength in the universe. Our nation is crumbling, and one reason is how 'God' has been taken out of the national anthem, out of the classrooms, and out of some households. He is King, no matter if we believe it or not. Let's shout it from the rooftops that God is our Father and Christ saved us all from ourselves and our sins.

> 24 For I will take you out of the nations; I will gather
> you from all the countries and bring you back into your
> own land. 25 I will sprinkle clean water on you, and you

will be clean; I will cleanse you from all your impurities and from all your idols. 26 I will give you a new heart and put a new spirit in you; I will remove from you your heart of stone and give you a heart of flesh.
Ezekiel 36:24–26, NIV

Even though our nation is crumbling, it does not mean that heaven is crumbling. It also does not mean that what God says to us is wrong. He promises to not abandon us, and He has not. Heaven is glorified when we proclaim His Good News to all. We are no longer on our own when we realize that we are a part of His Kingdom and family.

Countries have abandoned the Good News forever. God has been 'unwelcome' in many religions and most governments. This government appears to be heading down this same pathway.

We had a president that may have cared enough to allow God back into some of the places He was banned from. Our children are living in a special time. Nations are falling and people are dying, but God is still with us and has not forsaken us. We are His children. Our children are His children too.

He cleanses us through our minds, hearts, and souls. He will not allow us to move too far from Him unless we keep ignoring His Holy Spirit. We must turn back to Him and ask for forgiveness. We are not to idolize anything or anyone but God.

He is working on renewing our spirit and He is working on the spirits of our children. We are to understand His laws and remember that Christ died to fulfill these laws. Our hearts were made of stone and God softened them so that we could be encouraging toward our children.

Our children's hearts are being softened now too. When our hearts are soft, we know that we are to follow His Light and remain on the narrow path He has set before us and our children. Sharing this encouragement with our children is our humble honor.

Following the Light

Do we really think that it is easier to follow darkness? Do we get lost in the dark? Or do we get lost in the light?

We know that the Light is the right direction, but sometimes choose to remain in the dark. Trust me, I do this too. It is difficult to know why we do this. The only reason I have come up with is that we are human beings and must try living in the Spirit while we are still living in the flesh.

Yikes!

God sent His Son to earth as an example of how we are to live. I don't know about any of you, but boy do I fall short. However, this does not make us hopeless. In fact, we find hope in His forgiveness. Christ came to earth to save us all. Our children must learn this about themselves also.

1 Follow God's example, therefore, as dearly loved children 2 and walk in the way of love, just as Christ loved us and gave himself up for us as a fragrant offering and sacrifice to God.

3 But among you there must not be even a hint of sexual immorality, or of any kind of impurity, or of greed, because these are improper for God's holy people. 4 Nor should there be obscenity, foolish talk or coarse joking, which are out of place, but rather thanksgiving. 5 For of this you can be sure: No immoral, impure or greedy person—such a person is an idolater—has any inheritance in the kingdom of Christ and of God. 6 Let no one deceive you with empty words, for because of such things God's wrath comes on those who are disobedient. 7 Therefore do not be partners with them.

8 For you were once darkness, but now you are light in the Lord. Live as children of light 9 (for the fruit of the light consists in all goodness, righteousness and truth) 10 and find out what pleases the Lord. 11 Have nothing to do with the fruitless deeds of darkness, but rather expose them. 12 It is shameful even to mention what the disobedient do in secret. 13 But everything exposed by the light becomes visible—and everything that is illuminated becomes a light. 14 This is why it is said:

"Wake up, sleeper,
　　rise from the dead,
　　and Christ will shine on you."

15 Be very careful, then, how you live—not as unwise but as wise, 16 making the most of every opportunity,

because the days are evil. 17 Therefore do not be foolish, but understand what the Lord's will is. 18 Do not get drunk on wine, which leads to debauchery. Instead, be filled with the Spirit, 19 speaking to one another with psalms, hymns, and songs from the Spirit. Sing and make music from your heart to the Lord, 20 always giving thanks to God the Father for everything, in the name of our Lord Jesus Christ.

Ephesians 5:1–20, NIV

Immoral thoughts and actions might appear as a normal part of being human. However, they are to be put off like dirty clothes. Then we allow ourselves to be clothed with purity.

Only God can purify us and our children. We must learn to watch our language. This is one that I struggle with the most. Joking with people is not 'bad,' but joking about people and using coarse descriptions in these jokes is impure.

We must teach our children that greed is not success. Many people today have a hard time with this because the measures of success usually bring money to mind. However, godly success has nothing to do with money. We must remind ourselves and our children that money is the root of all kinds of evil (see 1 Timothy 6:10). However, if a person is godly and has money, there is nothing wrong with this, if they worship God only, not their money.

Our children are amid deceiving leadership right now. However, we are to teach them which words are His Truth. Lies from government, local and federal, are present in almost everything. Facebook is a dangerous place for our children because people can put whatever they want in their 'feeds' without punishment. Therefore, our children must hear from us as well as from social media, etc.

We are children of the Light...so are our children. We must remind them as often as possible. Pleasing the Lord is more important than pleasing people. However, we can please the Lord by showing our children how to be pleased and how to please the Lord. Instead of allowing our children (or ourselves) to walk in darkness, we must introduce them to the Light. God is their Father also.

Pray!

Christ shines His light on us all. Our children might appear to be in the dark, but they know where the Light is, and our prayers will make it difficult not to walk in His light. The wisdom of God is in their hearts, but they might not know it yet.

Pray!

As we know, we are living in evil times. Our children must have the hope of finding His Light. We must take every opportunity to share this Light with them. Encouraging them to seek His Kingdom first. Encouragement is the theme of this book, but it is more the theme of our lives with Christ in it. We must always give thanks to Him.

We must give thanks to God for our children and make sure to keep them in prayer. Whether they know God or not, they all need prayer. God's peace comes from listening and adhering to His Word.

God's peace is His gift to His children; us, and our children, and our children's children.

Grandchildren

How many of us have become grandparents? My husband and I are grandparents of six grandbabies at the writing of this book. We are blessed to have these precious jewels in our lives. I can honestly say that I make a much better Nana than I did a mommy.

Even though I tried, I failed often when it came to my children. And I am sure that I will fail at some point with my grandbabies. However, God's grace is sufficient (see 2 Corinthians 12:9). Nana and Pop Pop love their precious grandbabies.

Remember that grandchildren are the children of our children. Wow, what a mouth full! We are children of God. Our children are children of God and our grandchildren are children of God.

It goes to show us that we belong to a royal family and God is King. Therefore, we can go to the throne to ask for guidance with our children and our grandchildren—hoping to see our grandchildren and children more often, but knowing they are all right with God in their lives.

> 1 I will exalt you, LORD, for you rescued me.
>   You refused to let my enemies triumph over me.
> 2 O LORD my God, I cried to you for help,
>   and you restored my health.

231

3 You brought me up from the grave, O LORD.
> You kept me from falling into the pit of death.

4 Sing to the LORD, all you godly ones!
> Praise his holy name.
5 For his anger lasts only a moment,
> but his favor lasts a lifetime!
Weeping may last through the night,
> but joy comes with the morning.

6 When I was prosperous, I said,
> "Nothing can stop me now!"
7 Your favor, O LORD, made me as secure as a mountain.
> Then you turned away from me, and I was shattered.

8 I cried out to you, O LORD.
> I begged the Lord for mercy, saying,
9 "What will you gain if I die,
> if I sink into the grave?
Can my dust praise you?
> Can it tell of your faithfulness?
10 Hear me, LORD, and have mercy on me.
> Help me, O LORD."

11 You have turned my mourning into joyful dancing.
> You have taken away my clothes of mourning and clothed
> > me with joy,
12 that I might sing praises to you and not be silent.
> O LORD my God, I will give you thanks forever!
Psalm 30, NLT

I exalt the Lord. Even when I cannot see or talk to my grandchildren and/or children, I exalt Him. He alone is worthy to be praised.

While not seeing our grandchildren may affect our hearts, it cannot touch our souls. Our souls belong to God. He will help us to find joy, even when we miss our children and grandchildren. While it hurts when we miss our grandchildren, God will restore us.

God loves our grandchildren and children even more than we do. Hard to believe, I know, but it is true. When we miss our kiddos and grandkiddos, God lifts us up and comforts us. Sometimes when we miss them, we feel depressed or distressed. God is here and His desire is for us to be restored in their lives.

It might appear that God is upset and/or angry with us, but that is not why we are unable to visit our grandkiddos and kiddos. This world is lost and confusing. God's world is not. His favor will last throughout eternity. His joy will come in the morning. Remember, when we feel this way...

Pray!

It might appear that God has turned away from us. However, He might need to work on our grandchildren and children during these times away. He is always with us and with them.

We can trust Him with them more than we can even trust ourselves in their lives. Thankfully, He loves them even more than we do. As soon as we cry out to Him, He hears us and helps us.

God does not desire for us to fall into the grave. We would not be able to cry out to Him or praise Him from our grave. Therefore, He does hear our cries for salvation and the salvation of our children and their children. He shows us His mercy so that we can encourage our grandchildren even if we are not with them.

We mourn when we miss our grandchildren. However, He will turn our mourning into laughter. He will help us to sing and dance even when we miss them. We must not be silent anymore. We must shout praises to the Lord and wait for His comfort and joy to fill us up.

Many people need to hear from God and who need God to hear them. Our grandchildren need us to pray for them and their parents. We are also called to pray for and encourage people in our communities.

Pray!

Christine C. Sponsler

PART 4: Community Encouragement

12 This is my commandment, that you love one another as I have loved you. 13 Greater love has no one than this, that someone lay down his life for his friends. 14 You are my friends if you do what I command you. 15 No longer do I call you servants, for the servant does not know what his master is doing; but I have called you friends, for all that I have heard from my Father I have made known to you.
John 15:12–15, ESV

God has called us all to gather in His name; we are to lay down our lives for each other. We are not to envy or fight with each other. Encouragement embraces another believer. We might not know each other well, but God knows us all well. He calls us 'friends' because of Jesus' sacrifice.

*****

Be blessed and bless others today and every day.

Chapter 16: The Courage to Encourage Others

David also said to Solomon his son, "Be strong and courageous, and do the work. Do not be afraid or discouraged, for the LORD God, my God, is with you. He will not fail you or forsake you until all the work for the service of the temple of the LORD is finished.

1 Chronicles 28:20, NIV

6 "Be strong and courageous. Do not be afraid or terrified because of them, for the LORD your God goes with you; he will never leave you nor forsake you."

7 Then Moses summoned Joshua and said to him in the presence of all Israel, "Be strong and courageous, for you must go with this people into the land that the LORD swore to their ancestors to give them, and you must divide it among them as their inheritance. 8 The LORD himself goes before you and will be with you; he will never leave you nor forsake you. Do not be afraid; do not be discouraged."

Deuteronomy 31:6–8, NIV

13 Be on your guard; stand firm in the faith; be courageous; be strong. 14 Do everything in love.

1 Corinthians 16:13–14, NIV

We have the courage to stand firm against the enemy because God is with us. We can be reassured that God is our strength. We will find the courage to be an encouragement to others when we ask God for this courage. God desires that we encourage others to seek Him out. We are to do this all with His love.

*****

Christine C. Sponsler

Let's get out there and encourage others today!

Gathering in His Name

As we gather in His name, we are to love one another with the same love that He has shown us. That's a lot!

The love of the Lord includes forgiveness and mercy. We should be sentenced to death for we are sinners. However, Christ died to save us from this punishment.

Paul is not the only 'new' servant of the Church. We are now His servants. We are to encourage each other to remember this and support each other as we serve.

> 1 Paul, a servant of Christ Jesus, called to be an apostle, set apart for the gospel of God, 2 which he promised beforehand through his prophets in the holy Scriptures, 3 concerning his Son, who was descended from David according to the flesh 4 and was declared to be the Son of God in power according to the Spirit of holiness by his resurrection from the dead, Jesus Christ our Lord, 5 through whom we have received grace and apostleship to bring about the obedience of faith for the sake of his name among all the nations, 6 including you who are called to belong to Jesus Christ,
>
> 7 To all those in Rome who are loved by God and called to be saints:
>
> Grace to you and peace from God our Father and the Lord Jesus Christ.
>
> 8 First, I thank my God through Jesus Christ for all of you, because your faith is proclaimed in all the world. 9 For God is my witness, whom I serve with my spirit in the gospel of his Son, that without ceasing I mention you 10 always in my prayers, asking that somehow by God's will I may now at last succeed in coming to you. 11 For I long to see you, that I may impart to you some spiritual gift to strengthen you— 12 that is, that we may be mutually encouraged by each other's faith, both yours and mine.
>
> **Romans 1:1–12, ESV**

Christine C. Sponsler

Paul began as an enemy of the Church. Have any of us felt like we were the enemy of the church? I know that I have, and it hurts. It made me seek 'love' elsewhere.

I hope and pray that I never make anyone else feel this way. I don't want to put a millstone around my neck and jump into the sea (see Matthew 18:6; Luke 17:2). However, I would rather tie the millstone around my neck than to hurt a fellow believer.

Paul finally saw that Christ is the Messiah and he turned to God in repentance for His forgiveness. When he did, God used him to glorify His name. Christ died and was raised to conquer death and Paul began to understand this after his encounter with Jesus on the road to Damascus.

> Meanwhile, Saul was still breathing out murderous threats against the Lord's disciples. He went to the high priest 2 and asked him for letters to the synagogues in Damascus, so that if he found any there who belonged to the Way, whether men or women, he might take them as prisoners to Jerusalem. 3 As he neared Damascus on his journey, suddenly a light from heaven flashed around him. 4 He fell to the ground and heard a voice say to him, "Saul, Saul, why do you persecute me?"
>
> 5 "Who are you, Lord?" Saul asked.
>
> "I am Jesus, whom you are persecuting," he replied. 6 "Now get up and go into the city, and you will be told what you must do."
>
> 7 The men traveling with Saul stood there speechless; they heard the sound but did not see anyone. 8 Saul got up from the ground, but when he opened his eyes he could see nothing. So they led him by the hand into Damascus. 9 For three days he was blind, and did not eat or drink anything.
>
> 10 In Damascus there was a disciple named Ananias. The Lord called to him in a vision, "Ananias!"
>
> "Yes, Lord," he answered.
>
> 11 The Lord told him, "Go to the house of Judas on Straight Street and ask for a man from Tarsus named Saul, for he is praying. 12 In a vision he has seen a man named

Ananias come and place his hands on him to restore his sight."

13 "Lord," Ananias answered, "I have heard many reports about this man and all the harm he has done to your holy people in Jerusalem. 14 And he has come here with authority from the chief priests to arrest all who call on your name."

15 But the Lord said to Ananias, "Go! This man is my chosen instrument to proclaim my name to the Gentiles and their kings and to the people of Israel. 16 I will show him how much he must suffer for my name."

17 Then Ananias went to the house and entered it. Placing his hands on Saul, he said, "Brother Saul, the Lord—Jesus, who appeared to you on the road as you were coming here—has sent me so that you may see again and be filled with the Holy Spirit." 18 Immediately, something like scales fell from Saul's eyes, and he could see again. He got up and was baptized, 19 and after taking some food, he regained his strength.

Saul spent several days with the disciples in Damascus. 20 At once he began to preach in the synagogues that Jesus is the Son of God. 21 All those who heard him were astonished and asked, "Isn't he the man who raised havoc in Jerusalem among those who call on this name? And hasn't he come here to take them as prisoners to the chief priests?" 22 Yet Saul grew more and more powerful and baffled the Jews living in Damascus by proving that Jesus is the Messiah.

23 After many days had gone by, there was a conspiracy among the Jews to kill him, 24 but Saul learned of their plan. Day and night they kept close watch on the city gates in order to kill him. 25 But his followers took him by night and lowered him in a basket through an opening in the wall.

26 When he came to Jerusalem, he tried to join the disciples, but they were all afraid of him, not believing that he really was a disciple. 27 But Barnabas took him and brought him to the apostles. He told them how Saul on his

journey had seen the Lord and that the Lord had spoken to him, and how in Damascus he had preached fearlessly in the name of Jesus. 28 So Saul stayed with them and moved about freely in Jerusalem, speaking boldly in the name of the Lord. 29 He talked and debated with the Hellenistic Jews, but they tried to kill him. 30 When the believers learned of this, they took him down to Caesarea and sent him off to Tarsus.

31 Then the church throughout Judea, Galilee and Samaria enjoyed a time of peace and was strengthened. Living in the fear of the Lord and encouraged by the Holy Spirit, it increased in numbers.

32 As Peter traveled about the country, he went to visit the Lord's people who lived in Lydda. 33 There he found a man named Aeneas, who was paralyzed and had been bedridden for eight years. 34 "Aeneas," Peter said to him, "Jesus Christ heals you. Get up and roll up your mat." Immediately Aeneas got up. 35 All those who lived in Lydda and Sharon saw him and turned to the Lord.

36 In Joppa there was a disciple named Tabitha (in Greek her name is Dorcas); she was always doing good and helping the poor. 37 About that time she became sick and died, and her body was washed and placed in an upstairs room. 38 Lydda was near Joppa; so when the disciples heard that Peter was in Lydda, they sent two men to him and urged him, "Please come at once!"

39 Peter went with them, and when he arrived he was taken upstairs to the room. All the widows stood around him, crying and showing him the robes and other clothing that Dorcas had made while she was still with them.

40 Peter sent them all out of the room; then he got down on his knees and prayed. Turning toward the dead woman, he said, "Tabitha, get up." She opened her eyes, and seeing Peter she sat up. 41 He took her by the hand and helped her to her feet. Then he called for the believers, especially the widows, and presented her to them alive. 42 This became known all over Joppa, and many people

believed in the Lord. 43 Peter stayed in Joppa for some time with a tanner named Simon.

Acts 9, NIV

Then Paul belonged to God.

We also belong to God. I know, we are not possessions. Or are we? I would rather be God's possession rather than Satan's possession. We are to encourage each other with His love and kindness.

Paul was one of the first people to show us what this looks like. Reading everything that Paul wrote in the Bible explains how much God loves those whom He calls for His purpose.

Paul goes on to thank God for the Romans. How often do we thank God for each other?

Stop... thank Him right now. I'll wait.

Welcome back!

We are to pray for each other and share; cry with each other. And we are to encourage each other through Christ. Coming together was Paul's desire in this chapter and he has a good point; we are to gather and encourage each other often. Through hope and love, we are to strengthen each other through His Word. This will unify the Church.

Unified in Him

I know this text is beginning to look a lot like a study of Paul, but God did put His stories in the Bible for a reason. We are to find Paul as one of God's examples. Paul wrote a letter to the Church in Corinth. His dedication to Christ has changed many lives, from circa A.D. 50-54 until now, and then into the future. His stories are for enlightenment and encouragement.

Paul often begins his letters with opening lines which include greetings. Other times he gets right to the point of his letter. There are times when he finds churches struggling and other times when they are flourishing in the Lord.

His concerns are that the Church does not harm each other or go astray from God's Word. Paul is someone we can appreciate and look up to, but as he mentions in several places, he is not God and is not to be worshipped. With that being said, let's look at what Paul has to say here.

1 This letter is from Paul, chosen by the will of God to be an apostle of Christ Jesus, and from our brother Sosthenes.

2 I am writing to God's church in Corinth, to you who have been called by God to be his own holy people. He made you holy by means of Christ Jesus, just as he did for all people everywhere who call on the name of our Lord Jesus Christ, their Lord and ours.

3 May God our Father and the Lord Jesus Christ give you grace and peace.

4 I always thank my God for you and for the gracious gifts he has given you, now that you belong to Christ Jesus. 5 Through him, God has enriched your church in every way—with all of your eloquent words and all of your knowledge. 6 This confirms that what I told you about Christ is true. 7 Now you have every spiritual gift you need as you eagerly wait for the return of our Lord Jesus Christ. 8 He will keep you strong to the end so that you will be free from all blame on the day when our Lord Jesus Christ returns. 9 God will do this, for he is faithful to do what he says, and he has invited you into partnership with his Son, Jesus Christ our Lord.

10 I appeal to you, dear brothers and sisters, by the authority of our Lord Jesus Christ, to live in harmony with each other. Let there be no divisions in the church. Rather, be of one mind, united in thought and purpose. 11 For some members of Chloe's household have told me about your quarrels, my dear brothers and sisters. 12 Some of you are saying, "I am a follower of Paul." Others are saying, "I follow Apollos," or "I follow Peter," or "I follow only Christ."

13 Has Christ been divided into factions? Was I, Paul, crucified for you? Were any of you baptized in the name of Paul? Of course not! 14 I thank God that I did not baptize any of you except Crispus and Gaius, 15 for now no one can say they were baptized in my name. 16 (Oh yes, I also baptized the household of Stephanas, but I don't remember baptizing anyone else.) 17 For Christ didn't send

me to baptize, but to preach the Good News—and not with clever speech, for fear that the cross of Christ would lose its power.

18 The message of the cross is foolish to those who are headed for destruction! But we who are being saved know it is the very power of God. 19 As the Scriptures say,

"I will destroy the wisdom of the wise
   and discard the intelligence of the intelligent."

20 So where does this leave the philosophers, the scholars, and the world's brilliant debaters? God has made the wisdom of this world look foolish. 21 Since God in his wisdom saw to it that the world would never know him through human wisdom, he has used our foolish preaching to save those who believe. 22 It is foolish to the Jews, who ask for signs from heaven. And it is foolish to the Greeks, who seek human wisdom. 23 So when we preach that Christ was crucified, the Jews are offended and the Gentiles say it's all nonsense.

24 But to those called by God to salvation, both Jews and Gentiles, Christ is the power of God and the wisdom of God. 25 This foolish plan of God is wiser than the wisest of human plans, and God's weakness is stronger than the greatest of human strength.

26 Remember, dear brothers and sisters, that few of you were wise in the world's eyes or powerful or wealthy when God called you. 27 Instead, God chose things the world considers foolish in order to shame those who think they are wise. And he chose things that are powerless to shame those who are powerful. 28 God chose things despised by the world, things counted as nothing at all, and used them to bring to nothing what the world considers important. 29 As a result, no one can ever boast in the presence of God.

30 God has united you with Christ Jesus. For our benefit God made him to be wisdom itself. Christ made us right with God; he made us pure and holy, and he freed us

from sin. 31 Therefore, as the Scriptures say, "If you want
to boast, boast only about the LORD."
1 Corinthians 1, NLT

First, we see that Paul usually addresses other people in his greetings.
He is allowing the church in Corinth to know that he understands that
Sosthenes (the church chief ruler of the Synagogue), is also a part of his
letter.

We must remember to include all who have anything to do with what
we proclaim to our brothers and sisters. When we share God's Word with
others, we must include where we are receiving this information from so
that we do not take credit for someone else's words. God's Word is from
Him and He has used people such as Paul to write His words.

Then Paul dedicates his gratitude toward the people of the church by
including them in his letter. Paul appreciates the people of God now and
so should we. When people call upon the name of the Lord, we must be
thankful. Thankful that they know and love God, just as Paul is thankful
in this letter. Then he leaves a message of grace and peace for the church,
so they continue to serve the Lord.

Can you imagine receiving a letter from someone that you know, and it
reads that they are thankful to God for you? What a wonderful letter that
would be, right?

Our churches have gone through numerous decades of changes, mostly
good, since A.D. 54. Our churches are still blessed by God though. We
continue to serve with our spiritual gifts. God has given us His strength to
serve and encourage others. And our churches continue to await the Lord's
return.

Christ is going to return, whether we are ready or not. As Paul shows
his desires in most of his letter, we must show our desire for the church to
be ready for His return. We must share this love with as many lost people
as we can.

It might seem too difficult at times, but we are to live in harmony with
each other and love each other as Christ loves us. Division in the church
is nothing new. However, it must be met with just words so we encourage
our fellow believers, rather than discourage them.

Remember, we are not to be followers of our preacher, pastor, or priest.
We are to be followers of Christ who hear His message through these
leaders. Encouragement does not include worshipping people, only God.

As Paul mentions, he was not crucified, Christ was, and this makes Christ our Savior. Sharing this encouragement is how we dedicate our lives to God.

When we first heard the message of the Cross, we might have had doubt. However, we know that Christ died for our sins and was raised by God in three days to conquer death for all. We must encourage as many people as we can with this Good News every single day. Other people might believe that there is no God. We must strive to make Him known through our love and encouragement shared with the lost and doubters.

Scholars do not have the answers we are looking for unless they study the Bible too. We are not to look to the 'world' for wisdom because God is where wisdom is found. People may believe that Christ's death was simply the death of a prophet. However, we know that His death has saved us from our sins. Preaching and teaching this to as many people as we can is another way of encouraging others.

Our strength is nothing. His strength in us is the most powerful thing that we have. Christ is, and always will be, the power of God. We, as believers, know this and are given His power to help others realize this too.

God's plans are wise. Our plans can be when we rely upon His wisdom to attain our goals and plans. We are made strong through our weaknesses because then we must rely upon His strength.

We might have thought that we were wise prior to our dedication to the Lord. However, our wisdom cannot even touch God's wisdom. His is a wisdom that the world does not understand. We did not understand what His wisdom was until our salvation and we barely understand how vast it is now. The world might despise our beliefs and may even despise us for our beliefs, but we must share God's love with the world any way that we can.

We are united in the Lord. We must allow God to use us to unite as many people as possible. Encouraging each other to share His love and mercy.

This world believes that there is no hope, and we must proclaim otherwise. We must only boast about what God has done in our lives. We are nothing without Him. We must bear the burdens of each other to further encourage the church.

Bearing with Each Other

Christine C. Sponsler

What does it mean to bear with someone? God had to bear with us while we were out there in our fleshliness and ignoring His calling. He had to bear with us when we decided that drugs and/or alcohol were more important than He was. And He still must bear with us because we are only human.

We do have the Spirit in us. How often should we read the Word of God to find reminders of this Spirit that dwells inside of us? If you're anything like I am, it will be often. Weekly, daily, hourly, and often minutely.

His strength is ignored when I try to do things in my own strength. Yeah right, like that would ever work. It might appear to be working momentarily, but overall, only His strength always works. I must bear with myself as I remember that I am only human, and He is God.

> 1 We who are strong ought to bear with the failings of the weak and not to please ourselves. 2 Each of us should please our neighbors for their good, to build them up. 3 For even Christ did not please himself but, as it is written: "The insults of those who insult you have fallen on me." 4 For everything that was written in the past was written to teach us, so that through the endurance taught in the Scriptures and the encouragement they provide we might have hope.
>
> 5 May the God who gives endurance and encouragement give you the same attitude of mind toward each other that Christ Jesus had, 6 so that with one mind and one voice you may glorify the God and Father of our Lord Jesus Christ.
>
> 7 Accept one another, then, just as Christ accepted you, in order to bring praise to God.
> **Romans 15:1–7, NIV**

Our family, friends, and neighbors may need to find the strength to bear something difficult in their lives. When we try to help in our own strength, God can use this to show His strength. We mean well by bearing with people who need our help and God is glorified because we remind them how we happen to have the strength to help. God's love is our strength, and these encouraging words will help other people to rely upon His strength also.

There is only hope in Scripture and the promises that God makes throughout His Word. People might insult us, but we are to step back and ask God to help us to encourage the people who try to harm us with their insults.

Maybe they are hurting right now. Does this mean that it is all right for them to insult us? No, but we must be willing to return encouragement for their insults.

We are not to please ourselves anymore. God desires that everyone hears about Him. When they hear about Him, He desires that they choose to believe in Him, and that Christ is now their Savior. We must patiently continue to pray for our family members, friends, neighbors, and even our enemies, so they will know Him. We are to bear the burden of loving even those who insult us.

Our endurance through bearing with our families, friends, neighbors, and enemies will encourage people even if they do not realize it right at that moment. They will remember this encouragement when they are ready.

Jesus loves us all. Who are we to only love those who love us? We are to bear with our enemies, so they notice Jesus in us. The Holy Spirit will do the rest.

People who are hurting often hurt others. We must be willing to bear with others. We do this so that God will be glorified and known which will allow others to become ready for His return.

Be Ready

Are we ready to see the Lord? I know that we desire to see Him every day. But are we ready in our hearts? I hope that we are. It is difficult to live in this world.

We are not 'of' this world but live in it (see John 17:16; Ephesians 6:12). Yes, we are only human, but we are to live with the Spirit guiding us and encouraging us to live holy lives. Jesus said that we would not know when He would return (see 1 Thessalonians 5:2). Therefore, we must be ready and waiting for this day.

1 Now, brothers and sisters, about times and dates we do not need to write to you, 2 for you know very well that the day of the Lord will come like a thief in the night. 3 While people are saying, "Peace and safety," destruction will come on them suddenly, as labor pains on a pregnant woman, and they will not escape.

4 But you, brothers and sisters, are not in darkness so that this day should surprise you like a thief. 5 You are all children of the light and children of the day. We do not belong to the night or to the darkness. 6 So then, let us not be like others, who are asleep, but let us be awake and sober. 7 For those who sleep, sleep at night, and those who get drunk, get drunk at night. 8 But since we belong to the day, let us be sober, putting on faith and love as a breastplate, and the hope of salvation as a helmet. 9 For God did not appoint us to suffer wrath but to receive salvation through our Lord Jesus Christ. 10 He died for us so that, whether we are awake or asleep, we may live together with him. 11 Therefore encourage one another and build each other up, just as in fact you are doing.

1 Thessalonians 5:1–11, NIV

The coming of the Lord is described as He will come like a thief in the night. What this means is that we will not see it coming. If we were to know when our house would be robbed, we would do something to avoid this happening. However, we do not know the date or time that He will return. He does this because He desires a relationship with us now, not when we are 'ready' for His return.

Most women who give birth do not know the time that they will give birth. However, they wait, anticipating the new arrival. This is how we are to live. We are to be ready by anticipating His return and encourage others to do the same. As His children, we await His return, looking forward to seeing Him face-to-face.

There is also a reference to this which states that we are to be awake and ready for His return. This does not mean that we are to stay up all night, every night, but to be awake in the Spirit so that we are ready for His miraculous return. We live in the Light. We are to encourage others so that they see the Light also.

We have received salvation through Christ, and we are to share this with our family, friends, neighbors, and enemies. We are to use encouragement to brighten each person's days and light up each other's nights. Building each other up in Him will allow us to not be discouraging to each other.

Discouraging Words

Discouraging words are not always meant to be spoken. For instance, some people do not realize that what they say hurts other people. However, to figure out what is discouraging and what is encouraging, we must be willing to read the Bible for these answers. His Word will encourage us and this will help us to encourage others.

> 1 Truly my soul finds rest in God;
>   my salvation comes from him.
> 2 Truly he is my rock and my salvation;
>   he is my fortress, I will never be shaken.
>
> 3 How long will you assault me?
>   Would all of you throw me down—
>   this leaning wall, this tottering fence?
> 4 Surely they intend to topple me
>   from my lofty place;
>   they take delight in lies.
> With their mouths they bless,
>   but in their hearts they curse.
>
> 5 Yes, my soul, find rest in God;
>   my hope comes from him.
> 6 Truly he is my rock and my salvation;
>   he is my fortress, I will not be shaken.
> 7 My salvation and my honor depend on God;
>   he is my mighty rock, my refuge.
> 8 Trust in him at all times, you people;
>   pour out your hearts to him,
>   for God is our refuge.
>
> 9 Surely the lowborn are but a breath,
>   the highborn are but a lie.

If weighed on a balance, they are nothing;
   together they are only a breath.
10 Do not trust in extortion
   or put vain hope in stolen goods;
though your riches increase,
   do not set your heart on them.

11 One thing God has spoken,
   two things I have heard:
"Power belongs to you, God,
12 and with you, Lord, is unfailing love";
and, "You reward everyone
   according to what they have done."
Psalm 62, NIV

We are children of God adopted into His family. He does not discourage people. Therefore, we must learn how to not be discouraging. When we find rest in Him, He will help us to learn how to encourage people. He is our rock and our fortress, and He will not allow us to be shaken. We are firmly planted on His ground.

People can be cruel. We can be cruel and not even know that we are. Coarse words are acceptable in the world. However, they are not righteous.

People will try to topple us over, just to say they were able to do so. People will lie about us and appear to be 'getting away with it.' However, God is right here with us and will not forsake us. We will again find rest in Him.

Our hope is in the Lord. He is our salvation, and we are to encourage others to live inside of His salvation for them. God is our refuge a safe place to live. He does not abandon us, and we must not abandon each other. We are here for support for each other, and He delights in this. He pours out His love into our hearts so that we may pour out this love to others.

His power will always win. His love will always shine. We must be willing to share this with everyone we meet. Encouraging each other to remember that His power rules all.

Encouragement does not include the discouraging words that this world has become accustomed to. We must follow their discouraging words with His encouraging words instead. Our reward is in heaven and we want to see as many people find His salvation as possible so that we can continue to live in His community in heaven.

Loving Our Communities

Do any of us have neighbors that we just cannot get along with? I have had several that were a little loud or simply did not respect other people. However, I could have handled several of the incidents better had I relied on God to speak through me. Instead, I have been known to allow my flesh to speak too much. This causes me to feel guilty and then I repent, but the neighbor might not know that I have repented. Therefore, I have also been known to apologize as often as possible.

Trust me, the apologizing is not of my power; it is the Holy Spirit working inside of me. I saw apologizing as humiliating and the Holy Spirit reminded me that it was humbling. I do not mind being humble and if it means feeling humiliated, I am all right with that.

I am the type of neighbor who enjoys bringing cookies with her to welcome new neighbors. I have been met with weird looks at times and thanked other times. It should not stop me from being this type of neighbor because hopefully the new neighbors will see Christ in me.

> 1 Am I not free? Am I not an apostle? Have I not seen Jesus our Lord? Are you not the result of my work in the Lord? 2 Even though I may not be an apostle to others, surely I am to you! For you are the seal of my apostleship in the Lord.
>
> 3 This is my defense to those who sit in judgment on me. 4 Don't we have the right to food and drink? 5 Don't we have the right to take a believing wife along with us, as do the other apostles and the Lord's brothers and Cephas? 6 Or is it only I and Barnabas who lack the right to not work for a living?
>
> 7 Who serves as a soldier at his own expense? Who plants a vineyard and does not eat its grapes? Who tends a flock and does not drink the milk? 8 Do I say this merely on human authority? Doesn't the Law say the same thing? 9 For it is written in the Law of Moses: "Do not muzzle an ox while it is treading out the grain." Is it about oxen that

God is concerned? 10 Surely he says this for us, doesn't he? Yes, this was written for us, because whoever plows and threshes should be able to do so in the hope of sharing in the harvest. 11 If we have sown spiritual seed among you, is it too much if we reap a material harvest from you? 12 If others have this right of support from you, shouldn't we have it all the more?

But we did not use this right. On the contrary, we put up with anything rather than hinder the gospel of Christ.

13 Don't you know that those who serve in the temple get their food from the temple, and that those who serve at the altar share in what is offered on the altar? 14 In the same way, the Lord has commanded that those who preach the gospel should receive their living from the gospel.

15 But I have not used any of these rights. And I am not writing this in the hope that you will do such things for me, for I would rather die than allow anyone to deprive me of this boast. 16 For when I preach the gospel, I cannot boast, since I am compelled to preach. Woe to me if I do not preach the gospel! 17 If I preach voluntarily, I have a reward; if not voluntarily, I am simply discharging the trust committed to me. 18 What then is my reward? Just this: that in preaching the gospel I may offer it free of charge, and so not make full use of my rights as a preacher of the gospel.

19 Though I am free and belong to no one, I have made myself a slave to everyone, to win as many as possible. 20 To the Jews I became like a Jew, to win the Jews. To those under the law I became like one under the law (though I myself am not under the law), so as to win those under the law. 21 To those not having the law I became like one not having the law (though I am not free from God's law but am under Christ's law), so as to win those not having the law. 22 To the weak I became weak, to win the weak. I have become all things to all people so that by all possible means I might save some. 23 I do all this for the sake of the gospel, that I may share in its blessings.

24 Do you not know that in a race all the runners run, but only one gets the prize? Run in such a way as to get the prize. 25 Everyone who competes in the games goes into strict training. They do it to get a crown that will not last, but we do it to get a crown that will last forever. 26 Therefore I do not run like someone running aimlessly; I do not fight like a boxer beating the air. 27 No, I strike a blow to my body and make it my slave so that after I have preached to others, I myself will not be disqualified for the prize.

1 Corinthians 9, NIV

We can only hope to be 'good neighbors.' Sometimes our flesh shows through and we must apologize. When we do this, it should reveal Jesus in our actions. Paul reminded the people he taught that they are not to judge people. We must all be willing to share His love while working toward a stronger community.

Paul reminds people that we all work for the Lord. Soldiers do not work just to receive a paycheck. They work to sanctify our nation. God works to sanctify His Kingdom, and this will include our communities. We no longer live to fulfill the Law because we cannot do it. Christ died so that we could repent for our sins and approach God.

I like the story about not muzzling an ox while it is treading the grain. We tend to ask people to listen to God and do what He says to do and then turn around and forget it ourselves. This is what appears to be hypocritical to people who do not know him yet. Therefore, we must be careful not to be hypocritical.

Trust me, I hate it when I realize that I caught myself in a hypocritical act. However, no more guilt and shame because we have His grace and mercy.

Share this encouragement with others!

Material things might seem unimportant to some of us. However, Paul wrote to the Church of Corinth to let them know that it is not contrary to our beliefs to receive compensation for helping others come to know Christ.

We reap what we sow. He goes on to remind the church that he and his helpers chose not to reap from where they sowed so that the message of God could be heard. Listening to the Holy Spirit to better understand

255

when to reap from where we sow and when to gracefully give of our time and money will encourage people of our communities.

We all reap from what Christ sowed. Therefore, we have plenty to share and enough to give as gifts when something is needed in our communities. Sometimes we preach and teach as apprentices and might receive little to no pay for this. While other times we might preach and teach as the pastor of the church and receive compensation. Both are righteous and show His generosity.

Preaching the Gospel does not always reap monetary rewards. As a preacher, Paul reminds believers that he needs to be able to voluntarily preach the Gospel so that he can boast about God. He reminds believers that God will always supply us with what we need to be encouraging. We are either slaves to this world or slaves to God.

> When you were slaves to sin, you were free from the control of righteousness. 21 What benefit did you reap at that time from the things you are now ashamed of? Those things result in death! 22 But now that you have been set free from sin and have become slaves of God, the benefit you reap leads to holiness, and the result is eternal life.
> **Romans 6:20–22, NIV**

It is an eternal blessing to serve the Lord!

We are to treat our community with respect and show His honor toward them. Paul shares this by writing about how he became like the people who he was preaching to so that they could hear the message of the Good News more clearly. He stated that he became like the ones under the law to win the ones under the law, but without becoming under the law himself. We are to treat our community with the same respect. Do not ridicule peoples' beliefs, ever.

We can show our weaknesses to the weak so they can understand that they need to find God's strength. For the sake of the Gospel, we must be willing to hear what other people say. Whether they talk about another religion or another belief system, we must hear them and then be ready to respond gracefully (see 1 Peter 3:15). We are not to put people down for what they believe, but to lift them up to see the Truth, that God is their salvation and heaven and hell are real.

The next thing that Paul writes is one of my favorite metaphorical verses. He states that there is always one winner. We all run the race, but the fastest, most sustained racer wins. We must run as though we are going to win. We must support each other to win back our community. We must train ourselves and build each other up.

And we must also remember that the 'win' that we are focused upon is to be shared with as many people as possible. Our prize will last for eternity and we must share this with our communities so that more people will be running this eternal race. We must allow God to work in us and encourage others to do the same so that we can all declare His love for us and win the race. We will never be separated from His love.

Never Separated from God

Since we have been saved, we cannot be taken away from God. We can turn away, but nothing can take us away. When we turn away, He is still there and waiting to return to our lives. We are running the race and will most likely not turn away again, but we will sin again. No worries… well, sort of. He will still forgive us when we repent.

> 35 Can anything ever separate us from Christ's love? Does it mean he no longer loves us if we have trouble or calamity, or are persecuted, or hungry, or destitute, or in danger, or threatened with death? 36 (As the Scriptures say, "For your sake we are killed every day; we are being slaughtered like sheep.") 37 No, despite all these things, overwhelming victory is ours through Christ, who loved us.
>
> 38 And I am convinced that nothing can ever separate us from God's love. Neither death nor life, neither angels nor demons, neither our fears for today nor our worries about tomorrow—not even the powers of hell can separate us from God's love. 39 No power in the sky above or in the earth below—indeed, nothing in all creation will ever be able to separate us from the love of God that is revealed in Christ Jesus our Lord.
> **Romans 8:35–39, NLT**

Think about all that for a moment… nothing can ever separate us from God; nothing except our own choices. We can choose to walk away. However, this would not be wise.

We do have free will, but are we willing to use it for our own harm? Let's hope not. Since nothing can ever separate us from God, we need to not only remember this but share this joy with many people.

What does it mean that nothing can ever separate us from God? Does it mean that we are going to live life without any trials or troubles? No…what it does mean is that He is with us during those troubled times.

We will feel as though we are being slaughtered and tortured in life, but we can still stand on His promise to never leave us. We are the victors because of Christ's sacrifice and His ultimate love for us. Encourage others with this truth as soon as possible.

No death or end of a time can ever separate us from God. He is with us and will not forsake us. This is one of His many promises to us all.

No demon has any power over us anymore. We might suffer, but trust me, we are in good company because Christ endured the ultimate suffering for our salvation. Our community relies upon the people living inside of it. Therefore, sharing the love of God with the community will strengthen it.

We are asked to not worry about what tomorrow will bring… and sometimes we are faithful in this. However, there are times that our flesh takes over and we begin to worry.

It is up to all of us in our communities to stick together and support each other when these worries invade our hearts and trust. The faith to not worry so much is a declaration of His love. When we obey His command to not worry about tomorrow, He is faithful and will guide us.

The Declaration of His Love

God declared His undying love for us. He sent His only Son to die a criminal's death as a sacrifice for our sins. He loves us that much.

We must encourage others to love each other more. Our days are numbered here on earth, but there are no numbered days in eternity. We will be together, with Him, forever. This is another declaration of His love for us all.

1 The heavens declare the glory of God;

the skies proclaim the work of his hands.
2 Day after day they pour forth speech;
    night after night they reveal knowledge.
3 They have no speech, they use no words;
    no sound is heard from them.
4 Yet their voice goes out into all the earth,
    their words to the ends of the world.
In the heavens God has pitched a tent for the sun.
5 It is like a bridegroom coming out of his chamber,
    like a champion rejoicing to run his course.
6 It rises at one end of the heavens
    and makes its circuit to the other;
    nothing is deprived of its warmth.

7 The law of the LORD is perfect,
    refreshing the soul.
The statutes of the LORD are trustworthy,
    making wise the simple.
8 The precepts of the LORD are right,
    giving joy to the heart.
The commands of the LORD are radiant,
    giving light to the eyes.
9 The fear of the LORD is pure,
    enduring forever.
The decrees of the LORD are firm,
    and all of them are righteous.

10 They are more precious than gold,
    than much pure gold;
they are sweeter than honey,
    than honey from the honeycomb.
11 By them your servant is warned;
    in keeping them there is great reward.
12 But who can discern their own errors?
    Forgive my hidden faults.
13 Keep your servant also from willful sins;
    may they not rule over me.
Then I will be blameless,
    innocent of great transgression.

Christine C. Sponsler

14 May these words of my mouth and this meditation of my heart
be pleasing in your sight,
LORD, my Rock and my Redeemer.
Psalm 19, NIV

We live in uncertain times.
Hallelujah!
This means that the Lord is coming back for us. His glory is in heaven
and we will someday be with Him there. The uncertain times remind us
that He has not forgotten us.

When we read that the skies proclaim the work of His hands, it means
that His glory surrounds us, and we are reminded of this through the
beauty found in this world. Can you imagine what the beauty of heaven
looks like? It will be marvelous beyond what we can even imagine.

Nothing is deprived of the warmth and glow of the sun. And… nothing
is deprived of the warmth and glow of the Son.

God is heard through angel voices so that all His children know Him
and feel His love. We are running the course that God has laid out for us.
It is a beautiful thing to look outside and see God's beauty everywhere. He
has designed the earth and the beauty of heaven is far more intricate than
earth. We are given slight glimpses into the beauty which awaits us in
heaven.

God's law is perfect. But, you say, we are not to follow the law anymore.
Not exactly, we are to have faith that Christ fulfilled the law, and we are
saved.

The Lord's decree and commands are still relevant today and we must
follow them so that we can encourage each other. Our fear of God is pure,
and His acceptance of our fear is pure also.

He cares for us. We care for others with His love. His love, His laws,
and His hope are more precious than the purest gold. We get to share this
with each other forever.

Have any of us ever tasted honeycomb? It is one of the most pleasant
tastes that I have ever experienced. His decrees and commands are even
sweeter than the honeycombs. Thank about that… sweeter than one of
the sweetest tastes known to mankind.

Keeping His commands is a great reward. It allows us to live as though
we already know God and know that we will live in eternity with Him.

Praise God!

We must pray that God shows us our sins. Then repent and pray for His forgiveness of our sins, known and unknown. We must offer Him our praise and pray that they are pleasant to His ears and heart.

We must encourage each other to meditate and pray will also create a pleasing offering to God. Christ died to save us all, not just who we think is deserving because none of us are deserving.

Our love for each other must be strong. We rely upon His strength to make sure our love for each other is strong. We are called and commanded to love each other with the love of God.

He saved us and we are blessed with His love in our lives. Now we must share this love with others. He is our redeemer, and He asks us to love each other as He loves us. Loving each other as He has loved us might not be easy, but it is necessary to be encouraging to others.

Loving Each Other As He Has Loved Us

How do we show our gratitude? Do we need to show gratitude even when we are suffering? Does God hear our thankful prayers and songs?

All these questions are answered throughout His Word. We show our gratitude by obeying His commands. We need to show our gratitude so that we do not boast about our lives. He delights, hears, and enjoys our thankful hearts. He loves to hear from us always.

> 1 Before the Passover celebration, Jesus knew that his hour had come to leave this world and return to his Father. He had loved his disciples during his ministry on earth, and now he loved them to the very end. 2 It was time for supper, and the devil had already prompted Judas, son of Simon Iscariot, to betray Jesus. 3 Jesus knew that the Father had given him authority over everything and that he had come from God and would return to God. 4 So he got up from the table, took off his robe, wrapped a towel around his waist, 5 and poured water into a basin. Then he began to wash the disciples' feet, drying them with the towel he had around him.
>
> 6 When Jesus came to Simon Peter, Peter said to him, "Lord, are you going to wash my feet?"

7 Jesus replied, "You don't understand now what I am doing, but someday you will."

8 "No," Peter protested, "you will never ever wash my feet!"

Jesus replied, "Unless I wash you, you won't belong to me."

9 Simon Peter exclaimed, "Then wash my hands and head as well, Lord, not just my feet!"

10 Jesus replied, "A person who has bathed all over does not need to wash, except for the feet, to be entirely clean. And you disciples are clean, but not all of you." 11 For Jesus knew who would betray him. That is what he meant when he said, "Not all of you are clean."

12 After washing their feet, he put on his robe again and sat down and asked, "Do you understand what I was doing? 13 You call me 'Teacher' and 'Lord,' and you are right, because that's what I am. 14 And since I, your Lord and Teacher, have washed your feet, you ought to wash each other's feet. 15 I have given you an example to follow. Do as I have done to you. 16 I tell you the truth, slaves are not greater than their master. Nor is the messenger more important than the one who sends the message. 17 Now that you know these things, God will bless you for doing them.

John 13:1–17, NLT

Jesus is our ultimate example of what God desires from us. He washed His disciples' feet because He needed to show them that we are here to serve each other. He had authority over the earth and still demonstrated the servant attitude toward His disciples by washing their feet. This was an act of servitude and kindness and we are to do the same for each other.

Poor Peter could not understand what the Lord was doing and asked Him not to wash his feet. However, since Christ desired to show servitude, He insisted. Then, Peter demanded more from Him, not knowing the symbolism.

Not understanding sounds familiar. There are times when we do not understand why things are happening. However, we are simply to obey His commands and then learn from each struggle life will bring to us.

Unfortunately, Jesus already knew that Judas was ready to betray Him. Even though all His disciples were being cleansed by the Lord, Judas was being prompted to betray Jesus. This is both sad and a wake-up call for us all. We all fall short of the glory of God.

> for all have sinned and fall short of the glory of God, 24 and all are justified freely by his grace through the redemption that came by Christ Jesus. 25 God presented Christ as a sacrifice of atonement, through the shedding of his blood—to be received by faith. He did this to demonstrate his righteousness, because in his forbearance he had left the sins committed beforehand unpunished— 26 he did it to demonstrate his righteousness at the present time, so as to be just and the one who justifies those who have faith in Jesus.
>
> 27 Where, then, is boasting? It is excluded. Because of what law? The law that requires works? No, because of the law that requires faith.
> **Romans 3:23–27, NIV**

However, we did not betray Him to His killers... or did we? We all sin. It is difficult to determine what sin is 'worse' than another because it is all sin.

God desires that we repent for our sins. What I am about to say might be viewed as controversial; however, I feel it could be true. I believe that Judas' act of buying the field and hanging himself in it was a cry out to the Lord for forgiveness.

I could be wrong, but I had to write this in this space. We are all sinners, and we are all saved. Therefore, I believe this could be true about Judas.

Tangent over! Christ wants us to do unto others as He has done unto us. This is an extension of the Golden Rule, "do unto others as you would have them do unto you" (see Matthew 7:12; Luke 6:31). God will bless us for obeying this command. We are also to love each other just as Christ loves us. This proves that we are His.

We must encourage each other to show this love to as many people as possible. When we share His love, His light shines through and the Holy Spirit is present. Christ has revealed God's love to us; we must share this with our communities to bless and to honor them.

Christine C. Sponsler

Blessings and Honor

I use these three words as a signature in most of what I write. In school, in writing emails, and soon, in writing my blogs. The reason I am using it here is this... I truly hope that all who are reading this book are blessed and I hope that this book honors the encouragement of God.

Life is not easy, and Christians know this as well as nonbelievers. However, as believers, we have God to rely upon. We know that the love of God will get us through anything. We know that He is right here with us and is supporting us during our struggles. What does the world have to rely on? Hopefully, our encouragement.

> 1 How joyful are those who fear the LORD—
>   all who follow his ways!
> 2 You will enjoy the fruit of your labor.
>   How joyful and prosperous you will be!
> 3 Your wife will be like a fruitful grapevine,
>   flourishing within your home.
> Your children will be like vigorous young olive trees
>   as they sit around your table.
> 4 That is the LORD's blessing
>   for those who fear him.
>
> 5 May the LORD continually bless you from Zion.
>   May you see Jerusalem prosper as long as you live.
> 6 May you live to enjoy your grandchildren.
>   May Israel have peace!
> **Psalm 128, NLT**

Fear of the Lord is not the same thing as being afraid of Him. I know I wrote this before, but it is extremely important to remember this. Fear of the Lord shows wisdom (see Proverbs 9:10). Without fear of the Lord, we would become like Lucifer and believe that we are god. Scary thought, I know. We need God, not to be god.

We will enjoy the fruit of our labor, especially when we encourage another person to follow Christ. His ways are true and pure and bless us with the honor of His love. Our prosperity is not the same as the world sees prosperity and that is more than all right… it is another blessing. We do not have to try to fit in with the worldly ways anymore.

Our spouse, children, friends, neighbors, and even our enemies will find encouragement when we share His love with them. We are the encouragers of this world and we all hope to encourage others to come to know God. When we practice this, He is present and supports our efforts.

How many of us try to get our families together, and there are simply too many different reasons for why they cannot be present? When this happens…

PRAY!

Prayer may not always bring them together, but it will allow us not to feel hurt or distraught from their absence. We will find His blessings anyway.

The peace of this world is fleeting, at best. We can call upon the name of the Lord and find His peace for our lives and encourage others to do this also. We will share His inheritance with our loved ones. When we remember that He is God and we are not, we give Him glory and show His power to the rest of the world.

Glory and Power

Glory and power are the Lord's alone. His power guides us, strengthens us, and empowers us to be His encouragers. The glory of the Lord is shown throughout the Bible. However, we will travel into the Book of Revelations for a moment.

I know, the Book of Revelations…

YIKES!

It is with great honor and glory to God that we will be reading the words from John and hopefully grasping an understanding of how encouraging the Book of Revelations can be. We will focus on Revelations chapter 5 in its entirety. Let's get encouraged!

> 1 Then I saw in the right hand of him who sat on the throne a scroll with writing on both sides and sealed with seven seals. 2 And I saw a mighty angel proclaiming in a loud voice, "Who is worthy to break the seals and open the scroll?" 3 But no one in heaven or on earth or under the earth could open the scroll or even look inside it. 4 I wept

and wept because no one was found who was worthy to open the scroll or look inside. 5 Then one of the elders said to me, "Do not weep! See, the Lion of the tribe of Judah, the Root of David, has triumphed. He is able to open the scroll and its seven seals."

6 Then I saw a Lamb, looking as if it had been slain, standing at the center of the throne, encircled by the four living creatures and the elders. The Lamb had seven horns and seven eyes, which are the seven spirits of God sent out into all the earth. 7 He went and took the scroll from the right hand of him who sat on the throne. 8 And when he had taken it, the four living creatures and the twenty-four elders fell down before the Lamb. Each one had a harp and they were holding golden bowls full of incense, which are the prayers of God's people. 9 And they sang a new song, saying:

> "You are worthy to take the scroll
>   and to open its seals,
> because you were slain,
>   and with your blood you purchased for God
>   persons from every tribe and language and people and
>   nation.
> 10 You have made them to be a kingdom and priests to serve
>   our God,
>   and they will reign on the earth."

11 Then I looked and heard the voice of many angels, numbering thousands upon thousands, and ten thousand times ten thousand. They encircled the throne and the living creatures and the elders. 12 In a loud voice they were saying:

> "Worthy is the Lamb, who was slain,
>   to receive power and wealth and wisdom and strength
>   and honor and glory and praise!"

13 Then I heard every creature in heaven and on earth and under the earth and on the sea, and all that is in them, saying:

"To him who sits on the throne and to the Lamb
be praise and honor and glory and power,
for ever and ever!"

14 The four living creatures said, "Amen," and the elders fell down and worshiped.
Revelation 5, NIV

If you are reading this and know me, you will remember that this scripture is permanently a part of me. I have the Lion and the Lamb tattooed as a cover-up on my right arm. On my forearm are the Scripture verses listed on an ornate scroll. It is a sleeve, and it is dedicated to our Lord.

Can we truly imagine what it would be like to see the things described in this chapter? I know that it would be a revelation of His glory. Christ is the only one worthy to open the scrolls. His power is from God the Father and He was with God from the beginning.

In the beginning God created the heavens and the earth. 2 Now the earth was formless and empty, darkness was over the surface of the deep, and the Spirit of God was hovering over the waters.
Genesis 1:1–2, NIV

Christ is the Lamb of God. He is also the Lion of Judah. His love is deeper than we can even fathom. How awesome and wonderful He is.

The creatures mentioned in Revelation 5:6; 5:8 appear to be the same creatures mentioned in Revelation 4. They are an eagle a lion, an ox, and a man. When the scroll is unable to be opened, Christ (the Lamb) comes and opens the scroll. The scroll is in God's right hand and the prayers of believers were held in a golden bowl. All glory was given to God.

Every believer is represented when John mentions that the blood of the slain Lamb purchased the people from everywhere. The people of each tribe and nation are to serve as encouragers on earth. We are to follow in their footsteps and serve each other with His encouraging words. The Lamb of God purchased us through His blood.

The angels are watching over us while we are on earth and we must share this with as many people as possible. Many angels are present when the Lamb of God opens the scroll. Honor and glory are given to Christ (the Lamb) because He is worthy to be praised. With the praise, glory, and power of God, the four creatures said Amen and worshiped God.

This is encouraging!

Encouragement Extended

What have we learned from this book? How will we apply it to our lives? Does God truly watch over us and encourage us daily? Do we really need to get out there and encourage each other?

We have been called to encourage others. His desire is that everyone hears the Good News. We are to shout it from the rooftops, when necessary.

Do we have to worry about our lives in the way that the world worries? No, we live in this world, but are not of this world. Will worry help us in anyway?

Biblically speaking, we are not to worry about anything. God has our backs, and we must have each other's backs. We have learned that encouragement takes courage, love, joy, peace, hope, and His glorification.

We must apply this to our lives by getting out there and encouraging as many people as we can. God is always watching over us. We are His children. He is our Father. When we encourage each other, we will also find encouragement.

God has told us that we do not need to worry about anything. His grace is sufficient (see 2 Corinthians 12:9) and His love never fails (see Psalm 109:26; Romans 5:8). We are to remember these words instead of worrying. The Lord will protect us and watch over us. He will give us His strength to encourage others. It is encouraging to know that God is watching over us and that our worries should be given to Him.

> 25 "Therefore I tell you, do not worry about your life, what you will eat or drink; or about your body, what you will wear. Is not life more than food, and the body more than clothes? 26 Look at the birds of the air; they do not

sow or reap or store away in barns, and yet your heavenly
Father feeds them. Are you not much more valuable than
they? 27 Can any one of you by worrying add a single hour
to your life?

28 "And why do you worry about clothes? See how the
flowers of the field grow. They do not labor or spin. 29 Yet
I tell you that not even Solomon in all his splendor was
dressed like one of these. 30 If that is how God clothes the
grass of the field, which is here today and tomorrow is
thrown into the fire, will he not much more clothe you—
you of little faith? 31 So do not worry, saying, 'What shall
we eat?' or 'What shall we drink?' or 'What shall we wear?'
32 For the pagans run after all these things, and your
heavenly Father knows that you need them. 33 But seek
first his kingdom and his righteousness, and all these things
will be given to you as well. 34 Therefore do not worry
about tomorrow, for tomorrow will worry about itself.
Each day has enough trouble of its own."
Matthew 6:25–34, NIV

Our lives belong to the Lord. We are to offer ourselves up to Him and
ask for His guidance. He nourishes us. His love guides us. He clothes us.
He provides everything that we need.

We sometimes get caught up not knowing the difference between what
we want and what we need. He knows what we need and provides for us.
The desires of our hearts begin to align with His desires.

We are reminded of His love when we watch birds fly in the sky, eating
in our yard, or in nature. We do forget that we are even more important to
God, and He cares for us better than He cares for the birds. When we
worry about food or clothing, we are causing ourselves to live in doubt.
When we live in doubt, it is difficult to be encouraged or to be encouraging.

There are flowers in nature, and they do not have hoses leading to them.
However, they are still beautiful because of our God. When we forget what
He does for us, we show only a little faith, if any. He is faithful and we
must learn to be more faithful to Him. We must not worry about our food
or clothes so that God can use us to encourage other people.

Christine C. Sponsler

We must seek first the Kingdom of God and His righteousness to live inside of His protection and glory. We are to make plans, but not worry about tomorrow because tomorrow already has its own worries.

Today is enough to worry about. We must encourage each other today and always. Encourage each other to not worry so much so that we all can share in His encouraging words.

Chapter 17: Farewell and Stay Tuned

...but those who hope in the LORD
   will renew their strength.
They will soar on wings like eagles;
   they will run and not grow weary,
   they will walk and not be faint.
Isaiah 40:31, NIV

9 For God did not appoint us to suffer wrath but to receive salvation through our Lord Jesus Christ. 10 He died for us so that, whether we are awake or asleep, we may live together with him. 11 Therefore encourage one another and build each other up, just as in fact you are doing.

12 Now we ask you, brothers and sisters, to acknowledge those who work hard among you, who care for you in the Lord and who admonish you. 13 Hold them in the highest regard in love because of their work. Live in peace with each other.
1 Thessalonians 5:9–13, NIV

It is with a heavy heart and an elated heart that I must almost bid you all adieu. I am sad to see this book end but know that God is so good that there will be more. As mentioned before, there will be a testimony book. There is also a series to be explored about the life and times of hundreds of men and women who go through a Christian rehab center. Then they enter back into the world with His strength inside of them.

We are to renew each other through encouragement. We are to use His strength to approach others, especially those who are suffering without God in their lives. We are to remember that we are all sisters and brothers in Christ.

There are several more sections to this book following this 'good-bye' section. They include more encouragement and I hope you find them inspirationally encouraging.

Christine C. Sponsler

*****

We are to remember that our sins are forgiven… Forever!
Hallelujah!

Sins Forgiven...Forever

One of my favorite chapters of the Bible is Psalm 103. There are challenges and encouragement throughout the chapter. As we read God's Word with an open heart, He speaks directly to each of us.

We are His children, and He is our Father. He forgives our sins, and we are to forgive people who have sinned. We are all sinners, but with Christ's sacrifice, we can repent and be forgiven right away... forever.

1 Let all that I am praise the LORD;
  with my whole heart, I will praise his holy name.
2 Let all that I am praise the LORD;
  may I never forget the good things he does for me.
3 He forgives all my sins
  and heals all my diseases.
4 He redeems me from death
  and crowns me with love and tender mercies.
5 He fills my life with good things.
  My youth is renewed like the eagle's!

6 The LORD gives righteousness
  and justice to all who are treated unfairly.

7 He revealed his character to Moses
  and his deeds to the people of Israel.
8 The LORD is compassionate and merciful,
  slow to get angry and filled with unfailing love.
9 He will not constantly accuse us,
  nor remain angry forever.
10 He does not punish us for all our sins;
  he does not deal harshly with us, as we deserve.
11 For his unfailing love toward those who fear him
  is as great as the height of the heavens above the earth.
12 He has removed our sins as far from us
  as the east is from the west.
13 The LORD is like a father to his children,
  tender and compassionate to those who fear him.
14 For he knows how weak we are;

> he remembers we are only dust.
> 15 Our days on earth are like grass;
> like wildflowers, we bloom and die.
> 16 The wind blows, and we are gone—
> as though we had never been here.
> 17 But the love of the LORD remains forever
> with those who fear him.
> His salvation extends to the children's children
> 18 of those who are faithful to his covenant,
> of those who obey his commandments!
>
> 19 The LORD has made the heavens his throne;
> from there he rules over everything.
>
> 20 Praise the LORD, you angels,
> you mighty ones who carry out his plans,
> listening for each of his commands.
> 21 Yes, praise the LORD, you armies of angels
> who serve him and do his will!
> 22 Praise the LORD, everything he has created,
> everything in all his kingdom.
> Let all that I am praise the LORD.
> **Psalm 103, NLT**

Praise God that He gives us His forgiveness. Without it, we would be doomed to eternity without Him. We must be thankful for all the good He has done for us. He heals our brokenness so that we can encourage others with His Good News. We are renewed in Him daily.

The Bible uses the image of an eagle often. The image is of His majesty and our liberty. Have any of us seen eagles in nature?

I have, in Alaska. When they soar overhead, they are majestic and free. This is the symbol used when the psalmist writes about our youth being renewed. We are renewed when we are treated unfairly. Good things happen when we invite God into our lives.

God has been revealing Himself to His creatures since the beginning of man. He might appear as an angry God in the Old Testament, but the anger of God is righteous. He does not remain angry with us and we are to repent for things that anger Him.

He could deal very harshly with us. We have all sinned. He does not punish us for our sins because Christ was the ultimate sacrifice for our sins. He shows us unfailing love.

This next verse of Psalm 103 (12), is my 'life verse.' Our sins have been removed from us and there is no record of these sins. Do we fathom how far the east is from the west? It is unfathomable when thinking about the distance; just as it is unfathomable that He would ever bring up our sins after repentance (see Micah 7:19). He forgives those sins... forever.

We tend to bring those sins back up and wallow in our thoughts of who we were rather than who we have become... His children.

He is our Father... forever. We must always remember this. He shows us compassion and we need to receive it so that we can encourage others too. He knows that we are weak, and therefore He gives us His strength.

We are only here on earth for a little while. We will be with Him in heaven for eternity. This is encouraging and eternity is forever also. His love remains forever as well. I like this word, forever, because it means that we will never be without Him again.

That is encouraging!

The salvation for which Christ created is extended to our children, our children's children, and their children. Many generations will find Him through our encouragement. Our actions will draw people toward His salvation for them.

Hallelujah!

When we obey His commands and are faithful to His covenant, our children will become renewed too. They must turn to Him, but His promise says that even if our children turn away, they will return to Him because they know Him (see Proverbs 22:6). He is faithful. Praise His Holy name. We must praise God for the angels He has protecting us and our children.

Hallelujah!

We must praise the Lord and teach our children to do the same. Encourage each other with His promises and praise Him. His Kingdom is glorified when people acknowledge who He is, and we must shout it from the mountain tops often. We must learn to be grateful, no matter our circumstance.

Be Grateful in All Things

Christine C. Sponsler

Gratitude does not mean that we like our situation or circumstance. It simply means that we know that God is bigger than anything we go through. We must encourage each other to remember His promise that He will never leave or forsake us. Our family, friends, neighbors, communities, and even our enemies need to be encouraged.

We might not be near the people that we love, but we must pray for them. Call them with encouraging words and share our lives with them, if even from afar. It might feel as though God is far away, but He is right here with us every second of the day. We return to Paul as our guide toward being grateful in all circumstances, and not being anxious about anything.

> 1 Therefore, my brothers and sisters, you whom I love and long for, my joy and crown, stand firm in the Lord in this way, dear friends!
>
> 2 I plead with Euodia and I plead with Syntyche to be of the same mind in the Lord. 3 Yes, and I ask you, my true companion, help these women since they have contended at my side in the cause of the gospel, along with Clement and the rest of my co-workers, whose names are in the book of life.
>
> 4 Rejoice in the Lord always. I will say it again: Rejoice! 5 Let your gentleness be evident to all. The Lord is near. 6 Do not be anxious about anything, but in every situation, by prayer and petition, with thanksgiving, present your requests to God. 7 And the peace of God, which transcends all understanding, will guard your hearts and your minds in Christ Jesus.
> **Philippians 4:1–7, NIV**

Ever since the first days of the Church, there have been issues relating to believers against believers. Paul shares such a time with Euodia and Syntyche to have the same minds. Having the same minds toward each other and being more Christlike toward each other.

Paul desires to see his brothers and sisters behave more like Christ and love each other. This is encouraging because it reminds us that even if there are quarrels in the church, we are to remain encouragers.

We are to rejoice in our church family, even when we have differences of opinion. It might seem impossible to rejoice when we are upset, but we are to follow this command as best as we can.

Using gentleness to redirect anger issues in the church is encouraging. God is working in the situation to make it better, so an angry word might delay His work. Be an encourager, not a discourager.

We come to God with requests for each other all the time. He might be working on something in our heart, and we must hear from Him to change things or to simply obey. If we are too busy quarreling with each other, we could miss out on what He says. We do not want to miss anything He has to say to us.

Has anyone reading this ever felt anxious about anything? I know that I have and then I felt badly because I forgot to rely upon God. However, this usually brings me to prayer and meditation to strengthen my faith again.

We must be willing to give our anxieties to God. At times this feels impossible, but it is not. He is waiting to hear from us. Encouragement comes from knowing that we can give Him all our anxieties.

God's peace is nothing like the peace we search for from the world. We might attend a retreat to find His peace, but it does not mean that this world can offer us this peace. In other words, we must use the retreat to get closer to Him to find His peace.

His peace will guard our hearts against the world and allow us to live in His joy. God desires for us to repent and seek His forgiveness because Jesus died for our sins.

Jesus is the Lion of Judah!

Jesus is the Lamb of God!

The Lamb of God… Amen

Jesus died for our sins. He became the Lamb of God to be slaughtered in our place. We must rejoice in this and encourage others to rejoice with us. We are to share this Good News so that other people and nations will know Him. Hiding this news is discouraging because people need to hear about God to come to know Him.

Again… shout this from the rooftops!

Christine C. Sponsler

9 After this I looked, and there before me was a great
multitude that no one could count, from every nation,
tribe, people and language, standing before the throne and
before the Lamb. They were wearing white robes and were
holding palm branches in their hands. 10 And they cried
out in a loud voice:

"Salvation belongs to our God,
who sits on the throne,
and to the Lamb."

11 All the angels were standing around the throne and
around the elders and the four living creatures. They fell
down on their faces before the throne and worshiped God,
12 saying:

"Amen!
Praise and glory
and wisdom and thanks and honor
and power and strength
be to our God for ever and ever.
Amen!"
Revelation 7:9–12, NIV

The Book of Revelation is packed full of glorifying God. John wrote
the Book of Revelation on the island of Patmos near Asia Minor in circa
A.D. 96. He envisioned what the world and heaven will be like when Christ
returns. These visions were recorded in the Bible for our benefit. We are
to read the Book of Revelation and witness what John saw while searching
for God.

John saw many people from every nation, tribe, people, and language
worshipping the Lamb of God. They stood before the throne of God in
worship to Him.

What an awesome sight. We can only imagine what this looked like.
Then, we would multiply our vision of this by about a million to truly see
the glory of God.

Amen!

I simply cannot wait to see this in person. However, we still have things
to do here on earth. Things such as encouraging others to witness these

visions also. God is strength and wisdom. We are to praise Him forever and encourage others to praise His Holy name.

Blessings and honor to all the readers of this book. Keep watch for more books such as this one.

Christine C. Sponsler

Hope to Reveal More Soon

Well, hello and good-bye again readers. I hope to present another version of this book soon with more about the workplace, church environments, etc. Also, I will be presenting my testimony book as soon as possible. (See the Epilogue for a teaser.) God is so good, and I hope that each of you reading this book knows how much He adores you.
Hallelujah and Amen!

Part 5: Epilogue Family Testimony (condensed)

We are given one family (usually). When we are not sure as to where we fit in to this family, we can tend to stray. I know that I strayed. My grandmother was the only link that I wanted to my family. I was the 'black sheep,' and could not figure out how an 11-year-old could be labeled this way.

Rebellion was my next move. Since I could do no right, I learned how to do all wrong and became good at it and proud of it. I knew how to be 'bad' and I knew that I could no longer see the 'good' in myself. I did not care anymore.

I will not get too much further into what led me down a dark and evil pathway, but it has to do with molestation, rape, and witnessing death all around me.

I loved my grandparents and I know that they loved me. However, it was a little too late, I was only 14 when they saved me from drugs... or so we all thought. I was already on drugs and sneaking out, at age 11, to see my 22-year-old boyfriend. I met him on the weird chat line, I think it was called the 'hotline.'

I was only 11 years old when I first did cocaine and had sex. I was pretty much on the streets from the age of 11 to 14 years old. When my grandparents found me, they tried their best to show me right from wrong, and gave me rules to abide by, but I already had my own definition of what rules looked like.

My grandmother prayed for me all the time and that is why I am still here. His love for me was seen through the actions of my grandparents and I knew it.

I felt as though I had to take care of them for the rest of their lives. I was trying, all the while still on drugs, to care for them the best that I could. It was not good enough and I ended up in jail on a probation violation.

Grandma and grandpa were moved to a nursing home and I felt as though someone had shot me in the stomach. I had no idea that jail was where I was going to finally (25 years later) find God again. He was true to His promises, I simply walked away from Him. Now, I'm back.

During the time that I was in jail, my son was arrested for being present during an act of self-defense and was convicted of manslaughter. I thought I was going to die. He was simply acting like me. However, Jesus let me know that He had a plan for my son and me and it began with me leading the way for both of us to find His grace and mercy.

Also, while I was in jail, several rehab places came to talk to us women, but one stuck out to me… The Walter Hoving Home (WHH). I entered a different program for about a month, upon my release from jail. All this time, the Lord was guiding my sister to the WHH to refer me to them.

After this, I went back to my hometown simply to see my best friend and ex-husband. He looked yellow when I saw him, and I could not figure this out. Well, he died about six weeks later from cirrhosis of the liver and Hepatitis C, at the ripe old age of 37 years old. God had allowed me to say goodbye to him right then.

I continued with rehab, graduated, and subsequently worked there as staff on property. Then, after several years of schooling, I went back to mentor and counsel some of the new women. God has demonstrated that I am still loved by Him. He is still my Father, and I no longer must live in guilt and shame, but under His grace and mercy.

I would attend Monday night recovery classes at Village Church in Burbank, California and it was there that I met my husband, Ed.

We were best friends for about eight months and then started dating. He proposed to me at the Blue Bayou (Pirates of the Caribbean Restaurant) in Disneyland. We were married exactly one year after our first date. He is my blessing from God, and I know that I am loved and love him dearly.

My husband and I are filled with the joy of the Lord all the time now... well, almost all the time. We met while I was working for the WHH. We were married in the church that is associated with the school where I attended kindergarten and first grade. As I said, he is a blessing from God, and I am blessed to be a part of his family now.

We visited my (our) son while he was in prison and received custody of my (our) 14-year-old twins (they are now 25 years old) and my (our) middle son lived with us for years. We also adopted a son. Plus, when I was 17 years old, I adopted out my first son, who is in our lives now. God is good!

To find the details of this testimony, be ready for another text by Christine C Sponsler M.Div., MA, CLC

Christine C. Sponsler

References

American Bible Society. (1992). *The Holy Bible: The Good news Translation* (2nd ed.). New York: American Bible Society.

Lomax, J. A., Lomax, R. T. & Richardson, J. (1939) *Home on the Range*. Raiford, Florida, June 3. [Audio] Retrieved from the Library of Congress, https://www.loc.gov/item/lomaxbib000482/.

Merriam-Webster, I. (2003). *Merriam-Webster's collegiate dictionary*. (Eleventh ed.). Springfield, MA: Merriam-Webster, Inc.

One *Lyrics*. (n.d.). *Lyrics.com*. Retrieved February 15, 2021, from https://www.lyrics.com/lyric/4560654/Three+Dog+Night.

The Holy Bible: English Standard Version. (2016). Wheaton, IL: Crossway Bibles.

The New International Version. (2011). Grand Rapids, MI: Zondervan.

The New King James Version. (1982). Nashville: Thomas Nelson.

Christine C. Sponsler

Tyndale House Publishers. (2015). *Holy Bible: New Living Translation*. Carol

Stream, IL: Tyndale House Publishers.